Today's ISMS

WORKS BY WILLIAM EBENSTEIN

TODAY'S ISMS: *Communism, Fascism, Capitalism, Socialism (Fourth Edition)*

TOTALITARIANISM: *New Perspectives*

TWO WAYS OF LIFE: *The Communist Challenge to Democracy*

COMMUNISM IN THEORY AND PRACTICE

GREAT POLITICAL THINKERS: *Plato to the Present (Third Edition)*

MODERN POLITICAL THOUGHT: *The Great Issues (Second Edition)*

MAN AND THE STATE: *Modern Political Ideas*

THE NAZI STATE

THE GERMAN RECORD: *A Political Portrait*

INTRODUCTION TO POLITICAL PHILOSOPHY

POLITICAL THOUGHT IN PERSPECTIVE

FASCIST ITALY

CHURCH AND STATE IN FRANCO SPAIN

THE PURE THEORY OF LAW

THE LAW OF PUBLIC HOUSING

WILLIAM EBENSTEIN
University of California, Santa Barbara

Today's ISMS

fourth edition

COMMUNISM

FASCISM

CAPITALISM

SOCIALISM

PRENTICE-HALL, INC., Englewood Cliffs, N.J.

To the memory of Joy

PRENTICE-HALL INTERNATIONAL, INC., *London*

PRENTICE-HALL OF AUSTRALIA, PTY., LTD., *Sydney*

PRENTICE-HALL OF CANADA, LTD., *Toronto*

PRENTICE-HALL FRANCE, S.A.R.L., *Paris*

PRENTICE-HALL OF INDIA (PRIVATE) LTD., *New Delhi*

PRENTICE-HALL OF JAPAN, INC., *Tokyo*

PRENTICE-HALL DE MEXICO, S.A., *Mexico City*

Library of Congress Catalog Card Number: 64-14021

Printed in the United States of America   C-92446

Preface

The major conflict of our age is the struggle between aggressive totalitarianism and the free way of life. Not long ago the chief threat to liberty was fascism; today it is communism. The violence and terror of totalitarian communism and fascism, ranging from slave labor camps to genocide, reflect a fanatical ideology that brooks no compromise.

This book is a discussion of the main representatives of each side —communism and fascism on the totalitarian side, capitalism and socialism on the democratic. In a short book, it has seemed advisable to concentrate on the isms that shape the fate of the world rather than to discuss in detail the numerous other isms that are important, but that have not been decisive, in the struggle for men's minds. These lesser isms, whether philosophical, political, social, or economic, are therefore dealt with in this book only to the extent that they are related to the four major isms. The psychological roots of totalitarianism and democracy are given particularly close attention, since it is difficult to understand either system without understanding both the personality traits and psychological motivations to which each system appeals.

The key approach in this book is through the *way of life* concept rather than through one particular aspect, such as government or economics. Totalitarianism and democracy are more than specific social, political, or economic systems: they are two diametrically opposed ways of life, with contradicting beliefs and values, based on distinct and opposite conceptions of the nature of man. The scope and gravity of the present world crisis can therefore be fully grasped only by perceiving it, not as the mere result of conflicting political or economic ideas and practices, but as a conflict between two ways of thought and action encompassing the totality of social life.

WILLIAM EBENSTEIN

University of California
Santa Barbara

v

Contents

vi

PART 2. THE DEMOCRATIC WAY OF LIFE

3. Democratic Capitalism, 131

4. Democratic Socialism, 197

PART 1

The Totalitarian Way of Life

1. *TOTALITARIAN COMMUNISM*

2. *TOTALITARIAN FASCISM*

1

Totalitarian Communism

Before Marx, history was interpreted in several typical fashions. Some interpreters sought the key to history in the working of divine providence, and conceived of human development as but part of the unfolding of God's design of the whole universe. The main difficulty of this *religious* interpretation of history lies in the fact that God's will is unknown and unknowable to man's direct experience, and that whereas there is only one God, there are many contrasting human conceptions of God and his plans for mankind.

A second dominant pre-Marxist approach to the understanding of human history was *political:* great emperors, kings, legislators, and soldiers were viewed as the decisive forces in history, and historical writing was largely the record of kings, parliaments, wars, and peace treaties.

This political emphasis in human affairs has one main shortcoming: it tends to exaggerate the relative role that most people assign to government and politics in the total setting of their lives. It is natural that statesmen, politicians, and political philosophers consider politics the most important single element in human relations, and political remedies the most important answer to human troubles. But human nature and human problems are more intricate than politics; politics

3

is only one approach—and not always the most penetrating one—
among many others.

A third major approach, the *hero interpretation of history* (popu-
larized in modern times by Carlyle), is closely related to the political
one, inasmuch as most heroes in world history are conventionally
chosen from great kings, emperors, generals, legislators, founders of
new states, pioneering reformers, and revolutionaries. The main weakness of the hero interpretation is that it overstresses the role of individuals at the expense of larger cultural, religious, social, and economic circumstances, circumstances that form the background without which there can be no meaningful exercise of leadership. Although
it is undoubtedly true that leaders mold events, it is no less true that
events mold leaders.

The fourth pre-Marxist approach to the understanding of history
was through the impact of *ideas:* ideas were conceived (by Hegel, for
example) to be the principal causes of the historical process, and the
material conditions (social, economic, technological, military) of
society were thought of as essentially derived from, and caused by, the
great motivating ideas. This emphasis on ideas often also implied that
history was progressively evolving toward the realization of key ideas,
such as freedom and democracy.

While undoubtedly containing—like the other interpretations—
much that is valid, the exclusive emphasis on ideas as the main driving
force in history overlooks the fact that ideas not only generate events
but also reflect them. Therefore, to isolate ideas as the chief agent
of human action is to neglect the framework of circumstances; circumstances, after all, make some ideas possible and others not, and
it is circumstances from which ideas derive their vitality and practical
impact.

The study of history may also be focused on *war:* the phenomenon
of conflict is present in all phases of human development, and the
birth, rise, and decline of states are often directly connected with warfare. The shortcoming of the military interpretation of history lies in its
failure to recognize war as the result, rather than as the cause, of
events. There is no doubt that war often marks a turning point in the
life of nations and civilizations: yet the dramatic swiftness and de-
cisiveness of war should not draw our attention from the multitude of
psychological, ideological, and material factors that lead to war and
contribute to its complexity.

Marx's analysis of society was set forth through his *economic interpretation of history:* the production of the goods and services that
support human life, and the exchange of those goods and services, are

the bases of all social processes and institutions. Marx does not claim that the economic factor is the only one that goes into the making of history; he does claim that it is the most important one, the *foundation* upon which is erected the *superstructure* of culture, law, and government, buttressed by corresponding political, social, religious, literary, and artistic ideologies.

In a general way, Marx describes the relations between men's material conditions of life and their ideas by saying that *"it is not the consciousness of men which determines their existence, but, on the contrary, it is their social existence which determines their consciousness."*

In a nomadic society, for example, horses might be considered the principal means of acquiring and accumulating wealth. From Marx's viewpoint, this foundation of nomadic life is the clue to its superstructure of law, government, and dominant ideas. Thus, Marx would say that those who are the owners of the greatest number of horses in such a nomadic society would also be the political chieftains who make and interpret the law; they are also likely to receive the highest respect and deference from the tribe's members who own no horses. In the realm of ideas, the predominant social and cultural concepts would reflect the dominant economic position of the owners of horses. Even in religion the impact would not be missing: God might, for instance, be represented in the image of a swift and powerful rider, and the concept of divine justice and rule would be, in a sense, an extension and magnification of human justice as determined by the horse-owning chiefs.

In a settled agricultural society, the ownership of land would provide the clue to the political, social, legal, and cultural institutions and conceptions. In such a society, according to Marx, the landowning class is the real ruler of state and society, regardless of any divergent formal organization of authority. Similarly, the landowning class would also set the predominant social standards and values.

Finally, according to Marx, *in the modern industrial society of the last two hundred years the ownership of the means of industrial production is the master key:* the capitalists not only determine the economic destiny of society, but also rule it politically (regardless of formal and legal façades to the contrary), and set its social standards and values. The ultimate purpose of the law, education, the press, and artistic and literary creation is to maintain an ideology that is imbued with the sanctity and justice of capitalist property ownership.

Our understanding of history has gained immensely from Marx's economic interpretation. It is virtually impossible to write history today without some attention at least to the relation of economic forces and conflicts to political, military, and international issues.

In pointing out Marx's overemphasis on economics, however, one must not go to the other extreme of denying that economic interests play an important part in human affairs. The Marxian theory reduces man to an earth-bound beast with no spark of the lofty and divine; some anti-Marxian theories, on the other hand, have raised man to the level of an angelic being, having no contact with the earth, nearly divine in his goodness. Men are only too often inclined to dress up their selfish and material aims and actions in high-sounding moral or religious phrases.

Marx's economic interpretation suffers from the same defect that afflicts all theories that pretend to supply the master key to history: *excessive generalization and simplification.* Whenever a single factor (be it the hero, war, religion, climate, race, geography, and so forth *ad infinitum*) is required to do the work of explanation and illumination that can only be properly done by several factors, its burden proves too heavy. No single factor has been predominant throughout history, and which factor is the most important in a particular situation is a question of empirical inquiry.

In any event or series of events there is always a complicated pattern of many factors, and it is none too easy to disentangle them. It is difficult enough to state precisely what the component motivations of an action of one person are because one person's actions are often mutually contradictory and logically inconsistent. It is even more difficult to isolate the determinant components in a single action of a small group; and it is virtually impossible to generalize about large-scale collective actions and processes throughout the whole of history.

To take one practical illustration: the Marxist interpretation of *imperialism* is that it is primarily caused by economic interests and rivalries, and that war in the capitalist era is the culmination of such imperialist rivalries. There have undoubtedly been manifestations of imperialism in history, ancient as well as modern, whose origins can be traced to economic factors—some of the classical imperialist expansion of advanced capitalist nations like Holland, England, and France in the eighteenth and early nineteenth centuries can be attributed chiefly to economic forces. It is also possible to set forth examples of minor wars, in antiquity as in more recent times, that have been primarily motivated by economic interests and conflicts.

The economic interpretation, nevertheless, misses the core of the great and vital conflicts of history.

The Greeks who fought the Persians almost 2500 years ago did so, not primarily to protect Athenian investments and trade interests in Asia Minor, but because they knew that the victory of Persia would mean the end of Greek civilization. Persian victory would undoubtedly have entailed serious economic and financial losses for the Greeks, but the main effect would have been the destruction of the Greek way of life, its devotion to the search for truth, and its appreciation of human values. Because the whole fabric of Western civilization is unthinkable without its Greek source, Persian victory over Greece would have meant the spiritual and intellectual "Asianization" of Europe.

To take more recent illustrations, the core of the conflict in World Wars I and II was not the protection of British investments in Africa or of American loans to Britain and France, but the more fundamental issue of whether freedom—religious, intellectual, political, racial— was to survive, or whether totalitarian militarism was to rule the world. Again, there is no doubt that a German victory in World War I or II would have entailed profound economic losses for the vanquished, but the economic effects would have been relatively minor compared with the effects of forced reversion to a way of life based on a denial of the Western tradition.

Finally, the present conflict between communist imperialism and the free world cannot be explained in Marxian economic terms, according to which imperialism is the last phase of an advanced and mature economy with an abundance of capital that it seeks to invest in less developed areas. From the economic viewpoint, the Soviet Union and Red China are hungry for capital, suffering from its scarcity rather than abundance. Their imperialism is motivated by noneconomic drives: the *political* aim of world domination.

What makes communist imperialism so serious a concern to the rest of the world is precisely—contrary to Marxist logic—its noneconomic character: the fact that its main weapons are tanks and subversion. The Hungarian Revolution of 1956 clearly showed that Soviet imperialism can ultimately rely only on tanks and guns, and not on economic, or much less ideological, penetration. The repression of the Tibetan rebellion by Red China in 1959 and her conquest of Indian border areas in 1959-1962 showed that Red China, too, ultimately relies on armed force as the primary instrument of imperialist expansion.

What the Marxist-communist interpretation misses in the analyses of major conflicts is, first, the element of *power* (which is often the cause rather than the effect of economic advantage), and second, the clash of *value systems,* which are frequently more important to people than economic interests, regardless of whether the values concerned

are specifically political, religious, intellectual, or—in a wider sense—
the symbolic expression of a whole way of life.

In fact, where conflicts of interest are primarily economic, compromise will usually be relatively easy; it is where more deeply felt values
are at stake, such as individual liberty, freedom of religion, or national independence, that compromise becomes more difficult.

**DYNAMICS
OF SOCIAL
CHANGE**

Before Marx, basic social change was
thought to be the result of the work of
great political leaders, legislators, and
pioneering reformers. Marx rejects the
traditional emphasis on the force of
personality as the principal agent of
important social change, and looks for an explanation in impersonal
economic causes. The two key concepts that Marx uses in approaching the problem of basic social change are, first, the *forces of production* and, second, the *relations of production*. The clash between
these two is the deeper cause of basic social change, as expressed by
Marx in his *Critique of Political Economy* (1859): "At a certain
stage of their development the material productive forces of society
come into contradiction with the existing productive relationships,
or, what is but a legal expression for these, with the property relationships within which they have moved before. From forms of development of the productive forces these relationships are transformed into their fetters. Then an epoch of social revolution opens.
With the change in the economic foundation the whole vast superstructure is more or less rapidly transformed."

The Marxist conception of the *forces of production* expresses *man's
relation to nature,* and is essentially what we would call today technological and scientific *know-how*. Marx's notion of the *relations of
production* expresses *man's relation to man,* and encompasses all that
we would include today under the term *social institutions*. Seen in
these more modern terms, what Marx roughly suggests is that in every
social-economic system there is at first a balance between knowledge
and social organization, but gradually a disequilibrium or lag develops
between available scientific knowledge and existent social institutions.
Our scientific knowledge grows faster than our social wisdom.

This lag is the more modern, and broader, version of Marx's more
specific lag between the forces of production and the relations of production. Since the economic aspects of society are for Marx its chief

determining factor, it is not surprising that he reduces the general phenomenon of the lag between knowledge and wisdom to the more specific lag between forces of production and relations of production.

Thus, to provide an illustration in line with the Marxist pattern, when new productive forces developed within the productive relations of the feudal system, social revolution was, according to Marx, inevitable because the productive relations of feudalism (property relations, market controls, internal customs and tariffs, monetary instability) did not permit the utilization of the newly developing productive forces of industrial capitalism.

The capitalist system, having run its cycle, now shows the same tendency to rigidity, Marx holds, and it is due to meet the same fate when its productive forces (the capacity to produce) have outstripped its productive relations (law of private property, production for private profit). Like the social systems preceding it, capitalism thus will eventually stand in the way of scientific knowledge and will not permit technological resources to be fully employed.

What has doomed all historically known forms of economic organization, according to Marx, is the fact that when new productive forces develop, the existing productive relations—i.e., the existing social institutions—stand in the way of their proper utilization. Each system thus eventually becomes wasteful in terms of the creative potentialities that have developed in its womb but are not permitted to be born and grow. Only public ownership of the means of production can, according to Marx, bring into existence a new system of productive relations based on production for common use rather than for private profit that will match the tremendous forces of production actually or potentially known to man. In other words, man's capacity to produce will find full expression only in a social system in which production is limited by scarce resources and incomplete knowledge, and not by such faulty social institutions as production for private profit based on the private ownership of the means of production.

Marx's insight that man's knowledge of physical nature ("forces of production") grows faster than his wisdom in creating social institutions ("relations of production") is highly important in understanding a vital source of social tension and conflict both within and between nations.

What distinguishes Marx from non-Marxists is his insistence that *basic social change*—caused by the excessive lag between advanced scientific knowledge and retrograde social institutions—can be brought about *only by revolution;* whereas non-Marxists affirm that the necessary changes can be effected by peaceful means.

REVOLUTION

THE ONLY

WAY OUT

In the *Communist Manifesto,* Marx explains why revolution is the only method of basic social transformation. When technological know-how ("forces of production") begins to outstrip the existing social, legal, and political institutions ("relations of production"), the owners of the means of production do not politely step aside to allow history to run its inevitable course. Since the ideology of the ruling class reflects the existing economic system, the owners of the means of production sincerely believe that the existing system is economically the most efficient, socially the most equitable, and philosophically the most harmonious with the laws of nature and the will of whatever god they venerate.

Marx penetratingly denies that the individual feudal landowner or industrial capitalist obstructs social change out of selfish greed: the resistance of the ruling class to change is so obstinate—making revolution finally inevitable—precisely because it identifies its own values with universally valid ones. The ruling class will, therefore, mobilize all the instruments of the legal, political, and ideological superstructure to block the growth of the forces that represent the potentially more progressive economic system. For this reason, Marx states early in the *Communist Manifesto,* the "history of all hitherto existing society is the history of class struggles."

Marx could find no instance in history in which a major social and economic system freely abdicated to its successor. On the assumption that the future will resemble the past, the communists, as the *Communist Manifesto* says, "openly declare that their ends can be attained only by the forcible overthrow of all existing social conditions."

This is the crucial tenet of Marxism-Leninism, and the one that most clearly and irreconcilably distinguishes it from democracy.

Marx had no clear-cut notion of how the political transformation from capitalism to communism would come about. Though in the *Communist Manifesto,* as throughout most of his other statements on the problem, he believed in the need for revolution, he was occasionally less dogmatic. Speaking in 1872 at a public meeting in Amsterdam following the Congress of the International, Marx conceded that the working class can travel on different roads in its quest for power: "We know that we must take into consideration the institutions, the habits and customs of different regions, and we do not deny that there are countries like America, England, and—if I knew your institutions better I would perhaps add Holland—where the workers can attain their objective by peaceful means. But such is not the case in all other countries."

Marx never fully pursued the implications of this distinction, and the orthodox opinion of Marxism-communism has remained that fundamental social and economic change is impossible except by class war, violence, and revolution.

In the early eighteen thirties there occurred two major revolutions that Marx failed to appraise properly. In 1832, the passage of the Reform Act in England meant that the government of the nation would thenceforth be shared by the aristocracy and the middle classes, with the weight constantly shifting in favor of the latter.

At about the same time, the Jacksonian revolution in the United States effected a similar peaceful shift in class power, by bringing the men from the backwoods into American politics and successfully challenging the supremacy of the gentlemen from Virginia and New England who had treated the government of the United States as their God-given preserve.

These changes in Britain and the United States were more than just political victories: they inaugurated a permanent shift in the distribution of social and economic power in both nations, the kind of basic change that Marx had in mind. When revolution swept all over Europe in 1848, England was spared because the aims of the revolutions of 1848—winning for the middle class its proper share of social and political power—had already been peacefully obtained by the British middle class in 1832.

If Marx had accorded the political factor its due weight, if he had fully grasped the importance of the Reform Act in England and of the Jacksonian revolution in the United States, he might have realized that socialism, too, might be accomplished without violence in countries that possessed democratic traditions strong enough to absorb far-reaching social and economic changes without resorting to civil war. A recognition of the cultural and political factors in the equation of social change would have amounted, however, to a virtual abandonment of the central position of Marx: that history is the history of class wars, and that ruling classes always defend their positions to the bitter end.

When Marx allowed, occasionally, that in countries like England, the United States, or Holland, violent revolution would be unnecessary in transforming capitalism into the classless proletarian society, it was obvious that what the three countries had in common was *political democracy,* supported by democratic habits and institutions in all kinds of human relations, whether political or not. Whether the range of Marx's exceptions should now be enlarged or not thus depends on whether democracy has spread in the world since Marx's death.

In any case, Marx's concession that in a few politically advanced countries revolution might be unnecessary has always caused the communists a good deal of headache. Lenin took up the question in *State and Revolution* (1918), his best known and most influential political tract, claiming that by 1917 "this exception made by Marx is no longer valid" because England and the United States had developed bureaucratic institutions "to which everything is subordinated and which trample everything under foot." Between 1872 and 1917, both England and the United States broadened the suffrage and moved steadily in the direction of more political and social reform. In 1884, only one year after Marx's death, a British Liberal leader, Sir William Harcourt, stated, "We are all socialists now," indicating the acceptance of basic social and economic reform by all parties.

Since the plain historical record of the years 1872-1917 seemed to contradict Lenin's dogma, it was necessary to rewrite history. Far from admitting that England and the United States had moved toward more political and social democracy since 1872, Lenin maintained that both countries had become more repressive, authoritarian, and plutocratic. To Sir William Harcourt's "We are all socialists now," Lenin would have replied, "You are all bloodthirsty, militaristic lackeys of Wall Street."

Since 1917, the communist case has progressively become weaker. In the United States, there has been the peaceful revolution of social reform, which started early in the century with Theodore Roosevelt's Square Deal, was continued by Woodrow Wilson's New Freedom, and culminated in Franklin D. Roosevelt's New Deal.

In Britain, Lloyd George's "People's Budget" of 1909 gave the propertied classes a foretaste of things to come. In 1945, the victory of the Labor Party at the polls was more than a mere electoral triumph. Just as 1832 meant the incorporation of the middle classes into the government of the nation, 1945 meant the same thing for the working classes in Britain. Whether the Labor Party is henceforth in office or in opposition, the British working class will remain an active partner in the business of governing the nation.

In the light of these facts, the only way left open to communist interpretation is to rewrite history. In the communist mythology, the New Deal was not the revolt of the little man against Big Business, but a clever plot of Big Business to keep itself in power. Similarly, the communists deny that the British Labor Party is socialist, and claim that it is actually a front for the propertied classes.

The relentless communist insistence on revolution as the only way of basic social change violates Marxist doctrine at one central point. According to Marx, the conditions of man's existence determine his consciousness, and social change is, therefore, not the product of mere will and free choice. Where the conditions of society permit peaceful change from private to public ownership of the means of production, the use of force and subversion is, in a deeply Marxian sense, un-Marxian.

The communist dogma of universal revolution and dictatorship is in harmony with Marx's theory of consciousness only in societies in which the conditions of social and political life have created a general distrust in the possibility of peaceful change; it is out of harmony in nations whose democratic consciousness is the result, not of paper constitutions, but of the conditions of their existence. By insisting on universal revolution and dictatorship as the one and only method of change, communists in fact proclaim the un-Marxian doctrine that, regardless of historical, cultural, social, economic, and political conditions, a uniform consciousness—the creed of communism—can be imposed everywhere by sheer force.

There is a similar, reverse dogmatism maintained by anticommunist adherents of free enterprise, who would like to see it practiced in the whole world. They, too, violate elementary common sense and historical experience. Whether a society is likely to operate a capitalist economy is not a matter of pure logic and choice, but the result of historical environment, cultural heritage, social institutions, and political ideologies. Thus, in 1900 it would have been easy to predict that basic changes in Britain or the United States would occur without revolution, and that such changes would be accompanied by violence and revolution in countries like Russia or China.

At present, it is often possible to predict whether change will be possible with or without violence. Yet there are countries, such as Italy in Europe, or India in Asia, where prediction is difficult because the balance of democratic versus undemocratic habits and traditions is not easy to define. Clearly, in view of the fact that such borderline countries exist, no general prediction based on dogma—be it communist or anticommunist dogma—is likely to be accurate. Every prediction is a question of investigating each particular situation rather than of applying preconceived universal laws of development.

Usually, correct theory is a guide to effective policy, and faulty theory is punished by practical failure. Where the communist concept of revolutionary change is supported by the underlying facts of social and cultural development—as in the economically and politically backward areas of Europe, Asia, Africa, and South America—either communist revolution has succeeded or communist spearheads have penetrated the body politic in preparation for the conquest of power. Where the anticommunist position has been theoretically sound, where democratic conditions of existence make revolutionary change unappealing and unnecessary—as in northwestern Europe, North America, Australia, New Zealand, Uruguay, and Israel—anticommunist policy has been successful.

If the world today is divided into two, with one orbit led by the United States and the other by the Soviet Union and Red China, this political division generally follows the division into two ways of life: in one orbit, social change can be transacted more or less peacefully; whereas in the other, human relations are not yet established on a basis of consent. Where—as in Italy or India—these internal conditions are not clearly defined, the external political commitment is uncertain also.

The economic aid program is the indirect method of the United States to counteract communism by helping economically retarded nations so that they do not have to look to communist revolution as the way out. Subversion, infiltration, and civil war are the communist methods of preventing underdeveloped societies from evolving peacefully into more advanced social and economic conditions. If India, for example, can show the backward areas throughout the world that it can develop economically while retaining political liberty, it will win the race with China for leadership in Asia. If India stagnates economically, and China progresses, the communists will have convinced Asia that peaceful progress is impossible, and that totalitarian communism is the only road to economic and political-military power.

ECONOMIC CONTRADICTIONS OF CAPITALISM

The end of capitalism will be brought about, Marx argues, not by "subversive conspiracies" of professional revolutionaries, but by the same inexorable laws of social development and change that destroyed previous systems. Marx uses, first, the "grave-digger" theory: the more capitalism succeeds, the more capitalist enterprise is organized in *large-scale* units and the more it inevitably creates its own grave-digger, a class-conscious proletariat. Big Labor inevitably follows Big Business.

The capitalist class has no way of escaping the dilemma of rearing its own destroyer as it goes along: the *law of the falling profit rate* (which is not to be confused with the absolute amount of profit) makes that impossible. Marx's prediction of the declining profit rate was based on the assumption that, under the capitalist system of production, the entrepreneurial class would steadily accumulate more and more capital; the lessened scarcity of capital would then inevitably be reflected in the decline of the price (interest) and return (profit) of capital.

There can be no disagreement—because the facts speak too plainly —that the absolute amount of profits has risen immensely since Marx, and is constantly rising.

What about Marx's prediction that the *rate* of profit (and of interest) would go down because capital would become more abundant?

Here, too, the prediction has not come true. During the depression of the 1930's, the rates of profit and interest were low, and seemed to confirm Marx's forecast. Yet in the 1950's, as in earlier periods of prosperity, the rates of interest and profit again reached new highs, thus disproving Marx.

Contrary to Marx, the facts of economic history do not support his "law of the falling profit rate." Marx made his erroneous prediction because he looked primarily at the *supply* side of capital: more and more capital is constantly created and accumulated in the capitalist system, and increased supply of a good leads to a lower price—provided the demand remains the same. Yet this is exactly what did not happen. The reason for the high interest rates (price of capital) in the 1950's and 1960's is that, despite an all-time high in the supply of capital, the *demand for capital has grown even faster* since too many companies simultaneously want fresh capital for the improvement, expansion, and building of productive facilities.

The price of capital (interest) or return of capital (profit) are subject to the classical economic law of supply and demand, and not to any predetermined Marxian law of constant decline. Whenever the demand for capital outruns the supply, the rate of interest goes up, and the price of capital behaves like any other price.

The reason Marx overlooked the importance of the demand side in the capital market was his expectation (and hope) that the capitalist system would gradually lose its vitality and growth, thus requiring less new capital for investment. This, however, has not happened.

Finally, Marx also underestimated the role of technological progress. Capitalism not only constantly produces more capital, but *more efficient capital*. More available capital need not lead to lower rates of profit if the capital is more efficient.

In a stationary economy in which there is little or no technological innovation, more capital might automatically lead to lower rates of profit and interest. In a progressive economy in which the productivity of capital is constantly raised, profits and the rate of profit may go up although the absolute amount of available capital is also rising.

Moreover, technological innovation strengthens the demand side in the capital market because new technologies require large capital investments, thus counterbalancing the effects of increased capital on the supply side. The current capital investment needed to create a new job in the average American industry is well over $20,000, and it is much higher in electronics, chemicals, and petroleum. Therefore, as long as capitalism continues to progress technologically, the effects of increased capital resources will not, as Marx assumed, depress either the absolute volume of profit or the rate of profit.

Since Marx's main objection to capitalism was its inefficiency as well as its injustice, experience has contradicted his forecasts on that score, too. The per capita consumption in the United States is still about 4-5 times higher than in the Soviet Union. As to technological innovation, the capitalist countries still are in most cases the creators, and the communist, the borrowers and imitators.

Marx also stated that capitalists would seek to stem the impact of the law of the falling profit rate in two ways: first, they would constantly seek to "rationalize" industry, or make it technologically more efficient. This would eliminate the less efficient enterprises and would lead to concentration of economic power, large-scale industrial organization, and increasing proletarianization. Second, they would invest capital in underdeveloped countries, where the return for capital (profit) is still very high. This device, Marx points out, only delays, but does not avert, the inevitable doom. In the colonial country, too, capital becomes increasingly more abundant, a native capitalist class develops, threatened by its own proletariat, and the law of the falling profit rate makes the imperialist solution of the capitalist dilemma at home unfeasible.

Contrary to Marx, the flow of private investments from industrially advanced nations has not been guided primarily by the economic consideration of high profits, but by the political consideration of safety and stability. In 1963, American investments abroad were about $37

billion. The Western Hemisphere, in which American capital has traditionally felt safest, accounts for $22 billion, over half of which is in
Canada alone, and Western Europe accounts for $8 billion, half of
which is in Britain. In Asia and the Pacific, the trend of American
investments has been toward Australia, Japan, and the Philippines
rather than toward more underdeveloped nations like India and Indonesia. This is a typical illustration of Marx's underestimation of the
political factor in economics.

Another source of tension that undermines the vitality of the
capitalist system, according to Marx, is *unemployment*. In Marx's
own time, industry expanded at an enormous rate, and there was a
chronic shortage of labor. Yet Marx foresaw that the maldistribution
of wealth and income under capitalism would lead to periodic crises
of unemployment. The depression decade of 1929-1939 seemed to
confirm Marx's prediction, and there was severe unemployment right
up to 1939 when the preparation for war gradually eliminated it.

After World War II, the growth of welfare state policies in the
major capitalist countries led to the recognition of full employment as
a primary social objective. Also, the cold war, followed by hot war
in Korea, led to relatively full employment based, to a considerable
extent, on rearmament. Should the Western liberal capitalist societies
be freed some day from the burden of armament, it will be seen
whether the lessons of Keynesian economics combined with the objectives of welfare state policies will suffice to banish the scourge of
unemployment from free societies. In the United States, unemployment has been higher than in any other major economy, averaging
about six per cent in the decade of 1954-1963. Idle manpower
combined with idle plant resulted in an average annual loss of about
nine per cent of production during that period.

Marx also predicted that two other developments would distinte-
grate the capitalist system: the *concentration of economic power* and,
as a direct result, the *increasing proletarianization* of society. There
is little doubt that, compared with earlier stages of industrial development, the contemporary capitalist economy shows impressive features
of concentration. Yet it is doubtful whether the tendency toward concentration in the capitalist system keeps on forever, or whether after
a certain point the forces of competition begin to catch up with excessive concentration.

Also, Marx did not foresee that in advanced capitalist nations concentration of management might be mitigated by important counterforces: the spreading ownership of industry among large numbers of

persons through the holding of shares of corporate businesses, and the
growing control of business managements by government, public
opinion, and labor unions.

<table>
<tr><td>THE ROLE
OF THE
SALARIAT</td><td>Marx's prediction of the inevitable pro-
letarianization of society in a capitalist
economy has been very largely dis-
proved by events.</td></tr>
</table>

THE ROLE
OF THE
SALARIAT

Marx's prediction of the inevitable proletarianization of society in a capitalist
economy has been very largely disproved by events.

In the initial phases of industrial
development, under capitalism or any
other system, the industrial working class, Marx's "proletariat," constantly increases at the expense of artisans, landless peasants, and
other social groups whose members seek employment in the expanding factories and mines. In a later and more advanced phase of industrial development, however, the industrial working class begins to
decline in proportion to the total population, though it still continues
to increase in absolute numbers. What Marx did not foresee was the
enormous growth in an advanced economy that would create employment, but not of the proletarian type.

In the United States, for example, the volume of industrial production and the number of persons employed in industry have increased
tremendously since 1900, yet the proportion of the industrial work-

ing class in the total work force has consistently declined. This has been due to two reasons.

First, within industry itself, there has been an increasing shift of employment from blue-collar workers (Marx's "proletariat") to white-collar workers. In 1947, the percentage of white-collar personnel, or "salariat" (professional and executive employees, sales personnel, office workers), in manufacturing was 16 per cent of all employees; in 1962, white-collar personnel had risen to 26 per cent of all employees in manufacturing. The number of blue-collar workers in industry in 1947-1962 not only has sharply declined proportionately, but has not even maintained its absolute size, despite the tremendous increase of industrial production: whereas in 1947, the number of blue-collar (or production) workers in industry was 13 million, in 1962 it had dropped to 12.4 million. Both technological progress and automation have reduced the number of workers needed to produce a given quantity of goods, such as steel, coal, or automobiles.

COMPOSITION OF THE LABOR FORCE
IN THE UNITED STATES

By Occupation Group, 1910-1962

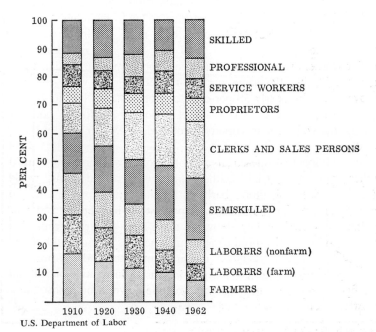

U.S. Department of Labor

The second reason for the relative growth of white-collar workers, or the salariat, is the rapid growth of employment in enterprises that produce services rather than physical goods, such as the government, motion pictures, radio and television, journalism, education, advertising, and the thousand and one new forms of service and entertainment made possible by the worker's increase in income and leisure.

This new type of economy is called *service economy* to distinguish it from the industrial economy that preceded it. Marx foresaw the transition from the agrarian to the industrial economy, but in all his writings there is not an inkling of the service economy that follows the industrial economy.

In 1870, about 75 per cent of all American workers were in industries that were producing goods. This percentage has gone down steadily over the years, until in 1962 only about 42 per cent of all workers were engaged in such industries. As the American economy becomes more productive, more and more people are engaged in service industries, providing for the amenities and luxuries of life rather than for its bare necessities.

By contrast, in 1962, 75 per cent of the Soviet labor force were producing goods, and 25 per cent, services—the relative composition of the American labor force in 1870. Yet the same trend operates in the Soviet Union, too, and as her economy progresses, the proportion of persons employed in the service industries is rising.

The intensity of the shift from blue-collar to white-collar employment in the United States becomes even more striking if we look at the absolute figures. Between 1947 and 1962, the number of blue-collar workers rose by only 3 per cent, or from 23.6 million to 24.3 million. During the same period, the number of white-collar employees rose by nearly 50 per cent, or from 20.2 million to 29.9 million. Thus, of the total increase of about 10 million in both categories, the white-collar workers accounted for 97 per cent of the new jobs.

In addition to white-collar and blue-collar workers, there are two other groups that fit into neither—farm workers and service workers (cooks, waiters, janitors, barbers, hospital attendants). These two groups are numerically not as important as blue-collar and white-collar workers, but they show the same over-all trend from goods-producing to service-producing employment as living standards rise. In 1953, service workers for the first time exceeded the number of farm workers, and are consistently increasing in relative and absolute strength, whereas farm workers have gone down in both absolute and relative strength.

The accompanying chart illustrates the growth of the salariat and other changes in the composition of the American labor force in the years 1910-1962. Most striking are the proportionate doubling of clerical and sales persons from 10.2 per cent of the total labor force in 1910 to 21.3 in 1962, the sharp drop of the combined total of farm laborers and unskilled industrial laborers from 29.2 per cent to 8.5 per cent, and the increase of the proportion of semi-skilled and skilled workers from 26.4 per cent to 30.5 per cent. Politically, the latter is very important because the skilled workers and the foremen generally look upon themselves as middle class and tend to be more conservative in their political outlook. In 1956, 56 per cent of skilled workers voted Republican, but only 46 per cent of unskilled workers did so.

The year 1956 was a milestone of American economic development; for the first time in American history, or in that of any nation, the *number of persons engaged in the production of goods* was *smaller than the number of persons employed in the performance of services.* Subsequently, the same changes occurred in the Swedish and British economies where more people now produce services than goods.

If we assume that leisure time will continue to expand, that government activity is going to stay on a high plateau and probably will increase, that people will earn more and spend more, then it may be safely predicted that the changes in the American economy from 1960 to 2000 will be along similar lines as in the years 1910-1960. In that case, Marx's prediction about the proletarianization of the labor force will be even more emphatically shown to be false since an increasingly larger proportion of the American labor force will be engaged in the performance of services rather than in the production of goods.

By contrast, where capitalism exists only in a rudimentary stage, as in the underdeveloped countries of Asia and Africa, the salariat is numerically and politically very weak, and communist infiltration stands a much better chance of achieving its objectives, as has been proved in the past.

What is politically important in this development is that *the salaried person tends to identify himself with the middle and upper class rather than with the working class,* even if his income is below that of the worker. This is wholly contrary to Marx's expectations and predictions. Marx assumed—necessarily, from his interpretation of human action—that the transformation of the independent middle class into a dependent salaried class would automatically change the outlook of the old middle class from bourgeois to proletarian. Yet the new middle class of the salariat has generally refused to join the ranks of the organized working class. In the Congressional elections of 1962, 49 per cent of white-collar employees voted for the Democratic party, as compared with 69 per cent of members of labor unions.

This refusal has been particularly marked in societies with rigid class lines; but even in the United States, with its more fluid class lines, the salaried man (or woman) who earns $400 a month is generally politically more conservative than the wage earner who earns $125 a week or more. Because salary earners have failed to identify themselves psychologically with the working class, they have very largely remained outside the ranks of organized labor. In the United States, the labor movement has been able to organize the workers in industry and to a lesser extent in agriculture, but has found it very difficult to organize teachers, clerks, civil servants, and other groups of white-collar employees.

The political problems posed by the rise of the salariat are not confined to industrial development under capitalism; they also appear under communism. In its first phase of industrialization, Russia witnessed a tremendous growth of her industrial proletariat. But as the Soviet Union entered a second phase of industrialization, a new salariat began to develop, with a way of life of its own, and with its own ideas, ideas different from those of the working class. Because under communism the state has been so much more responsible for developing industry than under capitalism, the number of government workers and white-collar employees has increased proportionately faster than the number of factory workers.

Despite communist denials, class lines are beginning to crystallize in communist Russia and the other communist states, and one important line of differentiation is that between white-collar and factory worker, a distinction not necessarily based on differences of income. The influence of the white-collar group—"intelligentsia" in Russia— is constantly rising at the expense of the working class, as can be seen in the changing social composition of Soviet political bodies, university students, and other key groups of social importance.

As long as the Soviet leaders adhere to Marxist-Leninist propaganda, they will find that time works against them, and that the slogans of Marxism-Leninism will not fit a society in which the white-collar class rather than the proletariat sets the style of life and thought. Thus, a class struggle along orthodox lines is beginning to take shape in communist societies undergoing industrialization, and— as in capitalist countries—proletariat and salariat do not generally find themselves on the same side of the barricades.

The first explosions in the communist world took place in Czechoslovakia and Poland in the spring of 1953; they were followed by the major rebellion in Eastern Germany of June 17, 1953, the uprising of Polish workers in Poznan in June, 1956, the Hungarian Revolution of October-November, 1956, and the victory of "national communism" in Poland late in 1956.

The driving force of rebellion in all these instances was not the bourgeois middle class, as might have been expected from the prophecies of Marxism-Leninism, but the industrial workers, who could no longer bear the ruthless exploitation by the communist bosses in the party and government.

This kind of class war—proletariat against salariat—was never foreseen by Marx and Lenin, and communists today cannot deal with it intelligently and effectively; they must deny its very existence as incompatible with their dogma.

LENIN'S
CONTRIBUTION TO
THE THEORY
OF COMMUNISM

The nature and deeper meaning of philosophical ideas can frequently be inferred from their appeal and impact. In the countries of Western Europe and the United States, the inevitability of revolution as preached by Karl Marx has had little impact; the liberal tradition in those countries keeps the door open for peaceful change. Although many social reformers have agreed with some of Marx's indictments of capitalism, they have refused to embrace a philosophy of class hatred and war to remedy social injustices. Where democratic habits and institutions prevail, the underlying psychological tie in social relations is sympathy and affection; in such a climate, men and women are unwilling to accept a philosophy of hatred and violence.

Particularly in the United States, Marxism has proved itself a failure as far as wide popular appeal is concerned. In the last century the frontier seemed to many to offer utopia here and now, whereas the Marxian utopia lay in the distant future, separated from the present by a sea of blood. Also, Marxism has made little progress in the United States because it attacks not only the economic foundations of capitalism, but the very heart of American democracy.

In only two major countries did the ideas of Marx take root in the nineteenth century: Germany and Russia. Despite the façade of representative institutions, imperial Germany was in fact an autocracy that did not permit genuine government by the people. The Germans followed the philosophy of Hegel (although Marx claimed that he had turned Hegel upside down). Hegel had asserted that the *state* was an objective reality, and that its laws, like those of nature, were susceptible of being *understood,* but not *changed,* by man. Marx followed the cast of Hegel's thought by claiming that the laws of *society,* in respect to its nature and evolution, have the same scientific validity that Hegel had claimed for those of the state.

By contrast, the liberal philosophical tradition of the West rejects the Hegel-Marx conception that human reason can only understand the laws of the state and society, and affirms the possibility of rational control and creative change of social and political institutions. The experience of free government is the psychological background for this affirmative, activist philosophy, whereas the experience of autocratic government in Germany provided the psychological background for the determinism of Hegel and Marx. In an environment of mental and political enslavement, man is prone to think of himself as being small and helpless, and his emotional pattern will find philosophical expression in determinism. Such a philosophy assures him that his own helplessness is not a personal misfortune, but a principle of world order.

In nineteenth-century Russia, conditions for the acceptance of Marxian ideas were even more favorable than in imperial Germany. Whereas the latter paid homage to virtue by at least adopting the forms and formalities of representative institutions, Russian tsarism long recoiled from such hypocrisy on the ground that pretenses, if practiced long enough, might easily turn into second nature.

Of all the major states in Europe, Russia was first in illiteracy, economic backwardness, religious obscurantism, oppression of minorities, political despotism, and social inequality. Marx's prophecy, clothed in the language of scientific magic, of the eventual liberation of man from bondage and oppression through revolutionary action, made a strong impression on Russian radicals. *Das Kapital,* Marx's *magnum opus,* was translated into Russian before any other language; oddly enough, the tsarist censorship permitted the publication of the work on the ground that it would not be read by many because of its difficult style.

Among the Russian followers of Marx, Lenin (1870-1924) was both the leading theoretician and the most agile and effective practical politician.

Lenin's contribution to the theory of communism, perhaps the only one he made, is to be found in his pamphlet, *What Is To Be Done?* (1902).

Just as Hitler openly revealed his intentions to the world in *Mein*

Kampf (and was not believed until it was too late), Lenin has left in his writings an accurate blueprint of communist goals and the strategy and tactics to achieve them. Much discomfort and sorrow could have been spared the world if the basic ideas of Lenin had been more widely known and accepted at their face value.

Lenin's most important single contribution to the theory of Marxism is his concept of the *professional revolutionary.*

Marx, tinged by nineteenth-century respect for man's capacity to think for himself, had assumed that the working class would *spontaneously* develop its class-consciousness in the daily struggle for economic existence, and that its leadership would largely come from its own ranks. Lenin had much less confidence in man, even if he

"Fellow-comrades and undercover agents of the F.B.I. . . ."

belonged to the select class, the proletariat. Communist activity, said Lenin, is to be carried on along two lines. First, workers are to form labor organizations with primarily economic objectives, operating openly, legally, and as publicly as conditions allow.

Side by side with such organizations, there are to be small groups of professional revolutionaries, patterned after the army and the police, highly select and entirely secret. Lenin did not care whether the professional revolutionary was of proletarian origin or not, as long as he did his job well. The organizations of the professional revolutionaries must be highly centralized, Lenin went on, and must constantly guide and supervise the open communist-led economic associations—the trade unions, the cooperatives, and the rest.

In particular, Lenin advised the professional revolutionaries to *infiltrate* and form cells in all existing social, political, educational, and economic bodies in society, be they schools, churches, labor unions, or political parties. Above all, he advised infiltration of the *armed forces,* the *police,* and the *government.*

Lenin also made it perfectly clear that communists should engage in *illegal* work even where legal Communist parties are permitted. He thought that legal opportunities should be utilized to the fullest extent, but he specifically advised communist activists to work through *front organizations,* constantly changing names and officers of organizations, and always keeping the ultimate objective in mind: revolutionary seizure of power.

In particular, the secret nucleus of professional revolutionaries is responsible for the recruitment and training of spies, saboteurs, and agents for all other activities relating to intelligence, foreign and domestic. When Gerhart Eisler first came to public attention in the United States in 1947, his name was unknown, not only to the general public, but even to communists. Yet Eisler had been the secret head of the American communists for years and was in charge of all party activities, legal as well as illegal. The official head of the party, William Z. Foster, was just a figurehead whose main function was to divert the attention of the public and the government from the real leader and his activities.

When the Canadian spy ring was broken up in 1945, it was established that several secret communist spy rings, each independent of the others, operated in Canada under the leadership of professional revolutionaries, many of whom had little connection with official, legal Communist party activities.

From the testimony of former communist agents it is evident that one of the first things a recruit into the inner ring of communist leaders has to do is to break all connection with overt Communist party or front groups, stop reading the party press, and lead the life of a solid, respectable bourgeois. There are bridges between the legal Communist parties and the inner rings of spies and agents of the professional revolutionaries since necessity often compels the choice of such agents from party ranks; ideally, however, the two sets of organizations are to be kept separate. Therefore what appears as the overt leadership of Communist parties is but a front for bosses à la Eisler, men who are unknown to the public and even to the ostensible communist leaders in many cases, and who report directly to Moscow.

Outlawing the Communist party is therefore no answer to the problem of how to deal with communism; the hard core of communist leadership and activity is always underground, even when the law permits Communist parties to operate above ground. Since there are always some links between the legal party and the inner nucleus of the professional revolutionaries, a legally functioning party is an asset, small as it may be, to counterespionage. It is probably for this reason that J. Edgar Hoover, director of the Federal Bureau of Investigation, has not advocated the outlawing of the Communist Party of the United States.

The Leninist approach to communist theory and strategy has been most effective in underdeveloped countries. Marx thought that communist revolution would first occur in economically advanced countries like Germany and England, where capitalism was mature—with one foot already in the grave, as it were. Lenin agreed with Marx that communist revolution was inevitable, but he asked: why wait until capitalism has matured? Why not smash it where it is weakest, that is, in economically backward areas like Russia and Asian or African nations. It is a tribute to Lenin's political genius that he saw the importance of underdeveloped countries over half a century ago, whereas today many people in the West still do not grasp the crucial role of the underdeveloped areas in the balance of world power.

Thinking about the spread of communism in military terms, Lenin argued that Western capitalism had to be attacked in its "soft underbelly" of Asia, Africa, and Latin America if a frontal attack on Western Europe and North America were not practical. It is a matter of record that communism has not spread significantly in the "mature capitalist societies" of Western Europe and North America, but has achieved its greatest successes of conquest of power or penetration in countries like China, Cuba, North Vietnam, Laos, and Indonesia. In such underdeveloped areas society is very poorly organized. Even the strongest organization—the government—generally rests on shaky foundations. The mass of the populations consists of poor peasants, living in isolated villages, with inadequate means of communication. There are few or no independent labor unions and practically no urban middle class—the backbone of anticommunist resistance in more advanced countries.

Where society lacks cohesion, the Leninist concept of the professional revolutionary is of strategic importance in the communist aim of conquest. All that is necessary for successful communist infiltration and conquest is a comparatively small force of well-organized revolutionaries who can deal skillfully with an unorganized mass. A small but disciplined army unit can control a numerically larger but undisciplined and unorganized civilian population. So, too, the communists believe that in the underdeveloped areas they can take control with a relatively small force, provided it is well organized and disciplined.

COMMUNIST
DOCTRINE AND
POLICY TODAY

Since Lenin's death in 1924, there has been no new addition or modification of basic Marxist-Leninist thought. Stalin, who ruled Russia from 1924 to his death in 1953, was stronger in practical administration and organizational ability than in theorizing. Most of Stalin's writings are but a rehash of Marx and Lenin, adapted to the momentary needs of his dictatorship. The core of the Stalinist summary of communist long-term strategy, largely followed by his successors today, consists in the concept of the *four basic tensions* underlying our present-day world:

(1) The tension between capitalists and proletarians everywhere
(2) The tension between imperialist states and colonies
(3) The tension between rival imperialist states
(4) The tension between communist states and capitalist states

This conception of the four basic tensions, far from being a mere exercise in semantic classification, actually provides a clear blueprint for communist strategy and tactics. It is virtually impossible to open a newspaper without seeing some evidence of communist application of these concepts to practical issues and policies.

(1) The *tension between capitalists and proletarians* is the classical conception of Marxism and goes back to Marx's belief in the contradiction between forces of production and relations of production. Capitalism today represents in communist propaganda the forces of production, the technological and scientific know-how, which cannot be fully utilized under the capitalist system of production for profit. The proletariat represents symbolically the relations of production, a new set of social institutions to be fully established after the overthrow of capitalism, allowing for the fullest use of all available knowledge and resources in a communist economic system, in which social institutions will aid, and not hamper, the productive process.

The great depression of 1929-1933 convinced the communists that capitalism is in a state of hopeless decay, and that the tension between actual production under capitalism and productive capacity under a communist organization of the economy must ultimately lead to a revolutionary solution. When after World War II a major economic crisis failed to materialize in the capitalist world, particularly in the United States, communists began to doctor facts and figures to prove that the prevailing prosperity was actually a depression, and that a really big depression was around the corner.

Communist propagandists have been even more disappointed by the phenomenal economic expansion of some leading capitalist countries, such as West Germany and Japan, that, in the 1950's and early 1960's, grew faster than both the Soviet Union and the United States. Communist opposition to the unification of Western Europe is based not only on politics and diplomacy but also on economics; the Common Market countries, France, Germany, Italy, Belgium, Holland, and Luxemburg, have shown that rapid economic progress can be reconciled with individual liberty and international cooperation—a contagious example to the enslaved peoples of Moscow's satellites in Eastern Europe. COMECON, the Council of Mutual Economic Aid of the Soviet Union and its European satellites, cannot match the Common Market for economic and political reasons. Economically, COMECON was intended from the beginning as an instrument of centralized planning primarily for the benefit of the Soviet Union. Politically, COMECON is an organization of totalitarian *governments,* not of free *peoples.* The existence of COMECON has not removed the iron curtain between the Soviet Union and its satellites. By contrast, the 170 million people of the Common Market can move as freely among their six countries as within one nation.

The main concern of communists with the tension between capitalists and workers is *political rather than economic.*

Thus, in formulating a policy for a strike, a communist will ask himself one primary question: will it aid the cause of the communist revolution? The welfare of the particular group of workers involved is secondary to the over-all objective of serving communism.

When Russia was a friendly nonbelligerent on the side of Nazi Germany in 1939-1941, the communists fomented strikes in Britain and the United States, not to help British or American workers, but to paralyze production in Britain and the United States, the two main opponents of Nazi Germany. The moment Russia was drawn into World War II by the German attack on June 22, 1941, communists everywhere opposed strikes as treason, exhorted workers to work sixty, seventy, and eighty hours a week, and called everybody a fascist who sought to protect the rights of the workers against the demand for all-out production.

Some trade unions in Britain and the United States for a long time failed to understand that communist zeal and devotion to unions had little to do with genuine concern for the workers' welfare, but was primarily a vehicle to further communist objectives.

Unions have fought for over two generations against company unions; they now refuse to be dominated by a new type of company union boss—the communist union leader who represents the Soviet Union rather than the workers in his own country. As a result, there has been a thorough housecleaning of communists in most labor unions in this country and in Britain in the last few years.

In the Soviet Union itself, the nature of labor unions as company unions is most clearly evident: the official task of Soviet labor unions is not to defend the interests of the workers against their employer, the state, but to impose the decisions of the boss, the state, on the workers. Strikes are, of course, illegal.

(2) The *tension between imperialist states and colonies,* although mentioned by Marx, was more clearly elaborated by Lenin, who lived in an age of colonial rebellion. Whereas Marx predicted the proletarian revolution in the most advanced industrial nations of the West, Lenin concentrated on the backward areas of the world as the most fertile soil for communist propaganda and eventual conquest.

When communists speak of colonies, they refer not only to territories legally dependent upon another state—the number of such dependencies had in any case approached the vanishing point by 1964 —but also to small, weak states that are in fact in the sphere of influence of the leading Western states. From the communist viewpoint, most states in Latin America or Africa are colonial although they are legally independent and sovereign. The communist strategy is always to help the colonial or weaker state against the West.

All over the globe communists take up the cause of anti-imperialism, as long as the imperialists are British, French, or American rather than Russian or Chinese. Thus, Cuba under Fidel Castro has been hailed by Moscow and Peiping as being truly independent because on both domestic and international issues the Castro regime rapidly moved into the communist camp. Similarly, when the Belgian Congo became independent in 1960, the Soviet Union quickly tried to turn it into a communist satellite. Pro-Western nationalist forces in the Congo are, in Moscow's eyes, nothing but "colonial lackeys of Wall Street imperialism."

Also, communists approach colonial tensions from a long-range viewpoint rather than in the light of the immediate interests of local Communist parties. Thus, in Iran the ultranationalist dictatorship of Mossadegh was supported by Moscow until his downfall in 1953, despite his anticommunism, because he sought to oust Britain and the United States from any sphere of influence in that oil-rich country. In Argentina, the fascist dictatorship of General Perón was also endorsed by the Kremlin until his overthrow in 1955 because he was anti-British and anti-American.

Finally, in more recent years the Soviet Union has showered Colonel Nasser, the militarist dictator of Egypt, with arms and all forms of diplomatic support although the Communist party is outlawed in Egypt. This is a minor consideration to the Soviet government, compared with the fact that Nasser is bent on wiping out Western influence not only in Egypt but in the whole Near and Middle East.

The communist line in all these cases is simple: whatever hurts the influence or prestige of the Western powers is good for world communism although local communists may have to take this long-term view from prison cells. An ultranationalist, anticommunist, fascist-type regime in a backward or weak state is looked upon by Moscow as but a prelude to communization, provided American or British influence can be kept out of the picture. Communist support for anticommunist regimes in weak states makes perfect sense in the light of long-range communist objectives.

It would be unwise, however, to underestimate the weapon the communists have in their hand when they exploit the slogan of anti-imperialism for their purposes. In Asia and Africa, the two main areas of imperialist domination and spheres of influence, imperialism has been traditionally identified with the West (Britain, France, Holland, and the United States); although the Western nations have been recently repenting and reforming, granting independence to their colonies, such repentance and reform come at a late date in the eyes of impatient Asians or Africans. The communist propagandists harp on the sins of the past, and the colonial peoples have a longer memory of their sufferings than do those who have perpetrated them. Also, a major asset of communist anti-imperialist propaganda is the fact that Western imperialism is a matter of experience, often bitter experience, to colonial peoples, whereas Russian or Chinese imperialism is unknown to them.

Paradoxically, as communist power spreads in Asia and other backward areas, it carries in itself a virus of immunization because communist reality so patently belies communist words. Thus, many Indians were rudely jarred from their neutralist feelings about communism when Tibet, a state bordering on India, was occupied by Red China in 1950. In 1959, the Tibetans revolted against their conquerors, but Red China crushed the revolt by massive armed force, just as the Soviet Union had done in Hungary in 1956. The Dalai Lama, the "god-king" of Tibet, fled to India with thousands of other Tibetans. Later in 1959, China invaded Indian border territory and annexed it despite Indian protests. India discovered the hard way that "coexistence" with communism requires more than paper agreements, and she began to look to the West for more diplomatic and economic help.

Russian brutality in suppressing the Hungarian Revolution in 1956 shocked many Asians into a rude awakening from neutralist pipe dreams. As the representative of Burma put it during the debate of the Russian intervention in Hungary at the United Nations: "Here, but for the grace of God, go we."

India and China now lead the struggle for the soul of Asia, and indirectly of all backward countries. China is following the communist totalitarian system, whereas India is trying to combine political democracy with a program of rapid economic development.

If India succeeds, world communism will lose a decisive battle. If India bogs down in a quagmire of lassitude, corruption, and economic stagnation, the field may well be clear for communism in India, to sweep from there to the rest of Asia. In her first five-year plan, Red China spent 44 per cent of total investment on industrial development, and only 8 per cent on raising the supply of consumer goods, such as food, clothing, and housing. By contrast, in India's first five-year plan, 44 per cent of the total investment went into increased production of consumer goods, and only 14 per cent on increased industrial production. If this ratio should keep up for the next twenty or thirty years, India may well lose the economic race with China although India is receiving billions in gifts, loans, and investments from the outside, mostly the United States, and China is not.

If India, with a population of 430 million, should ever become communist, the balance of world power would gradually, and irretrievably, shift to communism. In the general elections of 1952, the Indian Communist Party polled only 3.3 per cent of the popular vote; in the elections of 1957, this figure rose to an alarming high of 8.9 per cent, and the Communist Party was able to take over control of one state, Kerala, with a population of 14 million. In 1959, the President of India dismissed the communist state government of Kerala, on the ground that it was unable to govern peacefully in accordance with the Indian Constitution, and in 1960 an anticommunist coalition government was elected to office. In the general elections of 1962, the communists managed again to increase their share of the popular vote—to 10 per cent of the total vote. This increase in electoral strength occurred despite the large-scale invasion and conquest of Indian border territories by the Red Chinese armies in 1959-1962. The whole edifice of Indian illusions—that there was little to choose between communist and Western imperialism—collapsed. In 1963, India received large quantities of defense equipment from the United States (some of it rushed to India by air). While the Soviet Union, too, has aided India in her resistance against Red China, India has finally learned the hard way that her main hope of survival lies in close economic and military collaboration with the West.

(3) The *tension between rival imperialist states* goes back to Marx's theory of the decay of capitalism. When the rate of profit falls because of large accumulation of capital relative to the labor force, the capitalist looks for profitable employment of capital outside of his own country, and finds such opportunities in backward countries, countries in which capital is very scarce and labor abundantly available. However, as time goes on, investment opportunities in backward areas constantly shrink, and capitalists then look to their governments for aid. According to the Marxist-communist doctrine, the capitalist state is but the executive committee of the propertied classes, and therefore the flag willingly and eagerly follows trade. As capitalists from several countries collide in the same zone of influence and expansion, their governments become involved in a struggle for power.

War under capitalism is thus viewed by communists as a clash between rival imperialist forces motivated by the quest for economic expansion. World Wars I and II are interpreted by communists in this fashion, although if England was so anxious to preserve her commercial position in 1914, the communists have never explained why she did not go to war with the United States, which by 1914 had attained first place in industrial—and inevitably political and military —power. In 1939, American supremacy in industry, finance, and the resulting ability to wage war had become even more obvious, and communists again find it difficult to explain on Marxist grounds why England and France chose to fight Germany rather than the United States.

Speaking on February 9, 1946, at a so-called "election" meeting in Moscow, Stalin reiterated the old communist argument that World War II was "the inevitable result of the development of world economic and political forces on the basis of modern monopoly capitalism." Yet at the same time Stalin deviated from orthodox communist dogma by conceding that World War II was from the very outset "an anti-fascist war, a war of liberation, one of the aims of which was also the restoration of democratic liberties." Stalin also called the war one between "freedom-loving nations" (Britain, France, the United States, the Soviet Union) and the Axis states (Germany, Japan, Italy), who were "out for world domination and the establishment of a fascist regime throughout the world."

Stalin was apparently unaware that the main issue could be either that of rival capitalist imperialist states, as viewed by a Marxist, or that of national liberty versus fascist enslavement, as viewed by a non-Marxist; in the latter case, it mattered little whether the victims of fascist aggression were capitalist or communist. However, Stalin never relapsed into that kind of deviation again; early in 1946, there was still hope for a temporary understanding between Russia and the West, and therefore communist dogmatism was less rigid than it usually is.

After 1946, as soon as the cold war between Russia and the West started, communist spokesmen fell back into the old dogma that war in the era of capitalism is always the result of clashing imperialistic interests. On September 28, 1952 Stalin emphasized before the 19th Congress of the Communist Party that the old theory of the *inevitability of war between capitalist countries* still held good and had to be followed by party members.

Khrushchev, too, remains a faithful adherent of this communist analysis (or, hopeful expectation). The new (1961) Program of the Communist Party of the Soviet Union states that "the contradictions between the principal imperialist powers are growing deeper," and then specifies what the main sources of conflict in the noncommunist world are: "The Anglo-American, Franco-American, Franco-West German, American-West German, Japanese-American, and other contradictions are becoming especially acute. Fresh contradictions will inevitably arise and grow in the imperialist camp."

Although this assumption may seem unrealistic to noncommunists, communists not only believe in it but base their policy on it. Because they do not believe that capitalist states can work together peacefully and amicably, communists exploit existing tensions and create new tensions between capitalist states. Thus in Britain the main communist propaganda slogan is that America will fight to the last Englishman, whereas in the United States the communists ask why American boys should die for British imperialism. In France, the communists have managed to exploit the issue of wine versus Coca-Cola as one of French national independence versus American imperialism; if the communists find themselves unable to promote military conflict between the capitalist nations, at least they are trying their best to create dissension and confusion.

The successful creation of NATO (North Atlantic Treaty Organization) has been a thorn in the flesh of world communism not only because of its military value against communist aggression, but also because the very existence of NATO belies the communist myth that capitalist states cannot collaborate for common objectives. Similarly, Soviet Russia suffered another major diplomatic defeat in 1955 when the rearmament of Western Germany and her inclusion in NATO were ratified in both Bonn and Paris. This was done despite Soviet promises and threats, following the customary totalitarian policy of "divide and conquer."

By contrast, the disunity between the United States and her French and British allies over the Suez issue and the whole problem of peace in the Middle East was one of the great successes of Soviet diplomacy, starting with the seizure of the Suez Canal by dictator Nasser in July, 1956. The disunity between the United States and her Western European allies enabled Russia to become firmly entrenched in the Middle East for the first time in her history.

Later, in 1963, the Soviet Union scored another major triumph when France vetoed the entry of Great Britain into the Common Market. While General de Gaulle is staunchly anticommunist, his opposition to British entry removed a major source of anxiety in the Soviet leadership for the time being. With Britain in, the Common Market nations would surpass the Soviet Union in population and economic strength, not to speak of the dynamic psychological effects of such a community based on freedom. Without Britain, a united Western Europe is a source of constant concern, but not a fatal blow, to communist goals. Should the United States, too, some day become more closely associated with the Common Market (including Britain), it would be the ultimate in bad news to which the Kremlin could be exposed.

(4) The *tension between communist and capitalist states* is increasingly recognized by communists to be the most important of all four tensions. Marx had never given much thought to the question of coexistence between capitalist and communist states. He thought in terms of conflict as the vehicle of social development, but his concept of conflict related to domestic class struggles. Being steeped in nineteenth-century economic optimism, Marx may have hoped that tensions between states would eventually be resolved through economic means. Lenin and Stalin, however, faced with the realities of governing the first communist state and spearheading what they considered

to be a world revolution, gave a great deal of thought to the question of how communist and capitalist states can get along in one world.

As far back as 1924, when Russia was still on the defensive and struggling for her very existence, communist leaders developed a doctrine that was not taken seriously in the West, but that accurately anticipated future policies. In his *Foundations of Leninism* (1924), Stalin says that the world is divided into two hostile camps, "the world front of imperialism" and the "common front of the revolutionary movement in all countries." In particular, Stalin affirms that in the present stage of capitalism "wars cannot be averted," and he urges a *coalition between communist states in Europe and colonial revolutionaries in Asia,* such as the Soviet Union later practiced in China, Vietnam, Laos, and Korea.

In 1924, Stalin considered the Soviet Union as the "base for the overthrow of imperialism in all countries," and this idea of the *Soviet Union as the first phase of the inevitable communization of the world* has since then guided Soviet long-term strategy. In *Problems of Leninism* (1926) Stalin quoted with enthusiastic approval the following statement by Lenin: "We are living not merely in a state, but in a *system of states;* and it is inconceivable that the Soviet Republic should continue to exist for a long period side by side with imperialist states. *Ultimately one or the other must conquer."* Stalin also frequently quotes the Leninist statement that the Soviet Union should "attract to itself the oppressed classes of other countries, raising revolts in those countries against the capitalists, and in the event of necessity coming out even with armed force against the exploiting classes and their governments."

With a slight dash of humor, Stalin held out one hope for the capitalist states. War is not inevitable, if the capitalist countries are willing to surrender voluntarily without resisting communization. Stalin wrote that communism may spread to so many countries that the remaining capitalist states will realize the hopelessness of resistance, and that "encirclement" by communist states will make voluntary surrender "expedient." Put another way, the alternative to enforced slavery is voluntary slavery.

Before World War II was over, Stalin betrayed every pledge he had made to establish democracy in eastern and southeastern Europe. With the help of the Red Army, communist regimes were set up in Rumania, Bulgaria, Hungary, Poland, and East Germany. Leaders of proven democratic background and loyalty were imprisoned, exiled, or killed. In China and Indochina, communist revolutions were supported, with complete success in the former, and with partial success in the latter. In Greece, the communists started a civil war in December 1944, which ended in communist defeat after Yugoslavia broke with Moscow in the summer of 1948. In Malaya and the Philippines, communist guerrilla forces fought for years against the established regimes, causing much bloodshed and devastation. In France and Italy, the communists tried to stage general strikes on several occasions, presumably with the ultimate intent of transforming industrial strife into civil war.

In the Balkans and eastern Europe, the communists argued that there had never been political democracy and that the real choice lay between fascist totalitarianism and communist dictatorship. If such flimsy propaganda did have an effect on noncommunists for a time, its value was completely destroyed in Czechoslovakia in February 1948. Although the Soviet Union used the Czechoslovakian Communist Party as its tool, this was the first case of the subjugation of a truly democratic nation to communist dictatorship by armed force, represented by the threat of the Red Army standing on the borders of Czechoslovakia ready to intervene. Following Hitler's footsteps, Stalin repeated Hitler's technique of conquest. Just as Hitler's seizure of Prague was the beginning of his end, bringing about a rude and rapid awakening of the British and French governments and a determination on the part of those governments to resist further aggression, so the communist seizure of Prague in 1948 may someday be considered as the fatal blunder of world communism. For it was the communist seizure of Czechoslovakia that gave the prime impulse to the formation of the North Atlantic Treaty Organization, and that speeded up tremendously the rate of rearmament in the Western nations, particularly in the United States.

Above all, the communist aggression in Czechoslovakia showed that the only argument the communists respected was force. It was partly because of the Czechoslovakian experience that the United States, joined by many other members of the United Nations, determined to resist armed communist aggression in Korea in 1950 by force.

After the death of Stalin in 1953, Nikita Khrushchev, First Secretary of the Communist Party of the Soviet Union, gradually emerged as Stalin's successor, the chief spokesman of the Soviet regime in domestic and foreign affairs. In a major address before the Twentieth Congress of the Soviet Communist Party on February 14, 1956, Khrushchev stated that Soviet foreign policy was guided by the following five principles: peaceful coexistence; nonaggression; noninterference in internal affairs of other nations; mutual respect for territorial integrity and sovereignty; and equality and mutual benefit. In addition, Khrushchev declared that communization of noncommunist nations need *not always* be carried out *by force,* particularly where this could be done by parliamentary majorities. Significantly, no country has ever gone communist as a result of free elections.

Khrushchev's acceptance of the principle of peaceful coexistence suggested to many that communism had abandoned its objective of world revolution and world conquest, and that post-Stalin communism would be different from Stalin's foreign policy. Some optimists in the West went even so far as to hail Khrushchev's address as a "dawn of liberalism" in the Soviet Union.

Yet only nine months later, in October and November of 1956, the dawn of Soviet liberalism turned into the nightmare of the Hungarian tragedy.

Immediately after the Hungarian Revolution was suppressed, Khrushchev had this to say to a group of Western diplomats at a diplomatic reception in Moscow on November 18, 1956: "Whether you like it or not, history is on our side. *We will bury you.*"

On January 1, 1957, Khrushchev returned to this issue. "The imperialists call us Stalinists," he said in Moscow. "Well, when it comes to fighting imperialism, *we are all Stalinists.*" Made at a large gathering of diplomats, this statement clearly indicated that Stalin's "hard line" of keeping and expanding Soviet power in the world by brute force would continue to guide Soviet policy under the new rulers as it did under Stalin.

Although Khrushchev has, in public statements, more frequently spoken in favor of coexistence than Stalin did, his foreign policy has been more expansionist and daring than Stalin's. Stalin, following the tradition of the Tsars, concentrated on the expansion of Soviet power in areas in which Soviet land armies could be the decisive factor. By contrast, Khrushchev knows of no such limitations. In 1956, ignoring geographical frontiers, he firmly established communist influence in the Middle East through his deals with dictator Nasser of Egypt. In 1959, he—even more daringly—established a beachhead in the Western Hemisphere through his alliance with Cuba's communist regime of Fidel Castro. In 1960, Khrushchev attempted to bring the newly independent Congo into the Soviet sphere of influence. Although he failed in this attempt, Soviet influence is strong in West Africa (Ghana and Guinea) and noticeable in every part of the continent.

Of all these expansions of Soviet power, Cuba was the most important. It became the number one center of communist propaganda, infiltration, sabotage, and subversion in the Western Hemisphere. Emboldened by the inaction of the United States, Khrushchev introduced large numbers of aircraft capable of carrying atomic bombs as well as large quantities of missiles into Cuba in 1962. On October 22, 1962, the President of the United States announced that Cuba would be subjected to a blockade and that the Soviet missiles would have to be removed from Cuba—or else. After first denying that there were any Soviet missiles in Cuba, the Soviet government realized that the United States meant business. As a result, the missiles were shipped back to Russia, but about 30,000 Soviet "technicians" and soldiers were left behind in Cuba, as well as large quantities of Soviet weapons other than missiles. Thus, the threat of force by the United States saved peace and the existing balance of power between the communist and noncommunist world, temporarily at least. This was one of the rare and momentous occasions in the relations between democratic and totalitarian states when a leading democracy took the initiative in resisting the spread of aggressive imperialism before it was too late rather than travel the endless (and hopeless) road of appeasement.

Confident as Lenin and Stalin were of the ultimate triumph of communism throughout the world, Khrushchev is even more passionately convinced that Soviet superiority in military power, economic growth, scientific progress, and educational expansion will bring about the communization of the whole world without armed conflict. During his visit to the United States in the fall of 1959 he repeatedly assured the American people that the United States would eventually go communist, and on a trip to Austria the following spring he said that he wanted to see the red flag fly over the whole world in his own lifetime.

At a conference of top Soviet-bloc leaders in Bucharest in June 1960, Khrushchev explained that the "capitalist world" may well shrink to a few countries "no larger than buttons on a coat." Presumably these few remaining buttons could be sewed up for communism without much trouble—a new version of the Stalinist doctrine of the eventual peaceful surrender of noncommunist states—once they see how hopeless their situation is. In their final communiqué of June 27, 1960, Khrushchev and the other top communist leaders in the Soviet bloc made it clear that, where peaceful communist domination was not feasible, "revolution by nonpeaceful means" still remains the strategy of world communism.

On December 6, 1960, leaders of eighty-one Communist parties assembled in Moscow and issued a fundamental statement of policy about the relations of communist with noncommunist states. The leaders of international communism approved of "peaceful coexistence" for several reasons. First, it provides "favorable opportunities for the development of the class struggle in the capitalist countries and the national-liberation movements of the colonial and dependent countries." This means that, according to the communist concept of peaceful coexistence, communists are free to propagandize and subvert both advanced and underdeveloped countries without hindrance, whereas an Iron Curtain prevents democratic nations from doing the same in communist countries. Second, the communist leaders emphasized in the "December Declaration of 1960" that "peaceful coexistence of countries with different social systems does not mean conciliation" between communism and democracy, but an "intensification of the struggle" of all Communist parties for the "triumph" of communism. Almost the same language was used to describe peaceful coexistence in the new (1961) Program of the Communist Party of the Soviet Union.

What does peaceful coexistence mean in the competition between communist ideology and democracy? Those who had hoped that Khrushchev's slogan of peaceful coexistence would lead to an opening up of the Soviet Union to Western ideas were disillusioned by his major policy speech of March 8, 1963 on the relations of communism to art, literature, and ideology. Rejecting any free exchange of ideas with noncommunist states, Khrushchev said that "he who preaches the idea of peaceful coexistence in ideology objectively slides down to the position of anticommunism."

In sum, in the communist version of the phrase, peaceful coexistence means all forms of war short of nuclear war: local limited wars, guerrilla fighting in underdeveloped countries, and infiltration by subversion, propaganda, and espionage. In the communist view of world affairs, peaceful coexistence becomes an umbrella that permits communist imperialism to conquer the world by minor wars and subversion, particularly in the underdeveloped countries, whose "sacred struggle" and "just anti-imperialist wars of liberation" are promised full support in the 1961 Program of the Communist Party of the Soviet Union. By contrast, in this same communist interpretation of peaceful coexistence, the United States is supposed to refrain from any interference—however nonmilitary—in communist states. A communist take-over of a country in Asia, Latin America, or Africa by armed force or political subversion is called "national liberation," whereas American aid to any people enslaved by communism to regain their freedom would be "capitalist imperialism" that would have to be stopped by force, as Khrushchev has publicly stated on numerous occasions.

The limited nuclear test ban agreement of August, 1963 between the United States, Great Britain, and the Soviet Union fits the over-all Soviet strategy of expanding communist power and influence throughout the world by all means short of all-out nuclear war. Should the best of possible results of the test ban agreement ever come about, that is, gradual nuclear disarmament, the Soviet Union would then be provided with a shelter of nuclear security under which it could continue to spread its power by propaganda, infiltration, sabotage, and limited local wars fought with conventional weapons.

Khrushchev made himself clear on the ultimate goal of communism when he told an audience in Moscow on March 21, 1961: "We shall be happy only when the people of the world stand under the banner of communism." Returning to one of his favorite topics —that of "burying capitalism"—he said on June 20, 1962: "Capitalism is going to be buried. Only the new is growing. This is the law of life." In the middle of the public controversy with Red China, Khrushchev said this at a diplomatic reception in Moscow on February 15, 1963: "When we throw a last shovel on the grave of capitalism, we will do it with China."

SOCIAL-ECONOMIC CHANGES UNDER COMMUNISM

The first major attack in this century against the established social order occurred in Russia toward the end of World War I. The tsarist regime was overthrown in a bloodless revolution in March 1917, and it seemed as if Russia would have the opportunity to develop democratic institutions for the first time in her history.

The majority of the Russians wanted political liberty as well as fundamental social change. Inexperienced in the conduct of public affairs, however, and failing to understand the true nature and goals of communism, the new, democratic government of Alexander Kerensky allowed the Bolsheviks, led by Lenin and Trotsky, to subvert, and quickly destroy, the new democratic state.

Between March 1917 and November 1917, the Bolsheviks (the party was not known as the Communist Party until 1919) used three classical methods of gaining power, methods they were to repeat later in almost identical fashion in other countries.

First, they presented themselves in their propaganda as a people's party, dedicated to liberty, democracy, and social justice and opposed to all forms of reaction and social injustice. In an agrarian country like Russia, the communists emphasized the need for agrarian land reform, and encouraged the seizure of land by the peasants even before they were in control of the government. A generation later the Chinese communists proclaimed themselves (and were believed by many to be) no more than *agrarian reformers,* thus following the pattern of propaganda established by the Russian communists in 1917.

The second technique the Bolsheviks employed was *infiltration* of other political parties, trade unions, soldiers' councils, and local government authorities. In particular, the communists managed to infiltrate and gradually disrupt the Social Revolutionaries, the largest party in Russia, dedicated to political democracy and social reform and especially concerned with the question of the peasants. This technique of infiltration was again employed by the communists during and after World War II when they tried to take over socialist parties in a number of countries. Their most notable successes in that endeavor were in Italy and, to a lesser extent, in Czechoslovakia.

The third method used by the Bolsheviks in their revolution was *force.* In free elections in the summer and fall of 1917, the Bolsheviks polled about one-quarter of the total vote. Though this represented a far from negligible proportion, considering their fanaticism and frenzied activity, the Bolsheviks accepted the fact that in a free election they could not hope to win. In November 1917, therefore, the Bolsheviks seized the key positions of power in Moscow, and from there the revolution quickly spread all over Russia. Opposition to communist revolution sprang up spontaneously in various parts of the country, and a civil war ensued that lasted until 1921.

The ravages of World War I, followed by the devastations of the civil war, made immediate social reform impracticable. Lenin was realistic enough to see that the Russian people would literally starve to death if communist principles were imposed at that time. As a result, he inaugurated in 1921 the New Economic Policy, which permitted limited private ownership; this policy's main objective was to maintain and increase production on the farms and in the workshops and factories by retaining the old capitalist incentives of efficiency and profit. The application of the NEP for about seven years gave Russia a breathing spell, allowing the communist rulers to consolidate their power more effectively and giving the Russian people the temporary illusion that the bark of communism was worse than its bite.

But in 1928 Stalin decided that the time had come to put communist principles into practice, and he withdrew the temporary concessions earlier made by Lenin (who died in 1924). The First Five Year Plan, starting in 1928, aimed primarily at the rapid industrialization of Russia and secondarily at the collectivization of farming. In 1917 many peasants had sympathized with Bolshevism, not for reasons of theory or ideology, but because the Bolsheviks promised them the land they and their ancestors had tilled and coveted for centuries.

The reasons that motivated Stalin to force collectivization on the peasants were manifold. First, the communist rulers felt that agricultural production would be raised by mechanization and that this could be more easily effected in large-scale, collectivized farms than on small, individually owned ones. Second, individual ownership and operation of farms was a basic denial of a key principle of communism, namely that all means of production be transferred to public ownership. Collectivization would bring agriculture in line with industry, which was developed from the start on the basis of state ownership and operation. Third, the communist rulers saw in continued individual farm ownership a direct political and psychological threat to the acceptance of totalitarian political direction from the center.

The independent peasant had to be transformed into a dependent agricultural proletarian; as a member of a collective farm, the peasant was constantly working with others, talking to others, eating with others, and he could thus be more easily supervised and regimented.

Another reason behind collectivization was the need for labor for the newly developing industries in the cities; the required labor force could be obtained only by mechanizing agriculture and thus saving human labor. Finally, collectivization had an important military objective: in case of war, the collectives were to provide the nucleus for organized resistance behind the lines. In World War II, these military expectations were largely fulfilled: the Germans were never completely able to suppress Russian guerrilla activities behind their lines.

The cost of fundamental social and economic change in Russia was heavy. In the process of collectivizing the farms in the years 1929-1933 between four and five million peasants lost their lives or were uprooted from their homes and deported to slave labor camps in Siberia or the Arctic. To show their resistance to collectivization, the peasants slaughtered as much livestock as they could, so that by the time collectivization was accomplished livestock had greatly decreased in numbers. The number of cattle in the Soviet Union was 67 million in 1928, 34 million in 1934, 48 million in 1940, 58 million in 1950, and 82 million in 1962. Of the cattle, cows numbered 33 million in 1928, 19 million in 1934, 23 million in 1940, 25 million in 1950, and 36 million in 1962. During the same period of 1928-1962, the Soviet population increased by 70 million, from 150 to 220 million.

By contrast with Soviet figures for livestock, there were 57 million cattle in the United States in 1928, and 100 million in 1962. Of the cattle, there were 31 million cows in the United States in 1928, and 49 million in 1962. During the same period of 1928-1962, the population of the United States increased from 121 to 186 million, or by 65 million.

In fact, Russia is one of the few countries in the world in which standards of food consumption dropped in the four decades from 1913-1953. The per capita consumption of grain, potatoes, and beets rose during that period, whereas that of eggs, milk, and meat dropped. Advancing living standards invariably show a shift from bread, potatoes, and beets to high-quality foods like milk, butter, meat, and eggs. This is exactly what happened in the United States during the same period: the per capita consumption of wheat and potatoes dropped considerably, whereas that of meat, milk, and eggs rose sharply.

Since 1953, production of food in the Soviet Union has been considerably increased by putting new lands in Central Asia and Siberia under cultivation and by offering the peasants new incentives. By 1961, the Soviet Union attained 48 per cent of U.S. production in meat: proportionately still less than in 1913, when Russia produced 58 per cent of U.S. output in meat. Because of the persistent shortage of meat in the Soviet Union, Khrushchev publicly exhorted Soviet citizens to eat more horse-meat. Annual production of horse-meat in the Soviet Union is about 400 million pounds. The United States produces only about 50 million pounds of horse-meat annually, mostly for pet food. In the production of eggs, too, the Soviet Union was still well below one-half of U.S. output in 1961. Because the population of the Soviet Union is about 20 per cent greater than that of the United States, per capita consumption of better-grade foods is still considerably lower than that of the United States and other Western countries.

A comparative study of the consumption of better-grade foods per person in the Soviet Union and the United States shows that Soviet figures in 1958 were not only way behind American consumption in 1958, but were still far behind American consumption in 1890, as can be seen from the table below:

YEARLY CONSUMPTION OF BETTER GRADE
FOODS PER PERSON

	Soviet Union in 1958	United States in 1890	United States Consumption as Percentage of Soviet Consumption
Meat, poultry, and lard (kilograms)	38	89	234%
Milk (kilograms)	224	350	156%
Eggs (number)	105	293	279%

Source: Rand Corporation, 1961

One crop, however, shows a remarkable expansion under communism. From 1925 to 1929, the Russian production of potatoes was 4.5 times that of the United States. From 1955 to 1962, the Soviet Union produced about 7-8 times as many potatoes as the United States did.

Any visitor to the Soviet Union can verify the fact of bread and potatoes being the basic foods of people living under communism. Even in luxury restaurants (luxury by Soviet standards) catering primarily to visiting foreigners, huge quantities of bread and potatoes are served with every meal. According to official Soviet statistics, bread and potatoes made up 62 per cent of the average Russian diet in 1961.

A comparative chart on the cost of food in terms of man-hours illustrates the developments in the Soviet Union as well as their relation to American standards. Taking seven basic foods in the Soviet food basket, as applied to a family of four, we find that the Soviet worker had to work 26 hours in 1928, 38 hours in 1953, and 30 hours in 1962 in order to earn enough to purchase the basket. The American worker, had he bought the Soviet basket of food, would have had to work 12 hours in 1928, 7¾ hours in 1953, and 7 hours in 1962. Before the collectivization of agriculture started in the Soviet Union in 1929, the Soviet worker had to work more than twice as long as the American worker for the same amount of food; after 24 years of agricultural collectivization, he had to work (in 1953) five times as long; and in 1962, after 33 years of collectivization, the Soviet worker still had to work over four times as many hours as the American worker.

COST IN MAN-HOURS OF A WEEK'S SUPPLY OF FOOD
IN THE SOVIET UNION AND THE UNITED STATES

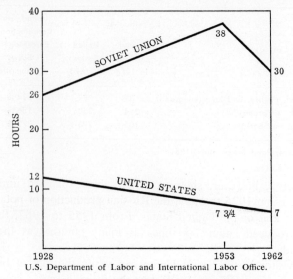

U.S. Department of Labor and International Labor Office.

Includes these quantities for a family of four:
bread: 22 lbs.; potatoes: 27 lbs.; beef: 8 lbs.;
butter: 1 lb.; sugar: 4 lbs.; milk: 5 qts.; eggs: 6.

Yet the chart does not tell the whole story. In the first place, the Soviet prices used in the chart are those of the government stores; in the open market, prices were (and are) from 50 per cent to 100 per cent higher than in government stores. To the extent that the Soviet worker trades in the open market, where foods are more often available and generally of a better grade than in government stores, he has to work even longer hours than the chart shows. Second, the chart relates to a Soviet food basket, heavily slanted toward large quantities of bread and potatoes. If one took the American food basket containing high-grade foods and luxuries, and consequently costing more, the chart would show a still greater gap between the number of man-hours.

As can be seen from the chart on the worktime required to purchase selected commodities in Moscow and New York in 1962, the Moscow worker has to work 600 per cent of the New York worktime for white bread, 400 per cent for potatoes, but 1000 per cent for eggs, 1100 per cent for butter, and 1900 per cent for sugar. The Soviet worker must work ten to sixteen times as long as the American worker for basic articles like shoes, dresses, suits, and shirts.

MOSCOW WORKTIME AS A PERCENTAGE
OF NEW YORK WORKTIME

IF NEW YORK WORKTIME = 100%, MOSCOW WORKTIME =

FOODS

Sugar, 1 kg. (2. 2 lb.)	1900%
Butter, 1 kg., second quality	1100%
Eggs, per 10	1000%
Beef, 1 kg., average quality	500%
Milk, 1 liter (1.06 qt.)	500%
Potatoes, 1 kg.	400%
Bread, 1 kg.	600%

CLOTHING

Shirt, men's, cotton	1000%
Suit, men's, wool, single-breasted	1050%
Dress, street, rayon	1400%
Shoes, women's., 1 pair, leather	1000%
Stockings, nylon	1100%

OTHER

Soap, 100 gm. cake, toilet (3 1/2 oz.)	1100%
Vodka, 1/2 liter (1.06 pt.)	450%
Cigarettes, 20	350%

Source: Joint Economic Committee, Congress of the United States, *Dimensions of Soviet Economic Power* (1963).

Looking at the farm picture as a whole, one discovers that the contrast between Soviet and American agriculture is the most striking of all segments of the two economies. In the United States, out of a total civilian labor force of 75 million in 1962, 5.2 million were employed in agriculture. In the Soviet Union, out of a total labor force of about 100 million, about 40 million depend on agriculture for their livelihood, about the proportion that existed in the United States in 1890. This figure does not include millions of urban dwellers who produce vegetables and potatoes on individual or collective garden plots outside many Soviet cities. In the United States, therefore, one person employed in agriculture feeds himself and fourteen other workers and their families on the highest standard in the world, and vast surpluses still accumulate which are given away or sold to the rest of the world. In the Soviet Union, one half of the population depending on agriculture for a living can barely feed itself and the other half of the people. The staple diet still heavily emphasizes bread, potatoes, and beets, while there is still a relative scarcity of better-grade foods. Items like coffee and chocolate, part of the ordinary diet of workers in Western countries, are still luxuries in the Soviet Union. Before 1914 Russia was one of the world's leading exporters of farm products; the collectivization of agriculture has turned her into an importer.

Government-imposed low prices for farm products induced many Soviet peasants to grow as little as possible in the early years of collectivization; as a result, there was widespread famine in the early nineteen thirties, particularly in the Ukraine, where peasant resistance was strengthened by the force of nationalism.

After World War II, the Soviet government decided to intensify collectivization and, between 1950 and 1960, the 250,000 collective farms were amalgamated into 50,000. The objective was to raise production and at the same time reduce the individuality of the peasant. In addition to these 50,000 collective farms (*kolkhozy*), there are 6,000 state farms (*sovkhozy*) in which the peasant is on a strict wage basis, just as in a Soviet factory. The peasant in the collective farm still has some share in the success or failure of the whole farm.

From the viewpoint of communist ideology, the state farms represent the highest possible form of agricultural organization and production because the peasant has been completely turned into a proletarian dependent on the state for his wage. Communist leaders hope that some day all collective farms will be transformed into state farms, but the Soviet government has not yet dared, for reasons of practicality, to go to such an extreme, although the amalgamation of collective farms into giant units clearly shows the ultimate goal in Soviet farm policy.

After more than thirty years of farm collectivism, the Russian peasant is still deeply opposed to communism in agriculture. Peasant pressure has forced the government to allow the member of the collective farm to devote part of his time to a small plot of land under his own personal management; he may then sell the products of his own effort on the open market at higher prices than are paid by the government (which is able to buy farm products at artificially low prices bearing little relation to the natural forces of supply and demand).

Although the peasant's own piece of land only amounts to an acre or so, it supplies him with nearly half of his income, and these dwarf holdings, amounting to only 3-5 per cent of all Soviet farm land, account for about one half of all Soviet milk, meat, and green vegetables, and for most of the output of eggs and potatoes. The peasants sell their personal produce in the regular "farmers' markets" found in most Soviet cities. It is not uncommon, however, to see individual peasants, more often women, arrive in the center of Leningrad or

SOVIET CAPITALISM: PEASANT
WOMAN SELLING FRESH
VEGETABLES IN THE
CENTER OF MOSCOW.

Photograph by the author

Moscow with a basket of fresh tomatoes or fruit and sell the produce in a few minutes to an eager crowd of buyers who are always on the lookout for items that are scarce or unavailable in government stores.

The superior efficiency of private farming over communist collective farming has also been amply demonstrated in the other communist states of Eastern Europe. In Hungary, for example, private farming on only 10.5 per cent of all farm land accounted for 63 per cent of Hungary's farm output in 1961. Not only the urban population in Hungary depends on private farming for its food. Ironically, even the farm collectives themselves received (in 1960) all their meat, fruit, and vegetables from the private farm sector!

The Soviet rulers know that as long as this remnant of private agriculture is permitted, the peasant will know from his daily experience that private farming is more efficient than collectivized communist agriculture. Yet so far the Soviet rulers have not dared to abolish this private element in farming because it contributes an important share to total farm production.

Psychologically, the Russian peasant has not been transformed into the proletarian that the communist rulers planned him to be. In the years after World War II, thousands of Russian peasants who had been deported to Germany as forced laborers during the war refused to go back home after having seen life outside the Soviet Union. Almost to a man, these peasants are opposed to collectivization and hope to own their own farms after communism is gone.

This sentiment of the peasants has been confirmed by events in Yugoslavia and Poland. After his break with Moscow in 1948, Tito allowed the peasants to decide whether they wanted to continue farm collectives or return to individual farming. The farm collectives rapidly disappeared, and Yugoslav production of wheat and rye in 1962 was about 50 per cent higher than under collectivization. In Poland, the Gomulka brand of national communism, brought into power by the October Revolution of 1956, also allowed the peasants to choose between individual and collective farming. In 1960, only 0.2 per cent of the Polish farm population lived on collective farms.

Yet all these peasants—whether in the Soviet Union or in other communist states—are not fanatical individualists. While irreconcilably opposed to collective farms, they eagerly accept cooperative farm institutions, such as Canadian, Danish, and New Zealand farmers have developed. There is a world of difference between collectivism and cooperation: the purpose of *collectivism* is to *destroy* the *individuality* of the farmer; the aim of *cooperation* is to *strengthen* the *individual farm*.

Interestingly enough, workers and professional people who have escaped from Russia have indicated in interviews that they wish to maintain public ownership in only the key industries after communism is destroyed, but want to return to private ownership in light industry, retailing, and some of the professions. These attitudes indicate the failure of completely dogmatizing the people in a generation of one-sided propaganda. Where economic activity—as in agriculture, light industry, and retailing—can be performed in the classical pattern of the individual owner-manager-worker, what little uncensored Russian opinion we have is opposed to the economic changes of communism. Only where ownership, work, and management are technologically not feasible in one individual unit—as in heavy industry and some public services—does public ownership seem to meet with approval.

In the field of industrialization, progress under Soviet communism has been immense, as was proved by Russia's ability to withstand the onslaught of Germany in World War II. Though Russia received some strategic supplies from the United States during the war, the bulk of the industrial production needed to defeat Germany came from Russian workshops and factories. Russian industrialization, from the First Five Year Plan, was conceived primarily as a means of increasing, not the material welfare of the people, but the power of the state. For this reason, the government consistently emphasized heavy industry as especially vital to the production of armaments and showed no great concern with the development of consumer goods industries.

The net result of economic change in Russia over a generation is not so much economic communism as a totalitarian state economy. In terms of sheer industrial power, Russia now ranks second in the world, preceded only by the United States. But this ranking is significant only in appraising the *power of the state to wage war* and not in reflecting the opportunity of the people to live the good life. Viewed from the latter angle, living standards in Russia are still way behind North America, most countries of Europe, Australia and New Zealand, and numerous other nations throughout the world.

At a meeting in Vladivostok on October 6, 1959, Khrushchev told a story about his meeting with a young mother in that city who told him how delighted she was about his visit: "Because you have come, they have brought shoes, fabrics, milk, and many other things into the shops. Come and see us more often. Then there will be more on sale in the shops." Complaints published in the Soviet press reveal that it takes three to four months to have shoes repaired, clothes cleaned or laundered, and that it is virtually impossible to have a radio set repaired. Long queues of customers in stores are a common sight.

Until recently appliances common in the American home were generally unknown in the Soviet Union; the government was too busy producing steel, tanks, military planes, missiles, and sputniks. In the last few years a start has been made toward producing some of the basic appliances. Yet, as the table below shows, the Soviet family is still a long way off from the standard of ownership of appliances that the American family takes for granted.

APPLIANCES OWNED BY 100 FAMILIES IN THE SOVIET UNION
AND THE UNITED STATES, 1960

	Soviet Union	U.S.A.
Radios	48	94
Television	10	89
Refrigerators	3.5	98
Washing machines	5	95

Source: Joint Economic Committee, Congress of the United States, *Dimensions of Soviet Economic power* (1963).

Radios are the only item that is fairly easily available at a moderate price in the Soviet Union because radios are considered by the government as an important means of propaganda. The other appliances are high priced and hard to get; consumers must usually wait several months or years before they can obtain them. In 1963, the waiting

period for refrigerators was 3-4 years. (*The New York Times,* August
17, 1963.) As a student of Soviet economic affairs observed: "Few of
these items would be salable in retail markets in the United States.
Appliances, on the whole, are poorly designed, crudely built, and subject to breakdowns. Soviet refrigerators have a small amount of usable
space in relation to their size and weight. The washing machines are
simple in design, usually with roller wringers operated by hand; some
have motor-driven centrifugal spinners; and a small part of the production have simple timing devices. Electric sewing machines have
been so unreliable that many housewives are returning to treadle machines while a good portion of the newer models rust in warehouses.
Even in the urban areas, the usefulness of appliances is limited by the
undependable nature of the Soviet supplies of electric power." (Imo-
gene Erro, in *Dimensions of Soviet Economic Power,* pp. 379-380.)
As to the production of automatic coffee-makers, dishwashers, clothes-
driers, home freezers, food mixers, or water softeners—to mention
but a few typical American appliances, the Soviet housewife has
hardly even heard of such things.

As to automobiles: annual Soviet production is a little over 100,-
000, and only about one out of every three hundred families owns a
car, one of the lowest ratios in the world. The waiting period for buy-
ing a car is about seven years, and top government officials, industrial
executives, and party bosses have first choice. In the United States,
annual production is over six million, to which about half a million
imported cars should be added. Fifty million American families own
over seventy million cars, and about twelve million families own more
than one car.

Yet the Soviet Union has plenty of resources and manpower to
produce the cars that many Soviet citizens would like to buy, but the
government has consistently refused. Why? During his visit to the
United States in 1959, Khrushchev gave two reasons. First, he noted,
an abundance of cars creates serious traffic problems. In his view, the
simplest way to solve the traffic problem is not to have any cars—
certainly the most radical proposal ever made to solve this problem.
The second reason given by Khrushchev is more to the point: "We
could do it tomorrow, but that means freezing capital. You go ahead
and do all that foolishness. It's for our benefit." Allen W. Dulles, then
Director of the Central Intelligence Agency of the United States, said
this on April 8, 1959: "While the Soviets last year were producing
only 1 automobile for every 50 we produced, they were turning out
4 machine tools to our 1."

A few days before the first sputnik was launched by the Soviets on

October 4, 1957, James Reston of *The New York Times* happened to travel by automobile from the Polish-Soviet border to Moscow. In a *631-mile* drive through the most advanced section of the Soviet Union, Reston counted *33 private passenger cars.* (*The New York Times,* October 1, 1957.) Sputniks and missiles have priority in Soviet economic policy over cars and dishwashers.

Of all the segments of the Soviet economy, housing has been the most neglected. Stalin's drive for industrializing Russia began in 1928, but in 1958, after thirty years, the average Russian had less dwelling space than before. In the late 1950's, the Soviet government made an effort to improve the housing situation, but so far the progress has not been too significant. At the end of 1961, the housing conditions of the city people finally reached the level of 1926. Fifty-four per cent of Soviet city families live in a single room, and twelve per cent of the families in only part of a room. Only twenty-four per cent of the families have a separate kitchen; thirty-seven per cent share a kitchen with several other families, twenty-two per cent have no kitchen, and eleven per cent use the kitchen for living space. The typical four-room apartment in a Soviet city houses four families, all sharing the kitchen and toilet facilities. Bathrooms of the American type are still a rarity. Even most new apartment houses built in the 1950's were designed for two to four families per apartment, each family occupying one room. The most recent apartment buildings have one- or two-room apartments for a single family, but such luxury is still a dream for the great majority of the Soviet urban population. By contrast, low-rent public housing in the United States, supported by public funds and meant for the lowest income groups, provides four times as much average living space per person as the average living space for *all* income groups in the Soviet Union. Moreover, even low-income housing projects in the United States have elevators, whereas in the Soviet Union many of the most recent buildings, four to six stories high, have no elevator.

Although nearly all American housing (about 99 per cent) is equipped with electricity, water, and sewage, only 90 per cent of Soviet *urban* housing is supplied with electricity, and about 33 per cent with water and sewage. In the countryside, only 39 per cent of Soviet housing has electricity, and running water and proper sewage facilities are still a rare luxury. Whereas 60 per cent of American urban housing has central heating, this convenience is available to only 4 per cent of Soviet urban housing.

Even the telephone is still a luxury in Russia. The United States has about eighty million telephones, the Soviet Union about five million.

Allowing for the larger Soviet population, the United States has twenty times as many telephones as has the Soviet Union. Telephone books, too, are not readily available in the Soviet Union, and trying to find a telephone number is a major adventure in red tape.

The Soviet emphasis on production rather than welfare or consumption is also illustrated by the Soviet attitudes toward the unemployed, the aged, and the women in the total setting of the economy. The Soviet policy on unemployment relief is one of the few instances in which a Biblical teaching is practiced: "He who does not work shall not eat." Soviet logic maintains that a person who loses a job can always find work if he is willing to take any job at any wage; therefore, there is no unemployment relief. The Soviets do not worry about the loss of pride and emotional disequilibrium a person might suffer if he has to take a lower-paying job of less prestige in an entirely different part of the country. Similarly, the pension for the aged is kept deliberately so low that old people keep on working as long as they are able. This is in sharp contrast to the outlook in the United States and other capitalist countries that penalize the recipients of old-age pensions if their earnings exceed relatively moderate amounts.

FEMALE PERCENTAGE OF THE LABOR FORCE
SOVIET UNION AND UNITED STATES, 1957

	Soviet Union	United States
Total	53	32
Major types of employment:		
Industry	45	26
Construction	31	3
Agriculture	59	19
Transportation and communication	32	18
Trade and supply	65	39
Government and administration	51	27

Source: Joint Economic Committee, Congress of the United States, Comparisons of the United States and Soviet Economies (1959).

With respect to the role of women in the labor force, the above table speaks for itself. Women compose 32 per cent of the labor force in the United States, as contrasted with the female percentage of 53 in the Soviet Union. The most conspicuous contrast of percentages is in construction; women constitute 31 per cent of the Soviet labor force, with 3 per cent of women employed in construction in the

United States. The visitor to the Soviet Union is struck by the large number of women that can be seen digging ditches, repairing roads, and building houses and factories. In numerous cases, one can see entire gangs of road workers composed of women.

The high percentage of women in the Soviet labor force is probably due to three factors. First, the husband generally earns too little to support his wife and family on his wage alone. Second, since entire families generally share one room, and four, five, or six families share one kitchen, there is not much incentive for women to stay at home. Third, the Soviet rulers deliberately encourage and cajole women to do any kind of work rather than to worry about dishpan hands or about how a woman of forty can look like a girl of twenty.

Although the Soviet national product is only about 40 per cent of that of the United States, Soviet annual investment in heavy industry and national defense is about equal to that of the United States. As a result, per capita consumption of the Soviet citizen runs to only about 20 per cent of American per capita consumption. Annual investment in new housing is twice as high in the United States as in the Soviet Union, although the available living space per person is already four times as high in the United States as in the Soviet Union.

The Soviet bias in favor of industrial and military power can also be seen in the uneven differentials of productivity in the Soviet economy. In agriculture, Soviet productivity (or the output per man in an hour) is only about 10 per cent of American productivity; in steel, about 50 per cent; and in electronics, about 66 per cent.

The price for this rapid industrialization has been steep. Millions of Soviet subjects have been employed for years in slave labor camps to provide cheap labor. The number of slave laborers in the two decades from the middle thirties to the middle fifties ranges from a conservative low estimate of five million to the more likely figure of about ten million. Since 1957 some of the camps have been closed, but, never having admitted their existence, the Soviet government has not divulged how many persons are still employed in "correctional labor" camps.

The Soviet worker is subjected to managerial authority such as has not been known in capitalist countries for over two generations. The communist promise of liberating the worker from capitalist oppression has turned into the reality of unlimited subjection to management, direct representative of the all-powerful state. All managerial authority is concentrated in a single chief. An official Soviet analysis of the position of the Soviet plant manager reads as follows: "His order is law for all his subordinates. The struggles against sentimentality, petty-

bourgeois disorder and disorganizing elements, and for high organization, iron labor discipline and Bolshevik order are all included in the
tasks of the single chief." (A. Arakelian, *Industrial Management in
the USSR,* 1950, p. 88.)

PROPORTION OF PRODUCER AND CONSUMER GOODS
IN SOVIET INDUSTRIAL PRODUCTION

(Per cent)

Year	Total	Producer Goods	Consumer Goods
1913	100	33.3	66.7
1928	100	39.5	60.5
1932	100	53.4	46.6
1937	100	57.8	42.2
1940	100	61.2	38.8
1950	100	68.8	31.2
1955	100	70.6	29.4

U.S.S.R. Council of Ministers, Central Statistical Administration, *The
U.S.S.R. Economy: A Statistical Abstract* (1956).

Economic change in the Soviet Union has failed to solve the problem of social justice, for the sake of which the change was ostensibly
undertaken in the first place.

During the first fifteen years of the Soviet regime, an attempt was
made to limit inequalities of income to a moderate range of differential; from the middle of the nineteen thirties on, however, with the in-
auguration of the era of purges, the last vestiges of equalitarianism
were wiped out and an entirely new policy was brought into being.
Wages based on performance rather than on fixed hourly rates became
the policy, a policy that labor unions in free nations had fought for
two generations as a system of inhuman exploitation.

The old-fashioned capitalist appeal for higher production compen-
sated by higher incomes was covered up with slogans like "socialist
competition," and workers were driven on to greater production
efforts by the policy of Stakhanovism, inspired by the alleged feats of
a coal miner named Stakhanov. Whereas the original concern in communist theory had been with problems of just distribution, Soviet
policy has in practice concentrated on maximum production. The *incentive of higher income* rather than service to the community has become the main appeal of Soviet social and economic policy, and the
philosophy of equality has been derided as "petty-bourgeois prejudice."

Stalin's conversion to the extreme incentive philosophy of primitive capitalism has been faithfully continued by Khrushchev. If anything, Khrushchev is an even more enthusiastic convert to the incentive theory. On December 1, 1958, Senator Hubert Humphrey had a lengthy talk with Khrushchev in Moscow. The conversation turned to the Chinese experiment of compulsory communal living, based on the principle, "From each according to his abilities, to each according to his needs." Khrushchev remarked: "You know that won't work. You can't get production without incentive." When Senator Humphrey said, "That is rather capitalistic," Khrushchev replied: "Call it what you will; it works." (*Life,* January 12, 1959.) President Eisenhower stated in his news conference of October 28, 1959, that during his conversations with Khrushchev at Camp David various economic issues were discussed. When Eisenhower made the point that the American economy had traveled a long way from the philosophy of laissez faire, Khrushchev remarked that the Soviets "are using the incentive system to increase production far more than we [in the U.S.] are," and that the American tax system "stifles increased productivity." The meaning of the words *communism* and *capitalism* becomes somewhat blurred when the head of communist Russia lectures the President of the United States about the virtues of the incentive system. Finally, Khrushchev even had a good word to say about profits when he addressed the Central Committee of the Communist Party on November 19, 1962. He urged that the Soviet Union copy what has proved successful in the "bourgeois capitalist" economies of the West: "We should remember Lenin's injunction to be able, if necessary, to learn from the capitalists—to imitate whatever they have that is good and profitable."

In line with Soviet anti-equalitarian policy, personal income taxes are among the lowest in the world. The Soviet government derives 85 per cent of its revenue from *sales taxes* and other indirect levies that proportionately hit the lowest income groups hardest. Only 15 per cent of the Soviet government revenue comes from income taxes. In the United States, the picture is the exact reverse: the United States government revenue is 85 per cent from income taxes, and 15 per cent from sales and other indirect taxes. In concentrating on sales taxes, the Soviets seek to *penalize consumption;* by contrast, heavy (and progressive) *taxation of incomes* in the United States—as in some other Western democracies—*hits the productive effort.*

The group with the highest incomes is the same in Russia as in the United States: business managers and executives. Yet, whereas the income tax in the United States goes up to 91 per cent, the top tax rate for Soviet executives is only 13 per cent. As to inheritance taxes: the top rate in the United States is 77 per cent; in the Soviet Union, inheritance taxes were abolished in 1942—another bonus to the affluent elements in Soviet society.

According to official Soviet propaganda the problem of social classes has been solved in Soviet society, because from the Marxist viewpoint there can be no class inequality except on the basis of the private ownership of the means of production.

Yet Soviet reality tells a different story. There are at least *four distinguishable classes*. In the first group—numbering a few hundred thousand families, perhaps as many as a million—there are the top government officials, party leaders, military officers, industrial executives, scientists, artists, and writers. The second group is made up of the intermediary ranks of civilian and military officials, collective farm managers, and some of the more affluent skilled workers and technicians in industry; this group forms the middle classes of Soviet society and numbers about two to three million families. The third class is made up of the bulk of the population, the mass of workers and peasants, numbering over forty million families. The fourth class includes the millions of slave laborers and other disadvantaged persons who, for political or other reasons, are placed outside the confines of ordinary society.

What is remarkable about social stratification in communist countries is that the *income spread between the different classes has been steadily widening,* while it has been continuously narrowed in the democratic nations of the West through taxation and other measures. Moreover, within the bulk of the population, the working class, the *difference between wages of skilled and unskilled workers* has been constantly on the increase in the Soviet Union, whereas in democratic nations this differential has been systematically reduced, largely owing to the pressure of free labor unions.

Before World War II, American skilled workers generally earned about two-thirds more than unskilled workers: at present they earn only about one-third more. By contrast, the Soviet skilled worker earns two to four times as much as the unskilled worker. The differential between skilled and unskilled worker is thus six to twelve times greater in the Soviet Union than in the United States.

The growing inequality between and within classes in communist states is one of the most explosive sources of unrest and revolt. The East German workers who rebelled in 1953 and the Polish and Hungarian workers who rebelled in 1956 objected less to the ideology of communism than to the brutal economic exploitation to which they were exposed, an exploitation that meant austerity for the masses of the people and affluence for a small privileged clique of party bosses and government officials. The reality of communist economics thus taught the workers that the mere transfer of property from private to public ownership did not in itself bring about a new society built on justice and equality.

HOW INCOMES VARY IN THE SOVIET "CLASSLESS" SOCIETY

	Monthly earnings (in rubles)[1]
Scientist (academician)	800-1,500
Minister (head of government ministry or department)	700
Opera star	500-2,000[2]
Professor (science)	600-1,000
Professor (medicine)	400-600
Docent (assistant professor)	300-500
Plant manager	300-1,000
Engineer	100-300
Physician, head	95-180
Physician, staff	85-100
Teacher, high school	85-100
Teacher, primary school	60-90
Technician	80-200
Worker, skilled	100-250
Worker, semiskilled	60-90
Worker, unskilled	27-50

[1] The official rate of exchange, as fixed by the Soviet government on January 1, 1961, is 1 ruble = $1.11. The actual purchasing power of the ruble is, however, slightly below the dollar.

[2] The top salary at the Bolshoi Theater has been reported as 500 rubles a month. Outside appearances increase the artist's income.

Source: *Monthly Labor Review* (April 1960)

As Aristotle said over two thousand years ago, the main question is not *who* owns property, but *how* property is used.

In our own day, the experience of communist economic change teaches again that the principal issue is not whether the government owns the means of production, but *who owns the government.*

This point has been forcefully expressed by a leading Yugoslav, Vladimir Dedijer. He describes the Soviet system as *totalitarian state capitalism,* "in which the exploitation of man by man is the fact of life." (*The New York Times,* May 25, 1957.)

SOURCES OF STRENGTH IN COMMUNISM

Among communism's sources of strength, the most important is probably the enormous *widening of the base from which the elite is recruited.* Before World War I, the Russian elite —in government, the army, business, science, and the arts—was drawn from a relatively small social group of upper-class and upper-middle-class background. There was a tremendous gap between the small governing classes of Russia, in intimate contact with western Europe, and the vast inchoate masses of peasants. The communist revolution, particularly in its first impetus, swept away distinctions of class, sex, or nationality and opened up a new world of opportunity for people who had hitherto been excluded from opportunity of any sort. Industrialization, perhaps the most dynamic key in creating new opportunities in science and government as well as in industry, formed a *new managerial class,* recruited on a very wide basis, for which there was no precedent.

A quick glance at the social background of the top leaders of the Soviet Union today gives us a fair idea of the Soviet leadership as a whole:

Leader	*Occupation of father*
Aristov	fisherman
Gromyko	artisan
Khrushchev	coal miner
Kosygin	poor worker
Kozlov	poor peasant
Mikoyan	worker
Podgorny	foundry worker
Polyansky	peasant
Shvernik	poor worker
Suslov	peasant
Voroshilov	railroad worker

These top leaders are typical representatives of the men who run Russia's industry, government, and armed forces. Those Westerners who have dealt with them agree that they are able and confident, full of drive and energy. In the United States, these men would be corporation executives, political and military leaders, and top government officials—the very same jobs they hold in the Soviet Union. Because their ideas and aims seem irreconcilable with Western ideas and objectives, many have been blinded to their high technical and executive ability.

The competition for leadership positions in the Soviet Union is more ruthless than in the democratic world, the premium for success greater, and the penalty for failure harsher. The successful manager who overfulfills his production quota is rapidly promoted and his rewards are—in relation to the rest of the population—more ample than in capitalist countries. The incentive system is more fully developed than in the United States; the bonus for the typical Soviet executive amounts to 25-50 per cent of his base salary. By contrast, only about half of American corporations have bonus schemes at all, and where bonuses are paid they typically amount to only 10-20 per cent of base pay.

The penalty for failure is also greater than in capitalist countries. Under Stalin, managerial failure could result in slave labor or even execution; in more recent years, the manager who fails in his production job is more likely to be fired and downgraded to a less responsible job. This harsh emphasis on performance may seem ruthless, but it works—if results are the only things that count.

In World War I, Russia sustained more losses from lack of medical facilities, faulty supplies, slow transportation, and other shortcomings of a technological nature than from direct combat casualties. In World War II, most of the generals who outmaneuvered and defeated the German General Staff were sons of serfs, workers, and small peasants; there is no doubt that in World War II Russia was able to draw on more of her people's talent than in World War I.

The less a position in the elite is directly tied up with politics, the more recognition can be given to talent and merit. As long as a leading surgeon, chemist, mathematician, engineer, or industrial executive keeps his mouth shut (politically speaking) and opens it only for the purpose of expressing his loyalty to the regime, he will generally (but not always) be left alone. The more a position in the ruling group is tinged with politics, the more criteria besides merit and talent become relevant and frequently decisive.

Rapid *industrialization* is the second main source of communist strength, in Russia as well as in other communized states. Before World War I, Russia was an overwhelmingly agricultural country; Russian industrial power was very low, ranking behind the United States, Britain, Germany, France, Japan, and Austria-Hungary. After World War II, Russia moved up to second place, preceded only by the United States. Industrialization in all communist states is concentrated on heavy industry, the base of military power.

In absolute figures, industry in Russia and the communist states still lags considerably behind the United States and her allies. But what is alarming is the rapid rate of industrial growth in the communist states, which considerably exceeds that of many Western nations. Even if it be argued that the communist states have now the initial advantage of backward countries undergoing rapid industrialization, and that their present rate of expansion cannot be indefinitely maintained, the Western nations will have to step up their own productivity and rate of industrial growth if the present balance of industrial power, still heavily in favor of the noncommunist states, is not to be lost.

If the free nations are to win the industrial race with communism, they will have to give more attention in their industrial programs to saving and productivity, and less to immediate consumption and "ice-cream" investments.

Fast economic growth is not something which automatically comes out of either communism or capitalism, but is the result of hard work and know-how. Within the communist group of nations, some have

Herblock in Washington "Post"

It's "split-level living" . . .

shown faster economic progress than others, and the same is true of the capitalist world. Specifically, the Soviet Union has no superior record of recent economic growth as compared with *all* major capitalist nations. While it is true that the Soviet Union has, in recent years, grown faster economically than the United States, other capitalist nations have done better than the Soviet Union. As the table below shows, during the decade of 1950-1960, the major economies of the world have shown a varied picture. The Soviet Union has a much better growth record than either the United States or Great Britain. Italy has grown almost as fast as the Soviet Union, and Japan and West Germany have grown faster than the Soviet Union. However, the eyes of the world are focused on the comparative economic growth of the Soviet Union and the United States, rather than on the comparative growth of the Soviet Union and Japan.

AVERAGE ANNUAL RATES OF ECONOMIC GROWTH
FOR SEVEN MAJOR ECONOMIES, 1950-1960

Country	Per cent
Japan	8.8
West Germany	7.5
Soviet Union	6.8
Italy	5.9
France	4.3
United States	3.3
Great Britain	2.6

Source: Joint Economic Committee, Congress of the United States, *Dimensions of Soviet Economic Power* (1963).

In gearing economic policy to the requirements of national power, the Soviet Union has made particularly strenuous efforts to close the gap with the United States in such key commodities as iron, steel, coal, petroleum, electricity, and cement. Increased production of these commodities also pays off propagandistically, because most underdeveloped countries look upon steel, for example, as a symbol of industrial progress and power. Part of the relative decline of steel production in the United States is due to the fact that other products such as aluminum and plastics increasingly replace steel in many uses; moreover, in an advanced economy like the American, people increasingly spend on services, amenities, and luxuries rather than on goods that use steel. Similarly, coal has declined in the United States because petroleum and natural gas have increasingly replaced coal as a source of fuel or energy. Moreover, absolute production figures of key commodities do not tell the whole story. In the United States, one-fifth of the output of steel goes into automobiles, and sizable amounts of steel are used in residential building, shopping centers, highway construction, consumer durables, and other facets of the good life, whereas in the Soviet Union steel is the foundation of heavy industry expansion and armaments. Similarly, although the Soviet Union produces nearly one-third of the electricity generated in the United States, these absolute production figures conceal the fact that, in terms of residential use, the American home uses eight times as much electricity as does the Soviet home.

Valid as these arguments may be from a strictly economic viewpoint, they make little impact—politically and propagandistically—in the underdeveloped countries. To them, steel is still the number 1 barometer of economic strength and progress, not the amount that people spend on eating out, entertainment, vacations, and other pleasant amenities that are little affected by steel production.

PRODUCTION OF SELECTED KEY COMMODITIES, 1950, 1961

		Soviet Union	United States
Pig iron	1950	19	60
(million metric	1961	51	65
tons)			
Steel	1950	27	88
(million metric	1961	71	89
tons)			
Coal	1950	261	502
(million metric	1961	375	402
tons)			
Oil	1950	38	266
(million metric	1961	166	356
tons)			
Natural gas	1950	6	193
(billion cubic	1961	61	355
meters)			
Electricity	1950	91	389
(billion kilowatt	1961	327	878
hours)			
Cement	1950	10	37
(million metric	1961	51	57
tons)			

Source: Joint Economic Committee and Department of Commerce

The third major area of Soviet strength is in *education and science*. The Soviet launching of the first sputnik on October 4, 1957 came as a bombshell to those who still had the illusion that Russia was largely a country of illiterate peasants. Yuri A. Gagarin's first manned orbital flight on April 12, 1961 showed that the Soviet lead in space exploration was still very impressive. Triumphs of this kind are the result, not of short-term crash programs, but of long, sustained effort over many years. According to the most authoritative American analysis, the increase in the years 1926-1952 of Soviet professional manpower was as follows: engineers, ten times; teachers, five times; and physicians, four times. (Nicholas DeWitt, *Soviet Professional Manpower,* National Science Foundation, 1955, p. 247.) Since 1952, the Soviet expansion in education has progressed at an even more rapid rate.

Looking at Soviet and American higher education in the three decades of 1928-1959 (for the Soviet Union) and 1926-1958 (for the United States), we find the following results: the Soviet Union trained during that period 1.8 as many engineers as the United States, 2.4 as many medical doctors, and 2.4 as many agricultural specialists as the United States. In the sciences (physics and mathematics, chemistry, geology, and biology), the United States trained 1.6 as many as the Soviet Union. The American lead is much greater still in the humanities and social sciences: in these fields, the United States trained 2.9 as many as the Soviet Union. In the grand total, the United States trained 1.7 as many in higher education as the Soviet Union, this over-all lead being largely due to the American heavy preponderance in the humanities and social sciences.

In 1960, Soviet schools graduated 111,000 engineers, as compared with 40,000 in the United States. The total pool of engineers and physicists is now greater in the Soviet Union than in the United States, and the gap is growing year by year. In the Soviet Union, 27 per cent of all college graduates are engineers, as compared with 9 per cent in the United States. Looking at all the sciences including engineering and medicine, the Soviet percentage is 57 as compared with the American percentage of 24 of all graduates.

In the field of medicine, 27,000 medical doctors were graduated in the Soviet Union in 1960, as compared with only 7,000 in the United States. The ratio of physicians to the population is 19 per 10,000 in the Soviet Union and 13 per 10,000 in the United States. The shortage of doctors is so severe in the United States that thousands of doctors have to be imported—many from poor, underdeveloped countries. In 1963, about one out of every four resident doctors in American hospitals was trained abroad. In New York City, half of the hospital

PROFESSIONAL GRADUATES WITH COMPLETED
HIGHER EDUCATION IN THE SOVIET UNION
AND THE UNITED STATES

FIELD	U.S.S.R. (1928–1959)	UNITED STATES (1926–1958)	COMPARISON
Engineering	1,117,800	620,300	U.S.S.R. : U.S.=1.8 : 1
Medical doctors...................	420,000	181,700	U.S.S.R. : U.S.=2.4 : 1
Farm specialists..................	389,200	166,400	U.S.S.R. : U.S.=2.4 : 1
Science majors:			
From universities 180,000			
From pedagogical institutes 250,000	430,000	704,400	U.S. : U.S.S.R.=1.6 : 1
Total, engineering, applied and theoretical sciences	2,357,000	1,672,800	U.S.S.R. : U.S.=1.4 : 1
All other fields (humanities, arts, social sciences, and teacher training)...............	1,772,300	5,198,600	U.S. : U.S.S.R.=2.9 : 1
Grand total	4,129,300	6,871,400	U.S. : U.S.S.R.=1.7 : 1

Source: Joint Economic Committee, Congress of the United States, *Dimensions of Soviet Economic Power* (1963).

staff is foreign, and in seven states (Arizona, New Jersey, North Dakota, South Dakota, Rhode Island, West Virginia, and Delaware) more than half of the resident physicians were educated abroad. Many of these foreign physicians come from countries lacking proper medical education.

Within the existing emphasis on engineering and science, priority goes to engineering rather than to basic scientific research. Before 1917, one Nobel Prize went to a Russian scientist (Pavlov, 1904). Since 1917, two and a half Nobel Prizes in science have been awarded to Russians. In basic scientific discovery, Soviet scientists have so far been behind small countries like Austria, Sweden, Switzerland, and Denmark, not to speak of major countries like the United States, Germany, Britain, and France.

The emphasis on engineering can also be seen in the greatest Soviet triumph—space satellites. From the launching of the first sputnik in 1957, the Soviets have maintained superiority in rocket power required to send heavy vehicles into outer space. The United States has launched more space satellites than the Soviet Union, but these vehicles were much lighter than the Soviet ones. While lacking the rocket power of Soviet satellites, American satellites have been gathering much more scientific information in the fields of cosmic radiation, meteorology, and communications.

Yet superior engineering in greater rocket power is one of the decisive elements in modern weaponry, particularly intercontinental missiles. Khrushchev had this to say at the United Nations on October 11, 1960: "Production of rockets now is a matter of mass delivery, like sausages that come out from the automatic machines. In our factories rocket after rocket comes off the assembly line." This purely military aspect of rocketry is more important to the Soviets than the basic scientific results obtained by American space research.

The Soviet commitment to education as a major goal of national policy is expressed in many ways. With a national income that is only about 40 per cent of that of the United States, the Soviets spend proportionately twice as much of their national income on education as is done in the United States. The Soviet professor receives eight times the wage of the average factory worker, whereas the American pro-

© 1960 *Harper's Magazine*

"How about 'Russian Scientists Say'. . . ?"

fessor receives only one and one-half times the American worker's pay. There is no tuition in Soviet universities and institutes of higher learning; 80 per cent of Soviet students receive monthly stipends ranging from twenty-four to seventy-five rubles; the latter figure equals the average pay of a factory worker. Students in fields such as mining, electronics, and chemical engineering receive the highest stipends, and an additional bonus of 25 per cent is given to those students who maintain a consistently excellent record.

The Soviet system of higher education tries to utilize the maximum of the available brain-power; the main method of recruiting talent is through written and oral examinations. By contrast, one-third of the top quarter of graduating high-school students in the United States does not go on to college—for economic reasons, in most cases.

Soviet leaders fully realize that the race for educational and scientific leadership may decisively contribute to the ultimate outcome of the struggle between East and West: "Whoever has the knowledge has the future at his feet." (Khrushchev, *The New York World-Telegram,* September 26, 1960.)

Finally, the most direct and dangerous source of communist strength lies in *military power*. Although the Soviet citizen consumes only one-fifth to one-fourth of the American standard of consumption, and although the whole Soviet national product is but 40 per cent of the American, the Soviet government spends about the same amount on military preparedness as does the United States.

The vast expenditures on building up military strength have paid off in communist imperialist expansion. Since the outbreak of World War II in September 1939, the Soviet Union has acquired an area larger than all the New England and Middle Atlantic States with a population of over 25 million. In addition to these outright annexations, the Soviet Union established by armed force dependent governments in the eastern European satellites, with a combined colonial population of over 100 million.

Never before in history has imperialistic expansion acquired so much in so short a time.

By contrast, the western powers have given freedom and independence to over 800 million people in former colonies since World War II.

USSR Annexed	Year	Area (square miles)	Population
1. Part of Rumania	1940	19,400	3,700,000
2. Estonia	1940	18,300	1,200,000
3. Latvia	1940	25,400	2,100,000
4. Lithuania	1940	23,000	3,000,000
5. Part of East Prussia	1945	5,400	1,200,000
6. Eastern Czechoslovakia	1945	4,900	730,000
7. Eastern Poland	1945	69,900	11,800,000
8. Part of Finland	1940	17,600	450,000
9. Tannu Tuva	1944	64,000	65,000
10. Japanese Possessions	1945	17,800	433,000
Communist Regimes Established			
11. Albania	1946	10,700	1,300,000
12. Bulgaria	1946	42,800	7,300,000
13. Czechoslovakia	1948	49,300	14,000,000
14. Eastern Germany (Including Soviet sector of Berlin)	1949	41,500	18,500,000
15. Hungary	1947	36,000	10,000,000
16. Poland	1947	121,100	26,500,000
17. Rumania	1948	91,600	17,000,000
18. Communist China (Not incl. Tibet)	1949	3,281,000	582,000,000
19. Outer Mongolia	1945	626,000	1,000,000
Communist China's Colonial Empire			
20. North Korea (With Communist China)	1948	48,500	9,000,000
21. North Vietnam	1951	72,000	12,000,000
22. Tibet (Annexed by Red China)	1951	469,000	1,200,000

SOURCES OF WEAKNESS IN COMMUNISM

The first source of weakness in communism is the stress on *conformity*. The most distinguishing quality of a leader is his courage to be different, to have new ideas, to be in a minority, even in solitude. Yet as time goes on, the leader in communist regimes is increasingly being replaced by the bureaucrat, the yes-man. The era of the purges in Russia in the middle nineteen thirties was the conflict between the leaders who had made the Revolution and the bureaucrats who administered it. Conformist as prerevolutionary Russia was, it was a paradise of diversity compared with the communist regime. Antigovernment parties of all types, including radical and socialist parties, functioned openly, and the press reflected all political viewpoints. *Pravda,* which became the official organ of the Communist party after the Revolution, started publication in 1912; it suffered occasional harassments, but it continued to be published.

Lenin, Trotsky, Stalin, and Khrushchev were all products of pre-communist Russia. Malenkov, Stalin's immediate successor, was the first Big Brother in Russia who was a product of communist rule. He proved not to possess the qualities of a leader; in 1955, he was removed as Prime Minister, and in 1957 he was purged by Khrushchev and exiled to Central Asia.

Under Lenin, orthodox conformity was required in social and political thought, but science and the arts were relatively unaffected. Under Stalin, the party line was applied to the physical sciences and the arts as much as to social science. After Stalin's death in 1953, requirements for orthodoxy were relaxed more in the physical sciences than in the arts. When Boris Pasternak received in 1958 the Nobel Prize in literature for his novel *Doctor Zhivago* (which was not allowed to be published in Russia), he was subjected to an organized campaign of vehement attacks and threats. Officially condemned as a traitor by the communist leaders, Pasternak was spared further humiliations by his lonely death in 1960.

Yet, despite the fate of Pasternak, a number of outstanding Soviet writers, particularly Ilya Ehrenburg among the older authors and Yevgeny Yevtushenko among the younger poets, continued to challenge the rigid party orthodoxies. The publication of *One Day in the Life of Ivan Denisovich,* by Alexander Solzhenitsyn, late in 1962 was perhaps the high point of the literary "thaw" permitted by the government. Although this story of life in a Soviet slave labor camp is cast in the form of a novel, the author wrote from personal experience, having spent the years 1945-1953 in such a camp. As the activities of the more liberally minded Soviet authors and artists grew, Khrushchev intervened again. In a major policy speech on the relation of the arts and literature to communism on March 8, 1963, Khrushchev attacked Ehrenburg and Yevtushenko by name, and repeated the old communist thesis that the Communist party regarded the press, radio, literature, painting, music, motion pictures, and the theater as "sharp ideological weapons." He continued: "In questions of art, the Central Committee of the Party will demand from every-one—from the most merited and renowned as well as from the young budding artists—unswerving adherence to the Party line." Khrushchev thus made it perfectly clear as to who is boss in Soviet artistic and intellectual activities.

In the field of biology, the Soviet agronomist Trofim D. Lysenko gained world-wide notoriety. Lysenko attacked all accepted biological knowledge by claiming that acquired characteristics can be inherited. When many biologists in the Soviet Union revolted against this theory, which is contradictory to all known and controllable facts, Lysenko addressed the Lenin Academy of Agricultural Sciences on July 31, 1948 on "The Situation in the Science of Biology." After damning traditional scientific biology, Lysenko made this statement: "The question is asked in one of the notes handed to me what is the atti-tude of the Central Committee of the Communist Party to my report. I answer: The Central Committee of the Party examined my report and approved it."

Thus, a question of utmost scientific importance was settled by the fiat of the Central Committee of the Communist Party rather than by the experimental method of the decadent capitalist scientists. Vavilov, the leading Russian geneticist and the outstanding opponent of Lysenko, was arrested in 1941 and exiled to Siberia where he eventually died.

After Stalin's death, Lysenko was attacked in several Soviet jour-nals and his influence declined for a while. But in 1957, the tide turned again in favor of Lysenko. Discussing (on April 10, 1957) the controversy between Lysenko and his opponents, Khrushchev authori-tatively stated before a scientific gathering: "If you asked me for which scientist I would vote, I would say without hesitation—for Lysenko." Since Khrushchev's one vote carries a great deal of weight in Soviet scientific circles, Lysenko's prestige was thus officially restored.

In the field of physics, the communists fully reached the Nazi level during the Stalin era. Just as the Nazis promoted a Nordic physics or mathematics, to be freed from Jewish or other non-German influences, the communists introduced their own party line into the natural sciences. Einstein was attacked by the Nazis for his Jewish physics; the communists attacked him for expressing bourgeois, idealistic con-cepts incompatible with truly proletarian dialectics. Western physicists like Niels Bohr and Heisenberg were attacked for harboring a "nar-row, reactionary outlook similar to Nazism," and were admonished to tread the "path indicated by Lenin and Stalin" along with communist or fellow-traveling scientists like Langevin and Joliot-Curie in France or Blackett and Haldane in Britain, all of whom have been cited by official communist spokesmen for special merit.

The fate of psychoanalysis under communism is another case in point. Until 1930, psychoanalysis was tolerated in the Soviet Union, having attracted considerable attention in Russia long before the Revolution. After 1930, psychoanalysis gradually fell into disfavor, and in 1936 the Communist party officially decided that psychoanalysis was incompatible with Marxism-Leninism-Stalinism. After having been branded by the Nazis as false because of its Jewish origin, psychoanalysis was condemned by communists as a web of false bourgeois concepts, and was finally assailed as an "ideological instrument of American imperialism!"

In the field of pure and applied philosophy, the communists have done much housecleaning, too. Their opposition to more conservative thinkers was to be expected, but eventually they took on progressive thinkers also. John Dewey, for example, has been roundly condemned for his pragmatic philosophy, which patient communist research has revealed to be yet another cleverly disguised instrument of American imperialism.

Another method of literary assassination is through enforced ignorance. After having talked to hundreds of Russians, a young American writer found that not one of them had ever heard of John Stuart Mill. (George Feifer, *Harper's Magazine,* December 1959, p. 43.) Any Western book, periodical, or newspaper introduced into Russia by a foreign visitor is eagerly snapped up by young Russians, who pass on such treasures from hand to hand.

Stalin felt as much at home with music as with the other arts. In January 1948 the Central Committee of the Communist Party of the Soviet Union decreed that all music must henceforth be popular, simple, and tuneful; at the same time the committee condemned the "formalism" of the best known composers in Russia, such as Shostakovich and Prokofiev. The attack was also directed against instrumental music in general and chamber music in particular, which, the composers were told, "the people did not care for," and the production of more vocal music was urged instead. In some instances, the communists not only have attacked modern art as "formalistic," "remote from the people," and "bourgeois"—the usual epithets—but have imitated the Nazis faithfully enough to charge some works of art with being "cosmopolitan."

Khrushchev, too, has come out as an authority on music and painting. Many Soviet citizens have become intensely interested in ab-

THE ART CRITIC

Courtesy Bill Mauldin and *Chicago Sun-Times*

stract painting and experimental music in recent years, such interest being heightened by the official policy of opposing such modern forms of art. In December 1962, the first abstract paintings by Soviet artists were publicly exhibited and immediately aroused enormous attention. After visiting the exhibit and seeing some of the abstract paintings, Khrushchev expressed his opinion that they could have been painted by a "donkey's tail." In his speech of March 8, 1963, he came out flatly against abstract painting and similar modern art forms, stressing the irreconcilability of communism with "abstractionism, formalism, and all other bourgeois distortions." A few weeks later, top Soviet leaders extended Khrushchev's dislike of abstract art further: even wallpapers and textile designs would have to be free from such "bourgeois decadence," since "everyday life of Soviet man must be cleansed of all vulgarity, commonplace, and abstractionism."

In the field of music, too, Khrushchev attacked modern styles in the

same speech, and picked out jazz as the typical example of undesirable music: "We stand for melodious music with content, music that
stirs the people and gives rise to strong feelings, and we are against
cacophony." Like Stalin, Khrushchev likes simple folk tunes, and
has no use for "decadent bourgeois" music like jazz or atonal music.

In literature, the communists have no use for the classical theme
"boy meets girl." Instead, officially approved communist art (called
"socialist realism") revolves around a new theme: "Boy and girl
meet machine, production rises, and all three live happily ever after."

For nearly thirty years, until 1956, Dostoevsky's novels were practically unobtainable in Russia, because his primary concern with individual guilt and responsibility proved to the Soviet rulers that he
was reactionary in his thinking and dangerous to the regime and, in
the language of Soviet literary critics, useful to the "lackeys of Wall
Street." Popular American writers such as John Steinbeck, John Dos
Passos, and Erskine Caldwell were attacked for writing books "hyenas
might have written if they could type."

Soviet thought control is augmented by a rigorous control of foreign radio broadcasts. In 1948, there were about a dozen jamming
transmitters in the Soviet Union and its eastern European satellites.
At the time of the death of Stalin, in 1953, the number rose to 1,500.
In 1958, after several years of Khrushchev's policy of "liberalization,"
there were about 2,500 jamming transmitters. This jamming equipment represents a capital investment of about 250 million dollars, and
the annual cost of operation has been estimated at about 100 million
dollars. The communists spend five to six times as much on jamming
foreign broadcasts as does the United States on its entire broadcasting program of Voice of America in all languages to all parts of the
world. Jamming is not limited to American broadcasts, but extends
to all countries that broadcast programs considered unsuitable by the
Soviet government. Factual news programs broadcast by the United
Nations have been frequently jammed, and even speeches of the
Soviet Foreign Minister at the United Nations have been jammed.

Since communist jamming activities concentrate on Russian language programs, foreign radio programs in English or French (particularly in English) are widely listened to behind the Iron Curtain.
As during the days of World War II, the British Broadcasting Corporation rates highest among Soviet listeners because its restraint,
objectivity, and truthfulness are generally admired. American programs (Voice of America and Radio Free Europe) enjoy the greatest
popularity for the excellence of the musical programs rather than for
their news and propaganada broadcasts.

Returning from a trip to the Soviet Union, Truman Capote, the American writer, reported in *The New York Times* (March 4, 1956) that a young Russian writer asked him who Freud, Proust, and Kafka were—he had never heard of them! By contrast, as soon as "national communism" under Gomulka was firmly established in Poland, Polish translations early in 1957 of George Orwell's *1984* and Arthur Koestler's *Darkness at Noon,* the two greatest novels on communist totalitarianism, were instantaneous and sensational successes.

One of the most hopeful aspects about communist indoctrination and thought-control is that they have proved much less effective than were believed to be. The remarkable thing about the Hungarian Revolution of 1956 was the predominant role of young people in the fight for freedom. Most of the fighters were in their teens or early twenties, all were products of communist monopoly in education and mass communication.

In Russia, too, forty years of communist indoctrination have not proved as successful as the Soviet leaders and the outside world thought. After Khrushchev's anti-Stalin speech before the Twentieth Congress of the Communist Party of the Soviet Union on February 25, 1956, there was a breath of fresh air, for a few months at least, and young people began to show strange feelings and interests. University students pinned foreign broadcast texts to bulletin boards, raised unorthodox questions in party-sponsored meetings, and otherwise made such a nuisance of themselves that the Communist Party of Moscow had to admit that "some sections of the student body have been subjected to the influence of unhealthy tendencies, and have occasionally come under the influence of ideas alien to the spirit of their motherland." (*Manchester Guardian Weekly,* January 3, 1957.) In Leningrad, too, *Pravda* became alarmed by the unrest among students, and demanded disciplinary action against the "politically illiterate demagogues" among the students, or those who spoke too freely, and showed the "influence of unhealthy tendencies" toward freedom of expression. Yet in spite of frequent harassments by police and university authorities, spontaneous student groups have spread from Moscow and Leningrad to many other Soviet universities. In these groups, an American visitor to the Soviet academic scene reports: "there is 'free' philosophy, not 'official' philosophy. They discuss books by Russell, Sartre, Camus: they listen to discussions on existentialism and totalitarianism, in which 'totalitarian society' is used to denote ambiguously the Soviet order." (Lewis S. Feuer, "Dilemma of the Soviet Intellectual," *The New York Times Magazine,* August 18, 1963, p. 80.) From time to time, the leaders of such groups are apprehended by the secret police, but the punishment is generally expulsion from the university or immediate military service, whereas in Stalin's times such students would have been shipped off to a Siberian slave labor camp. While such rebellious students still are no more than a small minority among Soviet youths, their influence is bound to grow if there is no return to the harsh methods of Stalinist repression. Whenever totalitarian rulers grant "a little freedom" to their subjects, they quickly discover that it cannot remain static and either grows or has to be repressed.

Despite Soviet anti-foreign, and particularly anti-American, hate propaganda over four decades, Soviet youth shows an insatiable hunger for foreign styles, fashions, and music, "particularly anything and everything American." (*The New York Times,* February 3, 1957.) Jazz, which had been forbidden for many years as the music of decadent American capitalism, became the rage of Soviet youth as soon as the ban was lifted in 1956. Louis Armstrong, Stan Kenton, Duke Ellington, and Erroll Garner are among the jazz idols of the Soviet hit parade. Frank Sinatra has had a devastating effect on the Soviet female contingent, from bobby-soxers to stately matrons, and Doris Day, Rosemary Clooney, and Patti Page have conquered the hearts of the male segment of Soviet youth. The pathetic craving of Soviet youngsters for Western "culture" is most dramatically evidenced by their enthusiasm for Elvis Presley, the secret weapon of the United States in the struggle with austere communism. Cut in Russia on discarded hospital x-ray plates, Presley records sell for as much as five rubles ($5.50 at the official rate of exchange).

The craze for American music, especially jazz, went so far that Soviet leaders felt it necessary to call a halt, and to propose a return to Stalinist standards and tastes in music, as in other fields. Dmitri Shepilov, top Communist Party propagandist (and former editor of *Pravda* and Minister of Foreign Affairs) warned Soviet composers on April 3, 1957, not to imitate "decadent western composers" and particularly American music, which he described as follows: "All this nervous and insane boogie woogie and rock 'n' roll are the wild orgies of cavemen. They are devoid of any elements of beauty and melody. They represent an uncontrolled release of base passions, a burst of the lowest feelings and sexual urges." Yet despite these warnings by Khrushchev and other leaders, jazz proved irrepressible. In 1962, the Soviet authorities—following again the theory of "a little freedom"—opened two "youth cafés" in which young people could listen to jazz over coffee or soft drinks. Yet two establishments for a city of six million quickly proved insufficient, and within a year jazz could be heard all over Moscow and some other major cities. Visiting Polish and Yugoslav bands cater to those who look for "progressive" jazz and even bolder new horizons in modern music still frowned on by the official tastemakers.

The craving of Soviet youth for foreign ways of feeling and acting is partly due to their pent-up curiosity after having been cut off from the outside world for so long. Partly, and perhaps more importantly, it is due to something deeper—a sense of dullness and frustration produced by Soviet conditions of living. Over and over, Soviet youth express their feeling to foreign visitors in these words: "It is so boring here. Life is so dull." (*The New York Times,* February 3, 1957.)

If the lack of freedom will not eventually make Soviet youth rebellious, the dullness and austerity of Soviet life perhaps will.

One form of such rebellion is the attempt to leave the Soviet Union without permission. It is extremely difficult for Soviet citizens to go abroad even for a short visit. During the five-year period of 1958-1962, for example, only 1,300 Soviet citizens were allowed by their government to visit the United States (nearly always traveling in groups), whereas 47,000 Americans visited the Soviet Union during the same period. When it comes to permanent emigration, Soviet citizens generally do not even bother to apply, as the desire to emigrate is considered evidence of hostility to the government. Thus, some more adventurous souls try to leave the country illegally. Under Stalin, this crime of treason was often punished with death. Under Khrushchev's more liberal approach, such attempts are still considered as crimes of treason, but the penalty now is merely a prison sentence of 6-10 years. (*The New York Times,* February 2, 1963.) What worries the Soviet authorities is that many of these would-be escapers from the Soviet Union are young people, and that many of these young people come from good families whose parents are party members. Another form of rebellion among some young people is in the economic field, such as black marketeering, theft of state property, and other serious economic offenses. In 1961, the death penalty was introduced for such crimes, and during the subsequent two years 100 persons were sentenced to death for "economic crimes." (*The Economist,* June 1, 1963.)

The *main weakness of communism,* however, is the *discrepancy between ideal and reality.* Its leaders proclaim lofty ideals for the renewal of mankind and yet use inhuman means, age-old instruments of oppressive despotism. One of the deepest insights of the liberal way of life is that *means and ends cannot be too sharply separated* from each other, and that the nature of the means employed in realizing an end will determine the character of the end itself. Communism acts in total disregard of this axiom, and purports to build a new fellowship of love and fraternity with the knout and the slave labor camp or "correctional camp," as it is now called.

One of the most powerful original messages of communism was its protest against social inequality and privilege based on class and caste. Yet in communist Russia a class system is being created that exceeds by far the class system Marx sought to supersede. In addition, communism has created the caste of political commissars, men who do not feel themselves accountable to man or God, men for whom the execution squad is the final method of persuasion.

Finally, the gap between promise and performance can be clearly seen with regard to the *freedom of nations*. The communist promise is international brotherhood and equality of all nations. In the Soviet Union itself, a fervent cult of the Great Russians has been built up in recent years; outside of the Soviet Union, the Russians have carried on a foreign policy that is openly and cynically imperialistic.

**REVOLTS
AGAINST
SOVIET COMMUNISM**

Titoism is a case in point. In 1948, Yugoslavia was more communized than any of the Soviet satellites in eastern Europe. Tito's crime in 1948 was not abandoning communism in favor of capitalism, but the much worse offense of trying to regain national independence for the peoples of Yugoslavia from Moscow. The Soviet Union mobilized all its resources of propaganda and subversion to overthrow Tito and his brand of national communism. At the time, few people thought Tito could defy Moscow successfully. Yet the unlikely happened, and Yugoslavia is still independent. Since 1955, the Soviet Union has come to realize that an independent Yugoslavia is here to stay, and has been compelled by the force of circumstances to come to a *modus vivendi* with the Tito regime. Yet Titoism is, by communist admission, a disease rampant throughout the communist world. No communist state or party is free from it. Titoism, or "national communism," reflects a people's natural desire to be free from foreign domination, an issue over which many empires have come to grief in the past.

Political and economic controls were relaxed in Yugoslavia following the break with Moscow. The peasants were given the choice of returning to individual farming, and the overwhelming majority of peasants chose without much hesitation to abandon the collectives. As a result, the production of food greatly increased, and Yugoslavia's economic development pushed forward at a rapid pace. Also, foreign books and newspapers are now obtainable in Yugoslavia—although in limited quantities—and there is a considerable exchange of students and teachers with Western countries, particularly the United States. Foreign movies are shown, and Western plays are performed on the Yugoslav stage. Travel abroad is difficult, but not impossible, and there has even been emigration to other countries, some legal and some illegal.

Yet the communist leadership in Yugoslavia reminds the people from time to time that there are limits to freedom in a communist state. The fate of Milovan Djilas is a case in point. Djilas was a life-long friend and one of Tito's closest friends and aides both during and after World War II. But in the early 1950's, Djilas began to express democratic ideas. He urged a free press and free public discussion, and he even dared to suggest that Yugoslavia be permitted to have more than one party. This was too much for the communist rulers. Djilas was tried in 1955 and sentenced to three years in prison. In 1957, a book by Djilas entitled *The New Class* was smuggled out of Yugoslavia and published in New York. In his book, Djilas exposed communism as nothing more than an instrument of the communist ruling class (the "new class") for the exploitation and domination of the Yugoslav people. A new trial followed in which he received another seven years of imprisonment. Released from prison in 1961 for reasons of health, Djilas went to work on another book, *Conversations with Stalin,* describing the talks he had had with Stalin in 1944-1948. The book was published in 1962 in New York; Djilas was tried again, and this time he received nine years of prison. A communist from early boyhood, Djilas spent three years in prison under the anticommunist regime of Yugoslavia before World War II. Under communism, he has found out how much more efficient communist repression is than that of the preceding system he helped to destroy.

After Tito's rebellious break with Moscow in 1948, the next major explosion took place on June 16 and 17, 1953, in East Germany. Food conditions had steadily deteriorated under Soviet exploitation and East German communist mismanagement, and there was less food than during World War II. Even bread and potatoes, the staple diet of communist economic planning, were scarce.

The spark which fired the smouldering resentment of the people was a government announcement on May 28, 1953, that workers' wages would be cut further unless they produced at least 10 per cent

EAST BERLIN 1953

more than in the past. On June 16, building workers on Stalin Avenue in East Berlin started a spontaneous strike, and marched toward government headquarters. The strike spread quickly throughout East Germany on that day and the next, and in many communities the workers were in command of the situation, occupying police offices, liberating political prisoners, and setting government and Communist party buildings on fire. Many members of the police either took a wait-and-see attitude, or even went over to the rebels. Before long, the rebels demanded, in addition to more tolerable living conditions, free elections, free labor unions, and the end of Soviet domination.

Hesitating at first to intervene directly, the Soviet forces quickly realized that the communist regime would soon be overthrown completely, and thousands of Soviet tanks moved into the major strongholds of rebellion, suppressing it in a few days. Several hundred Germans died in the uprising, hundreds were wounded, and about 50,000 were imprisoned.

The East Germans continued to show their distaste for communist rule in the one way still left open: mass flights into West Germany through the escape hatch of free West Berlin. In the years 1950-1961, about four million East Germans fled to West Germany, or nearly one-fifth of the entire population of East Germany. What made this mass exodus particularly painful to the communist government was the fact that the refugees included disproportionately large numbers of young people, skilled workers, and professional people. The Soviet government realized that, should the mass flight of East Germans into West Germany continue for another decade or two, East Germany would soon become a country without people, and all that might be left would be the Soviet occupying army and its loyal puppet government of Walter Ulbricht. As a result, the East German government sealed off the borders between East and West Berlin on August 13, 1961 by hastily erecting a barbed-wire and concrete barrier. During the first two years of the Berlin Wall, only 16,000 East Germans managed to escape from the prison into which East Germany had been turned, and at least sixty-five were killed while trying to escape, mostly to West Berlin. More perhaps than any other action of communist policy the Berlin Wall has come to express, before the whole world, the nature of communism as a vast prison.

Exactly three years after the uprising in East Germany the Poles revolted. On June 28, 1956, thousands of workers of the Stalin Steel Works in Poznan went on strike early in the morning, and moved toward the center of the city, chanting "bread, bread, bread," singing Polish national songs, carrying the old Polish national flags, and refusing to disperse despite the tank formations quickly brought into the city by the communist authorities. Before long, the striking workers occupied the Communist party headquarters and the radio station, and set the city prison on fire after freeing the prisoners. In the ensuing battle with army and police, a battle that lasted for several days, about 200 Poles lost their lives, thousands were wounded, and many more thousands arrested.

Militarily, the rebellion was successfully repressed, but politically it unleashed a chain of events which is still in the making. In October 1956, Wladyslaw Gomulka was elected First Secretary of the Polish Communist Party. This announcement came as a bombshell, because Gomulka was known as the leader of Titoism or "national communism" in Poland and had spent several years in prison for that crime.

For a while, the Russians considered full-scale occupation of the country and the re-establishment of Stalinism by force. But the Poles stood their ground, and Poland had won, for the time being, its struggle for some degree of national independence, although its government continued to be communist dominated.

One of the first steps of the new leadership was to release Cardinal Wyszynski, the symbol of Catholic resistance to communism, from prison, and to permit religious instruction again in public schools. Poland became the only country behind the Iron Curtain to have a Catholic university (in Lublin) as well as a network of Catholic schools from kindergarten to secondary school. Since 1960, the government has closed some of the Catholic schools and harassed the others through harsh tax measures, but on the whole the position of the Catholic Church still remains strong, more so than in any other communist regime. Two figures testify to the strength of the Catholic Church in Poland. Before World War II, the country had 31,000 priests and 7,251 churches and chapels. In 1962, there were 53,000 priests and 10,981 churches and chapels. (*Survey,* July 1963, p. 167.)

The peasants were given by Gomulka the choice of leaving the collective farms, and they made full use of the opportunity; only a very small portion of the land remains in state and collective farms. As a result of the return to private farming, food production rose, leading to improved living conditions of the urban population as well. In industry, too, the harsh controls over workers were relaxed, and industrial production moved steadily forward from its previous low.

Since the triumph of Gomulka in October of 1956, Poland has steadily, though cautiously, moved away from Stalinist totalitarianism to a mixture—as yet unsettled in its final proportions—of authoritarianism in government and relative liberty in thought, religion, and literature. The Polish people, who have always considered themselves the last outpost of Western civilization on the European Continent, the cultural boundary between Europe and Asia, are desperately looking to the West for encouragement and inspiration.

As in Yugoslavia, many Western books and newspapers are obtainable in Poland. Modern tendencies in painting and music are eagerly discussed and practiced, and American jazz is played as enthusiastically as anywhere in Europe. Novelists, poets, and philosophers in Poland have been able to express more liberal views than even in Yugoslavia. Numerous Polish teachers, writers, and students have visited Western countries, including the United States, and American scholars and students have visited Poland. They all find deep eagerness among the Polish people to maintain close contacts with the Western world.

In foreign policy, the new Polish government has tread softly, because "Poland's neighbors are not Australian shepherds," as Poles are being reminded by their leaders. Poland is a member of the Warsaw Pact, the Moscow-sponsored military counterpart to NATO, including Russia and the east European communist-run states. She realizes that she can no more offend Russia openly and directly than can Finland, which also, though democratic and independent, must refrain from any foreign policy that could be construed as anti-Soviet by the Kremlin.

Yet in 1957 the Polish government took the bold—for a communist country—step of sending a mission to the United States to obtain economic and financial aid. In granting nearly one billion dollars in the years 1957-1963, the United States took a calculated risk, since Poland might revert to Stalinism some day, and since such aid allows the Soviet Union to divert resources from Poland to more aggressive purposes. Should Poland continue on her path of internal freedom, American aid might strengthen her ties with the West and show the Polish people who is exploiting them and who is helping them in an hour of need.

For the time being, totalitarianism of the Stalinist type is dead in Poland, but as yet it is uncertain how much liberty the individual citizen will be permitted under the Gomulka regime, or a regime led by any other "national communist." For a few years after the changes in 1956, freedom of religion and freedom of speech and the press were relatively high. From 1960 on, the government has gradually nibbled away at these liberties, without daring to abolish them in a single stroke. In industry, controls over workers have been tightened, and in farming the government still tries to induce the peasants to give up "capitalist" farming, since it is well understood that in the long run Poland cannot remain economically half communist and half free —collectivist in its industry and capitalist in its agriculture.

This new revival of authoritarianism has also been felt in the relations between church and state. Increasingly, the government has attacked church leaders on the ground that they teach loyalty to their church rather than to the government. In his Lenten sermon on March 19, 1961, Cardinal Wyszynski answered Gomulka's accusations: "I tell you, you Caesars, you will bow to your God, and you will serve only him. Satan is mighty, but man will not bow his head before him. Man was created not just to be a consuming animal; man is called to something higher."

The events in Poland in 1956 immediately raised hope and passion in Hungary. On October 23, 1956, university students, quickly joined by thousands of industrial workers, held a mass meeting in Parliament Square. Expressing their sympathy for the Polish fight for freedom and independence, they put forward a series of demands, including among others: the evacuation of Russian troops from Hungary; free elections; free labor unions and the right to strike; revision of workers' wages and a complete reorganization of the economy; the immediate release of political prisoners and the return of Hungarians deported to the Soviet Union; removal of the statue of Stalin; and, finally, reorganization of the compulsory system of farm collectives.

The political police turned a peaceful meeting into bloody rebellion by firing on the students and workers. The fighting quickly spread throughout the whole country. The workers declared a general strike, and the freedom fighters were soon joined by the regular Hungarian army and police. On the communist side, the Hungarian political police were joined by powerful Russian tank forces. Yet the incredible happened. The freedom fighters won their struggle, and on October 29, 1956 Hungary was free. Political authority was exercised by the representatives of popular organizations, and almost at once dozens of democratic newspapers began to be published. Communists were nowhere to be seen, and statues of Stalin were publicly burned. Also, political prisoners were set free. The best known among them was Cardinal Mindszenty, who had been imprisoned since 1948.

However, this period of Hungarian freedom and independence lasted for only five days. On November 3 close to 200,000 Soviet troops and 5,000 tanks moved into Hungary to suppress Hungarian freedom. After a week of heavy fighting, the revolution was put down. Prime Minister Nagy was kidnapped by the Russians and later executed. Over 35,000 Hungarians were killed in the fighting, and many more wounded. Many thousands were deported to Siberia, and over 200,000 managed to escape to Austria. The physical destruction of the towns was worse than that suffered by Hungary in World War II, when she was a major battleground for many months.

Despite their military defeat by Soviet tanks, the Hungarians learned several lessons. First, the spectacle of rebelling workers trampling and burning the red flag as the symbol of oppression destroyed the myth, once and for all, that Soviet communism represents the cause of the workers. Throughout the whole Hungarian Revolution, the Hungarian Workers' Council, and local workers' councils across the nation, were the center of anti-Soviet and anticommunist activity.

Second, the Hungarian Revolution proved that Moscow-sponsored regimes of eastern Europe are not national governments, but stooges of the Kremlin. Without the overwhelming force of 200,000 Russian troops and 5,000 tanks, the Hungarian Revolution would have decisively triumphed as there was very little resistance on the part of the few native communists.

Third, the Hungarian Revolution revealed the inefficacy of communist indoctrination. The revolution was touched off by university students—the products of communist education and indoctrination.

Pavlov, the great Russian physiologist of the nineteenth century, discovered in his experiments with dogs the phenomenon of conditioned reflexes through continued repetition of the same stimuli. The communists have tried to apply Pavlovian techniques to humans, in order to transform man into a conditioned reflex machine, behaving automatically and unthinkingly in accordance with a predetermined pattern inculcated in him by his masters.

The evidence of the Hungarian Revolution, particularly as supplied by the resistance of youngsters in their teens and early twenties, suggests that—despite Pavlov and communist indoctrination—there is still a difference between man and dog.

Finally, the Hungarian Revolution gave the death-blow to the theory, obsessively clung to by the free world, that revolution in a totalitarian police state is impossible. According to this theory, revolution was possible in the eighteenth or nineteenth century because the government did not then possess the powerful weapons of suppression available to it in this century. The Hungarian Revolution has proved that the mind of man is still king, as it has always been, and that totalitarian despotism of the twentieth century cannot rely exclusively on terror and torture any more than could despotism in the past.

During the first years after the crushing of the Hungarian Revolution and the installation of the puppet government of Janos Kadar, it seemed to many, inside and outside of Hungary, that the heroic effort of the Hungarian people had been all in vain. Harsh measures were imposed by the Kadar government on the political, economic, and intellectual fronts, and Hungary seemed for a while more Stalinist than the Soviet Union itself. Yet, in the end this reasoning—an implied defense of inert submission to communist totalitarianism—proved wrong. The very fact of the Hungarian Revolution—failure or no failure—encouraged tendencies toward more national independence in other communist states. From 1960 on, Albania has been able to defy the Soviet Union completely by unreservedly siding with Red China in her conflict with the Soviet Union. Rumania, always held up as a perfect example of unquestioning obedience to her Soviet overlords, has recently developed strong ideas of autonomy in the field of economic planning, refusing to be integrated into an over-all eastern European economy along strictly Soviet ideas.

In Hungary herself these changes have been most marked. Although the active rebellion was put down, the Kadar government gradually realized that Soviet bayonets and tanks were not enough if Hungary was to develop economically and regain some sort of political stability. By 1963, this movement of relaxing the most oppressive controls gathered considerable momentum; thousands of political prisoners were released under a general amnesty, and the government eased its stringent controls in industry and farming. Writers and artists were given greater freedom of expression, and noncommunists were appointed to important positions. Whereas the previous slogan had been "He who is not for us is against us," the new official slogan became "He who is not against us is with us." In the summer of 1963, about 50,000 Hungarians were permitted to visit Austria, and large numbers travelled to other European countries as tourists. In the field of foreign relations, Hungary has tried, since 1963, to improve her relations with the Vatican and the churches in Hungary, and particular efforts have been made to improve relations with the United States. By the end of 1963, Hungary was next to Poland the least oppressive of the communist regimes in eastern Europe. In her foreign policy, she continues to follow, like Poland does, the line laid down by the Kremlin.

The reverberations of the Hungarian Revolution were not confined to Europe, however. In 1959, the Tibetan people revolted against Red China, which had conquered Tibet by armed force in 1950. Red China had to fight heavy battles for several weeks before the rebellion was put down. Thousands were killed, and over 40,000 Tibetans, including the Dalai Lama, their "god-king," fled into neighboring countries, mostly into India.

The Hungarian Revolution provided a conclusive answer to the variety of Soviet reactions to deviations of satellites from the Moscow line. Why did the Soviet Union tolerate the changes in Yugoslavia and Poland toward "national communism" of a more liberal variety, while it suppressed by military force the uprisings in East Germany, Poznan, and Hungary? Specifically, why did it allow, at almost the same time in the fall of 1956, the changes in Poland, the most important of the satellites, while it ruthlessly suppressed the changes in Hungary, a much less important satellite?

The answer to these questions may be found in this consideration: in both Yugoslavia and Poland, the changes were brought about *from the top*. They were palace revolutions within the top leadership of the Yugoslav and Polish Communist Parties, whereas the movements in East Germany, Poznan, and Hungary stemmed *from below*. The Soviet people themselves are used to palace revolutions within the communist leadership; by allowing Titoism and Gomulkaism, the Soviet leaders demonstrate to the Soviet people that changes in a communist state can only come from the top. Had the Soviet Union given in to the popular pressure and uprisings in East Germany, Poznan, and Hungary, such examples might have set a dangerous and provocative precedent for possible changes in the Soviet Union itself. By tolerating Tito and Gomulka and saving them from true popular democracy, the Soviet leaders think of their own necks.

THE SINO-SOVIET CONFLICT

The most explosive conflict within world communism is as yet to come: Red China against the Soviet Union. Basically, it is a struggle over power, but like every power struggle it has other elements as well.

First, there is the issue of nationalism, or Chinese against Russians. For over three hundred years, Russia has expanded her empire in Asia, frequently at the expense of China. Russia has, therefore, traditionally feared the prospect of a strong and united China ruled by an effective central government, the kind of government that communist totalitarianism has established in Red China since 1949. From the traditional Chinese viewpoint, the Russians are meddlesome troublemakers, imperialist expansionists, and—by the standards of the ancient Chinese civilization—a horde of crude barbarians. In the eyes of the Chinese, Russians are not (as they appear to some Westerners) semi-Asiatic or semi-Oriental, but full-fledged Europeans and, as such, barbarians by definition.

Even under Stalin, Titoism showed that the force of nationalism was stronger than the myth of "international proletarian solidarity and fraternity." If the nationalism of little Yugoslavia could prevail against Stalin, the nationalism of a great power like China, the Chinese feel, is even more destined to prevail against a mere Khrushchev. Marx or no Marx, over 700 million Chinese will not forever accept the idea that the 220 million motley peoples of the Soviet Union are the leaders of the communist world. The Chinese are quite familiar with the Confucian saying, "When two men ride on a horse, only one can sit in front." The Chinese are determined that they, not the Russians, will sit in front.

Closely connected with the traditional force of nationalism is the issue of population and resources. Over 700 million Chinese inhabit a densely populated area, with an annual increase of population running to about 12 million people. By contrast, the 220 million inhabitants of the Soviet Union live in a much vaster territory, and the annual increase of population is only about 3 million. On the

Russian side of the common border, the land is empty, and the population very sparse. On the Chinese side, the land is overcrowded. This growing gap between the Soviet ratio of people and resources on the one hand and the Chinese ratio on the other may some day lead to Chinese expansion at the expense of Soviet territory.

In particular, the Chinese have publicly proclaimed in recent years that they do not recognize the imperialist treaties and conquests at the expense of China in the past. This is of particular concern to Russia, since she took more territory from China than any other imperialist power. The major areas in dispute include vast Far Eastern stretches of land, from the mouth of the Amur River down the Pacific coast of Siberia and reaching west as far as Lake Baikal. Today, this area of 5.5 million square miles is inhabited by 9 million Soviet citizens. The Chinese feel that, with more intensive cultivation of the soil, at least 100 million Chinese could live there—albeit on a lower Chinese standard of living. Next, Red China has also shown desires for the "liberation" of formerly Chinese territories in Soviet Central Asia, covering an area of about 0.5 million square miles and 10 million people. This is rich land with a great potential in food and fibers. Finally, there is Outer Mongolia, with nearly one million square miles and only one million population. A Chinese province from 1686 to 1911, it became a Russian protectorate in 1912-1919, and again a Chinese province in 1919-1921. In 1921, Outer Mongolia became an independent state in form, but in fact completely dominated by Moscow.

While the Soviet leaders have repudiated many of the internal policies of the tsars, they are not willing to give up the fruits of tsarist conquest, be it in favor of the Chinese or of anybody else. So far, the Red Chinese have publicly stated that they do not wish to settle the issue of these disputed areas by force, but by peaceful negotiation at "the appropriate time," that is, when China is strong enough to bargain effectively with the Soviet Union. Chinese maps now indicate the area of the country before and after the foreign imperialist grabs of Chinese territory. By coincidence, Russia always appears in these maps as the foremost imperialist, helping herself to more Chinese territory than any other imperialist state of the past. Since such maps are published in the officially prescribed school books in Red China, a whole generation is growing up eager to regain the lost territories.

Far from dismissing these territorial ambitions of the Red Chinese as idle speculation, the Soviet government has taken them seriously. In 1963, the Soviet government began a drive to double the population of the disputed areas in the east within a decade, and supplemented this campaign with detailed economic plans designed to attract, and provide for, a rapidly growing population. Even if this project of doubling the population of the Soviet Far East were to succeed, the Chinese population is multiplying so much faster than the Soviet that it is doubtful whether the Soviets can ever match the Chinese population pressure by transferring its own population in sufficiently large numbers to match the Chinese density of population in even an approximate manner. In the meantime, the Red Chinese have embarked on an intensified settlement program at two crucial frontiers with the Soviet Union: Northern Manchuria and Sinkiang. The Soviet authorities are aware of this Chinese pressure on their borders, and Soviet border guards in the Far East and Central Asia have been alerted against "enemy violators." (*The Economist,* March 16, 1963.)

Soviet fears of a resurgent China have also been seen in the economic field. During the first years of the communist regime in China, from about 1950 to 1957, Soviet aid and advice were significant in the total economic planning of Red China. After 1957, tensions gradually developed, and the Soviets took measures against Red China where they could be most painful: in the economic sphere. In 1959, the first repatriations of Soviet advisers, experts, and other technicians took place; by the middle of 1960, these repatriations were about finished. Interestingly, Soviet aid to Red China—even in the early years of closest cooperation—never included the atomic field, a precautionary measure for which the Soviet leaders later could claim much credit in their country. However, the Soviet Union did not only cut off all technical aid after 1960. In some instances, the departing Soviet technicians even took with them the plans of the projects they were engaged on, as was the case in the huge Sanmen Narrows Dam on the Yellow River.

Moreover, the Red Chinese also had to suffer a considerable decline of trade with the Soviet Union and its satellites after 1959. Soviet-Chinese trade in 1959 amounted to about two billion dollars. By 1962, this figure dropped to 680 million dollars, or by about two-thirds. The Chinese trade with the Soviet satellites suffered similar declines. Since Chinese imports from the Soviet Union and its satellites included such vital items as arms, machinery, and industrial raw materials, the sharp Soviet bloc curtailments of exports to Red China have hit her very hard. Also, the Red Chinese will not forget so soon that even during the three catastrophic years (1959-1962) of the Chinese economy the Soviets insisted on Chinese repayment of earlier loans in the form of foods and consumer goods (such as textiles), in both of which China was desperately short. Paradoxically, while in theory Red China tries to appear more virulently anti-Western than the Russians, she has tried to increase her trade with the noncommunist world since 1959, and by 1962 such trade already surpassed that of 1959. While the United States maintains an absolute embargo on trade with Red China, several western European and other noncommunist nations have shown themselves more receptive to such Chinese overtures—both for economic reasons and possibly also on the political speculation that intensified Chinese trade with noncommunist nations might make the chasm between Red China and Russia even more serious.

Diplomatically, too, the Soviet Union and Red China have different interests, for reasons of geography if for no other. For the Soviet Union, the problem of Germany and the more specific issue of Berlin are the key problems in Europe—in both of which Red China has shown very little interest. By contrast, Red China's number one issue in Asia is the conquest of Formosa—a matter which is of little concern to Russia. In the struggle between India and Red China, the Soviet Union has not even pretended to be a neutral. From the beginning of the Chinese aggressions against India in 1959, the Soviet Union at first refused to side with the aggressor, and later openly aided India with jet fighters, transport planes, helicopters, and other equipment. She has also aided India in building her own factory producing Soviet-type jet fighters. At the opening of an Indian trade fair at Moscow on July 20, 1963, Khrushchev not only made a personal appearance—in itself an intended slap at Red China—but even went so far as to say that the Soviet Union and India stood "side by side" on international problems, "particularly the problem of securing peace."

The case of India illustrates the two divergent approaches of Red China and Russia to the goal—shared by all communists everywhere —of spreading communism throughout the world, particularly the underdeveloped world. The Soviet approach under Khrushchev has been that the first objective is to get a foothold in an underdeveloped country through economic aid, propaganda, and subversion, with the immediate objective of neutralizing and minimizing Western (particularly American) influence as rapidly as possible. If subsequent events develop along hoped for lines, then the Soviet approach fully envisages Soviet support for local civil wars and minor international wars fought with conventional weapons.

By contrast, the Red Chinese approach to the problem of communizing the underdeveloped countries is different. In the first place, the Chinese argue that Soviet economic aid should only go to communist states (like China herself) or those well on the road to becoming communized, but not to "capitalist regimes" like India or Egypt. As to the spreading of communism in underdeveloped countries, the Chinese urge Soviet support for more direct—that is, armed —action. After the Soviet withdrawal of missiles from Cuba in October 1962, the Chinese communists attacked Khrushchev as an "adventurist" and a "coward" for having embarked on an important project of spreading communism, only to "chicken out" before the American "paper tiger." When the Soviets replied that the paper tiger had "nuclear teeth," the Chinese remained unconvinced and told the Cubans that they had been sold out by the Russians to the "American imperialists."

The Soviet Union hopes to communize the world through leadership in economics and science, propaganda, subversion, and minor wars short of all-out nuclear war. The Chinese position is that such a nuclear world war is not inevitable, because the West is unlikely to strike back with nuclear weapons if pushed harder than the Soviets are willing to do. However, the Red Chinese reason, should the risk of nuclear war materialize, such risk must be accepted, because nuclear war would see, not the end of mankind, but of capitalism, on

Drawing by Alan Dunne. © 1949 The New Yorker Magazine, Inc.

"Karl Marx say . . ."

the ruins of which communism would triumph everywhere. For the Chinese, a loss of 200 million people in a nuclear conflict would still leave enough Chinese to carry on. For the Soviet Union, a similar loss of 200 million people would mean the destruction of the whole country, and Soviet leaders are, therefore, less comfortable about the prospect of nuclear warfare.

The two illustrations of India and Cuba also show that differences are not primarily based on different interpretations of communist dogma. In a general way, the Soviet approach toward the communiza- tion of the world expresses the attitude of a country that has ac- quired much self-confidence and that feels that time is on its side. By contrast, Red China has accomplished relatively little, as measured by the standards of other great powers (like the United States or the Soviet Union), either in the field of economic development or scien- tific leadership. She is, therefore, in a hurry and willing to take greater risks in direct action. Moreover, in the case of India the national interests of China and Russia would be different and very likely op- posed, even if Lenin had never laid down any guidelines for com- munizing the world. Both Russia and China have one major interest with respect to India: to see to it that India not become subservient to China (as viewed by Russia) or to Russia (as viewed by China). By aiding India in her self-defense against Chinese imperialism,

Russia today is doing no more than trying to preserve the balance of power in Asia, just as in Europe Britain has for centuries sided with the states that were threatened by a hegemonious power on the European continent.

The competition between China and Russia is taking place on all continents, both within communist states as well as within communist parties in noncommunist states. In Europe, Albania, the poorest of the communist states, has come under the influence of Red China. In Asia, Africa, and Latin America Red China portrays herself as the true leader of the poor, have-not nations, whereas Russia is pictured as being too busy with keeping what she has, and not dedicated enough to world revolution. In Asia, Red China leads over the Soviet Union in North Korea and North Vietnam, whereas Soviet influence is paramount in the communist regime of Outer Mongolia. Among the Asian communist movements, Soviet influence is dominant in Ceylon and India, although in both cases there are strong pro-Peking factions.

Many Asian Communist parties deliberately adopt an attitude of nonalignment in the Sino-Soviet conflict in order to obtain greater freedom of action by playing one side against the other. Some of the Asian, African, and Latin American parties are truly neutral between Moscow and Peking; others are nonaligned, but favoring to some degree one side or the other. In some cases, the local Communist parties have been rent by internal dissension over the Sino-Soviet issue to such an extent that factions and splinter groups have developed threatening the unity of the movement as a whole.

From the beginning of 1963 on, the Chinese communists have persistently played on one major theme in their conflict with Russia, a theme that has particular relevance in the underdeveloped countries: color. A mockery of anything even remotely related to Marx or Lenin, the theme of race and color may well become the most powerful weapon in the hands of the Chinese against the Russians. Fully aware that the majority of the world's people are nonwhite, and that in most underdeveloped countries the colored vastly outnumber the whites, Red China is trying to create the image of Russia as but another white imperialist power, seeking to impose its will on the poor, nonwhite masses in Asia, Africa, and Latin America. Thus, when the Soviet Union signed the partial nuclear test ban agreement with the United States and Great Britain in the summer of 1963, Red China refused to join, because she was eager to get ahead with her own atomic weapons program. Yet very soon she publicly attacked the agreement as another example of the Russians joining with the white imperialist "haves" against the "toiling masses" of the non-whites throughout the world.

In spite of all the tensions and conflicts between Red China and the Soviet Union the nations of the free world should not forget that the Sino-Soviet conflict is not over the issue of whether to bury the noncommunist nations, but *how* to bury them. Freedom will survive only if the policies of the free nations are flexible enough to cope with both the Chinese and Soviet methods of communist expansion.

THE ISSUE OF COMMUNISM

The communists, following Lenin and Stalin, assert that the issue which divides the world, and for which there is no peaceful solution, is the clash between individual, capitalist enterprise and public, collective ownership of the means of production and distribution in industry and agriculture.

This communist analysis of the world situation is concurred with, oddly enough, in capitalist countries by some extreme conservatives, men who claim to be the most uncompromising foes of communism. Such men constantly acknowledge the validity of the communist party line by asserting that the preservation of free enterprise is the supreme goal of the free world, and that the main threat of communism lies in its opposition to private enterprise.

Yet to accept this communist-conservative interpretation of the present world struggle is to fall into an erroneous analysis of the facts and an even more disastrous formulation of policy. The partial socialization of basic industries in Britain and in the Scandinavian countries has proved that varying forms of industrial ownership and organization do not in themselves constitute a source of conflict. The staunchest allies of the United States are Britain and Norway in Europe, Australia and New Zealand in the Pacific, and Israel in the Near East —nations with the strongest socialist movements in the world. The Anglo-American alliance after World War II, culminating in the North Atlantic Treaty Organization, is the closest association of the United States and Britain ever formed in time of peace, and on the British side it was initiated and carried through by the socialist Labor government.

Socialists in Britain, as in other countries, understand that their disagreement with certain aspects of American capitalism, or even with capitalism in general, is a minor issue compared with their disagreements with totalitarian communist imperialism.

What makes communism an issue of peace or war is not its opposition to capitalism, but its determination to impose its philosophy by force of arms. *The proper division of the world, therefore, is not between communism and capitalism, but between nations that prepare for aggressive conquest and nations that honestly and sincerely wish to maintain peace.*

The internal economic system—be it capitalism, socialism, a mixed economy, or communism—is of no necessary relevance to the main issue of world peace and the right of nations to be free.

Similar to the error of confusing communism with anticapitalism is the equally common error of confusing it with *antidemocracy*. However understandable the emotional and intellectual revulsion of free men from communist despotism and cruelty, they must not lose sight of the fact that communist antidemocracy is no more the main issue than communist anticapitalism. Numerous antidemocratic regimes throughout the world are gladly accepted by the free nations as allies in the struggle against communism, just as they were welcomed earlier in the struggle against fascism. Many Latin American states are governed by antidemocratic (or, at least, nondemocratic) regimes. Turkey has had for over forty years various forms of dictatorship; if the main division of the world were between democracy and dictatorship, Turkey (as many another nation) would be a weak candidate for the democratic side, yet she is helping to resist imperialist aggression.

From a practical viewpoint, the identification of communism with antidemocracy and anticapitalism plays right into the hands of the communists, since both capitalism and democracy (as understood, for example, in the United States) are not typical, but rather exceptional, in the world at large. If Western policy were to limit admission to the alliance of the free nations to a select group of a few countries happily matching the economic and political institutions of Britain or the United States, the resulting group of states would be hopelessly inadequate in meeting the threat of communism.

From the viewpoint of international ethics and common sense, the main interest one country has in another is the latter's willingness to preserve the peace. Only when autocracy is accompanied by aggressive imperialistic designs does it become a danger to the world. And then what is dangerous in it is its aggressiveness, not its autocracy, and the two should not be confused.

If the free nations draw the line sharply between themselves and the communist orbit, the issue can be presented in the age-old terms of human liberty versus serfdom and slavery. Thus expressed, the issue will be clear wherever men and women prize liberty, and communist propaganda will fail in its attempt to picture the world struggle as one between Wall Street and the peoples of the world. If the free world would thus commit itself to the fight for human liberty against communist aggression as the main issue of the present crisis, there is little doubt of the ultimate outcome of the struggle.

FOR FURTHER READING

Abramov, Fyodor, *The New Life: A Day On a Collective Farm*. New York: Grove Press, Inc. (Black Cat Books), 1963.

Almond, Gabriel A., *The Appeals of Communism*. Princeton: Princeton University Press, 1954.

Barnett, A. D. (ed.), *Communist Strategies in Asia: A Comparative Analysis of Governments and Parties*. New York: Frederick A. Praeger, Inc. (Praeger Paperbacks), 1963.

Bauer, Raymond A. and others, *How the Soviet System Works*. New York: Random House, Inc. (Vintage Books), 1961.

Bergson, Abram and Simon Kuznets (eds.), *Economic Trends in the Soviet Union*. Cambridge, Mass.: Harvard University Press, 1963.

Berlin, Isaiah, *Karl Marx*. New York: Oxford University Press, Inc., 1948.

Brumberg, Abraham (ed.), *Russia Under Khrushchev*. New York: Frederick A. Praeger, Inc. (Praeger Paperbacks), 1962.

Cantril, Hadley, *The Politics of Despair*. New York: Collier Books, 1961.

Clarke, Gerald, *The Coming Explosion in Latin America*. New York: David McKay Co., 1962.

Crankshaw, Edward, *The New Cold War: Moscow v. Peking*. Baltimore: Penguin Books, 1963.

Cross, James E., *Conflict in the Shadows: The Political Nature of Guerrilla Warfare*. Garden City, N.Y.: Doubleday & Co., 1963.

Crossman, Richard, *The God That Failed*. New York: Bantam Books, Inc., 1952.

Daniels, Robert V. (ed.), *A Documentary History of Communism*, 2 vols. New York: Random House, Inc. (Vintage Books), 1962.

Djilas, Milovan, *Conversations With Stalin*. New York: Harcourt, Brace & World, Inc., 1962.

Djilas, Milovan, *The New Class.* New York: Frederick A. Praeger, Inc. (Praeger Paperbacks), 1959.

Draper, Theodore, *Castro's Revolution: Myths and Realities.* New York: Frederick A. Praeger, Inc. (Praeger Paperbacks), 1962.

Ebenstein, William, *Great Political Thinkers,* 3rd ed., chap. 23. New York: Holt, Rinehart & Winston, Inc., 1960.

————, *Modern Political Thought,* 2nd ed., chap. 9. New York: Holt, Rinehart & Winston, Inc., 1960.

————, *Political Thought in Perspective,* chaps. 24, 25. New York: McGraw-Hill Book Co., Inc. (McGraw-Hill Paperbacks), 1963.

————, *Totalitarianism: New Perspectives.* New York: Holt, Rinehart & Winston, Inc., 1962.

Freemantle, Anne (ed.), *Mao Tse-tung: An Anthology of His Writings.* New York: Mentor Books, 1962.

Galbraith, John K., *Economic Development in Perspective.* Cambridge, Mass.: Harvard University Press, 1962.

Goodman, Elliot R., *The Soviet Design for a World State.* New York: Columbia University Press, 1960.

Granick, David, *The Red Executive.* Garden City, N.Y.: Doubleday & Co. (Anchor Books), 1961.

Griffith, William E., *Albania and the Sino-Soviet Rift.* Cambridge, Mass.: M. I. T. Press, 1963.

Heilbroner, Robert L., *The Great Ascent: The Struggle for Economic Development in Our Time.* New York: Harper & Row, Inc. (Harper Torchbooks), 1963.

Hodgkin, Thomas, *African Political Parties.* Baltimore: Penguin Books, 1962.

Hodgkinson, Harry, *Double Talk: The Language of Communism.* London: Allen & Unwin, 1955.

Holt, Robert T. and John E. Turner (eds.), *Soviet Union: Paradox and Change.* New York: Holt, Rinehart & Winston, Inc., 1962.

Hook, Sidney (ed.), *World Communism: Key Documentary Material.* Princeton: D. Van Nostrand Co. (Anvil Books), 1962.

Hsie, Alice Langley, *Communist China's Strategy in the Nuclear Age.* Englewood Cliffs, N.J.: Prentice-Hall, Inc., 1962.

Inkeles, Alex and Kent Geiger (eds.), *Soviet Society: A Book of Readings.* Boston: Houghton Mifflin Co., 1961.

James, Daniel, *Cuba: The First Soviet Satellite in the Americas.* New York: Avon Books, 1961.

Joint Economic Committee, United States Congress, *Dimensions of Soviet Economic Power.* Washington, D.C.: Government Printing Office, 1963.

Koestler, Arthur, *Darkness at Noon.* New York: Mentor Books, 1948.

Kolarz, Walter, *Religion in the Soviet Union.* New York: St. Martin's Press, 1961.

Laqueur, Walter and Leopold Labedz (eds.), *The Future of Communist Society*. New York: Frederick A. Praeger, Inc. (Praeger Paperbacks), 1962.

Lessing, Pieter, *Africa's Red Harvest*. New York: The John Day Company, 1962.

Lichtheim, George, *Marxism: An Historical and Critical Survey*. New York: Frederick A. Praeger, Inc. (Praeger Paperbacks), 1962.

Loh, Robert, *Escape from Red China*. New York: Coward-McCann Co., Inc., 1962.

Masaryk, T. G., *The Spirit of Russia*, 2nd ed. New York: The Macmillan Co., 1955.

Matthews, Herbert L. (ed.), *The United States and Latin America*, 2nd ed. Englewood Cliffs, N.J.: Prentice-Hall, Inc., 1963.

McNeal, Robert H., *The Bolshevik Tradition: Lenin, Stalin, Khrushchev*. Englewood Cliffs, N.J.: Prentice-Hall, Inc., 1963.

————, (ed.), *Lenin, Stalin, Khrushchev: Voices of Bolshevism*. Englewood Cliffs, N.J.: Prentice-Hall, Inc., 1963.

Miller, Margaret and others, *Communist Economy Under Change*. London: André Deutsch, 1963.

Monahan, James and Kenneth O. Gilmore, *The Great Deception: The Inside Story of How the Kremlin Took Over Cuba*. New York: Farrar, Straus & Co., 1963.

Monat, Pawel and John Dille, *Spy in the U.S.* New York: Harper & Row, 1962.

Moraes, Frank, *The Revolt in Tibet*. New York: The Macmillan Co., 1960.

Nove, Alec, *The Soviet Economy*. New York: Frederick A. Praeger, Inc. (Praeger Paperbacks), 1962.

Nutter, Warren and others, *Growth of Industrial Production in the Soviet Union*. Princeton: Princeton University Press, 1962.

Pasternak, Boris, *Doctor Zhivago*. New York: Mentor Books, 1959.

Royster, Vernon, *Journey Through the Soviet Union*. New York: Dow Jones & Co., 1962.

Schapiro, Leonard (ed.), *The U.S.S.R. and the Future: An Analysis of the New Program of the CPSU*. New York: Frederick A. Praeger, Inc. (Praeger Paperbacks), 1963.

Schram, Stuart A., *The Ideology of Mao Tse-tung*. New York: Frederick A. Praeger, Inc. (Praeger Paperbacks), 1963.

Schwartz, Harry, *Russia's Soviet Economy*, 2nd ed. Englewood Cliffs, N.J.: Prentice-Hall, Inc., 1960.

Sigmund, Paul E., Jr. (ed.), *The Ideologies of the Developing Nations*. New York: Frederick A. Praeger, Inc. (Praeger Paperbacks), 1963.

Solzhenitsyn, Alexander, *One Day in the Life of Ivan Denisovich*. New York: Bantam Books, 1963.

Spulber, Nicolas, *The Soviet Economy: Structure, Principles, Problems*. New York: W. W. Norton & Co., 1962.

Staar, Richard F., *Poland, 1944-1962*. Baton Rouge: Louisiana State University Press, 1962.

Strausz-Hupé, Robert and others, *Protracted Conflict*. New York: Harper & Row (Harper Colophon Books), 1963.

U.S. Office of Education, *Soviet Commitment to Education: Report of the First Official U.S. Education Mission to the U.S.S.R.* Washington, D.C.: Government Printing Office, 1959.

Vali, Ferenc A., *Rift and Revolt in Hungary: Nationalism Versus Communism*. Cambridge, Mass.: Harvard University Press, 1961.

Wetter, Gustav A., *Dialectical Materialism*. New York: Frederick A. Praeger, Inc. (Praeger Paperbacks), 1963.

Whitney, Thomas P. (ed.), *The Communist Blueprint for the Future: The Complete Text of All Four Communist Manifestoes, 1848-1961.* New York: E. P. Dutton & Co. (Dutton Paperbacks), 1962.

Wiles, P. J. D., *The Political Economy of Communism*. Cambridge, Mass.: Harvard University Press, 1962.

Yevtushenko, Yevgeny, *A Precocious Autobiography*. New York: E. P. Dutton & Co., 1963.

Zagoria, Donald S., *The Sino-Soviet Conflict, 1956-1961*. Princeton: Princeton University Press, 1962.

Zawodny, J. K., *Death in the Forest: The Story of the Katyn Forest Massacre*. Notre Dame: Notre Dame University Press, 1962.

2

Totalitarian Fascism

SOCIAL
BACKGROUND
OF FASCISM

Communism was the first major twentieth-century totalitarian revolt against the Western, liberal way of life; *fascism* was the second. Stripped to its essentials, fascism is the totalitarian organization of government and society by a single-party dictatorship, intensely nationalist, racialist, militarist, and imperialist. In Europe, Italy (1922) was the first to go fascist, followed by Germany (1933). In Asia, Japan went fascist in the nineteen thirties, gradually evolving totalitarian institutions out of its own native heritage. In the Western Hemisphere, a semi-constitutional government of a landed oligarchy was destroyed in Argentina in 1943 in a revolt of dissatisfied officers, and a fascist dictatorship was subsequently built up under the leadership of Colonel (later General) Perón, lasting until its overthrow in 1955.

Clearly, then, whereas communism is the form of totalitarianism typically linked with poor and underdeveloped nations (Russia in Europe, China in Asia), fascism is the form of totalitarianism that typically grows in wealthier and technologically more advanced nations (Germany in Europe, Japan in Asia). In the Americas, Guatemala, one of the poorest and most backward nations, for years encouraged the growth of communism until the pro-communist regime of President Arbenz was overthrown in June 1954; Cuba under Fidel Castro is a more recent example of communism in the Americas.

Fascism, on the other hand, saw its most intense development in Argentina, the wealthiest of the twenty Latin American republics.

Whereas communism is very largely the product of predemocratic and preindustrial societies, fascism is *postdemocratic* and *postindustrial:* fascism is impossible in countries with no democratic experience at all. In such societies, dictatorship may be based on the army, the bureaucracy, or the personal prestige of the dictator, but it will lack the element of mass enthusiasm and *mass support* (not necessarily majority support) characteristic of fascism. Moreover, although no fascist system can arise in a country without some democratic experience (as in Germany or Japan), there is not much likelihood of fascist success in countries that have experienced democracy over a long period, for example, Switzerland, Scandinavia, Holland, England, or the United States.

Paradoxically, experience has proved that, in general, the more violent and terroristic fascist movements are, the more popular support they tend to have. Thus fascism in Germany was both the most brutal and the most popular political movement; in Italy fascism was less popular and less brutal. Such fascist dictatorships based on mass support are not to be confused with traditional dictatorships such as existed in Europe in several countries during the nineteen thirties, particularly in the Balkans and eastern Europe. The present authoritarian dictatorships in Spain and Portugal, too, are essentially traditional, relatively moderate, and rest on the established forces of the bureaucracy and army.

In Latin America, there also are numerous dictatorships, but they are not fascist (with the exception of Argentina from 1943 to 1955) because they typically rest on the personal magic of one man, usually a general. Relying as he must on the good will of his army, the Latin American dictator has no need for, and rarely has, the mass support that characterizes fascism. Popular political movements hardly enter the picture.

The second condition essential to the growth of fascism is a considerable degree of industrial development. There are at least two principal points of contact between fascism and relatively advanced industrialization. First, fascist terror and propaganda require a good deal of technological organization and know-how. Second, as a system of *permanent mobilization for war,* fascism cannot hope to succeed without considerable industrial skills and resources.

It may be argued that the connection between fascism and modern industry goes even deeper. Every industrial society brings about social and economic tensions. Such tensions can be dealt with in one of two ways: the liberal way or the totalitarian way. The liberal society recognizes the variety of economic interests and their necessary conflict (such as between labor and management, agriculture and industry, skilled and unskilled workers), and seeks to reconcile such conflicts by the experimental method of peaceful, gradual adjustment. The totalitarian fascist state either denies that there are divergent social interests (abhorring as it does the notion of variety, especially in the form of departures from state-imposed uniformity) or, if it half-heartedly concedes the existence of divergent social interests, it resolves such differences by force.

The difference between communism and fascism on this point may be briefly (and with some oversimplification) formulated in this way: communism is the totalitarian way of *industrializing a backward society;* fascism is the totalitarian method of *solving conflicts within an industrially more advanced society.*

In its social background, fascism has particularly appealed to two groups: first, a numerically small group of *industrialists* and *landowners* who are willing to finance fascist movements in the hope of thereby getting rid of free labor unions. Industrialists are not, as a class, any more fascist-minded than other social groups; in countries with strong liberal and democratic traditions, for example, industrialists are no better and no worse than other people as far as their faith in the democratic process is concerned. But where democracy is weak, as in Germany, Italy, or Japan, it takes only a few wealthy industrialists and landowners to supply fascist movements with ample funds. In *I Paid Hitler* (1941), Fritz Thyssen, one of Germany's wealthiest steel manufacturers, has given a typical account of the support, running into many millions of dollars, that the Nazis received in the nineteen twenties and early thirties from German big business and finance.

Where the pressure of public opinion is strongly democratic and liberal, individual industrialists who are inclined toward fascism will find that supporting fascist groups is bad business; but where democratic traditions are weak, leaders of big business like Thyssen and Krupp in Germany, or the Mitsui trust in Japan, will find it possible to side openly with the cause of fascism.

The second main source of fascist support—and numerically by far the most important—comes from the lower middle classes, mostly in the salaried group. Many persons in this class dread the prospect of joining (or rejoining) the proletariat, and look to fascism for a salvation of their status and prestige. The salaried employee feels jealous of big business, into whose higher echelons he would like to rise, and fearful of labor, into whose proletarian world he would hate to descend. Fascism very cleverly utilizes these jealousies and fears of the salariat by propagandizing simultaneously against big business and big labor. Although such propaganda is neither logically nor politically consistent, its very inconsistency both reflects and appeals to the confusion of the salaried class, uncertain as that class is where to turn politically.

Paradoxically, organized labor frequently contributes to this uncertainty and demoralization of the salariat without meaning to do so. For psychological reasons, white collar workers are generally unwilling to organize into unions. As a result, the *incomes of workers,* particularly those organized in unions, *have tended to improve much faster than the incomes of salaried employees.* As the gap between the economic status of workers and that of salaried persons widens, the latter become more and more resentful of losing what they consider their rightful place in society, and may turn to fascism, which promises to keep unions and other upstart organizations under control. The leaders of organized labor may point out that the weak economic position of salaried persons is their own fault, and that such persons are in error in refusing to organize and bring pressure upon their employers; such arguing points, however, though they may be logically valid, are psychologically ineffective. In times of prosperity the divergence between labor and the salaried class may not be too upsetting politically, but in times of crisis and depression the smallest class antagonisms may turn into political dynamite.

Another important social group that has shown itself particularly vulnerable to fascist propaganda is the military. Even in a strong and well-established democracy, professional military people tend to overestimate the virtues of discipline and unity; where democracy is weak, this professional bias of the military becomes a political menace. Thus, in the early stages of Nazism in Germany, the military class of the nation either openly supported Hitler or at best maintained an attitude of benevolent neutrality. The top military leaders of Germany knew that a high proportion of Nazi bosses were criminals and unscrupulous psychopaths, yet they supported the Nazi movement as a step toward the militarization of the German people. In Italy, too, fascism in its early stages received considerable support from army circles, and in Japan fascism developed with the active and enthusiastic support of the army, which had every reason to be the main pillar of a regime committed to imperialist expansion. In Argentina, semi-constitutional government was overthrown in 1943 in a revolt of the "younger offi-cers," under Perón, who set up his own brand of fascism, named *peronismo* after him.

Yet it should be pointed out that the military often also play a leading part in getting rid of fascist and other kinds of dictatorial government. Perón himself learned this lesson in 1955, and the same thing has happened to several other Latin American dictators since the end of World War II. Once fascism is established, people often look to the army as one of the last remaining bulwarks of decency and legality. Therefore, fascism (as is also true of communism) in-dulges in periodic purges of the armed forces, because fascist leaders realize that the army is one of the few institutions left that enjoy genuine popular respect.

Although fascism is not a direct or necessary result of economic depression, as Marxist-communist theory suggests, there is a relation between the two. In times of depression, fear and frustration under-mine faith in the democratic process, and where the faith in rational methods weakens, fascism is the potential gainer. The small business-man blames big business for his troubles; big business puts the blame on the unreasonableness of the labor unions; labor feels that the only way out is to soak the rich; the farmers feel that they are not getting enough for farm products and that they are made to pay too high prices for manufactured goods; city people envy the security of the farmers ("always something to eat and a roof over your head"); and —worst of all—there is the large mass of unemployed people.

What democratic nations have failed to understand sufficiently is that the worst feature of unemployment is not economic suffering (which can be mitigated by adequate relief), but the feeling of being useless, unwanted, outside of the respectable ranks of society. It is among these spiritually homeless that fascism makes serious inroads during a depression: by putting an unemployed person into a uniform, a fascist movement makes him feel that he "belongs," and by telling him that he is a member of a superior race or nation, such a move-ment restores some of his self-respect.

This sense of not belonging is, in a way, characteristic of life in modern industrial society in general. Industrialization and urbaniza-tion have debunked and frequently destroyed traditional values, with-out always providing adequate substitute values in their place. The disorientation and confusion resulting from these effects of industriali-zation provide the social and psychological background of fascism and its attempt to restore the old, preindustrial way of life in a modern nation.

It can thus be seen that the Marxist interpretation of fascism in terms of class (identifying fascism with capitalism in decay) is not borne out by the facts. *Fascism cuts across all social groups;* wealthy industrialists and landowners support it for one reason, the lower middle classes for another, psychopaths and criminals for another still. Finally, there are the many nationalists and chauvinists in every country who prove themselves vulnerable to every promise of conquest and empire. In terms of explicit programs, fascist movements must make the most contradictory promises to satisfy all their adherents; such contraditions are one main weakness of fascism. Yet in terms of implicit psychological background, fascism looks within all social groups for the great common denominators, *frustration, resentment,* and *insecurity.* These psychological attitudes can easily be turned into hatred and aggression, against both internal and external "enemies."

Because these social and psychological attitudes are not the monopoly of any one social class, fascism manages to appeal to large masses of people in some countries. When Adolf Hitler joined the Nazi party in 1919, he was Member No. 7. Yet within fourteen years Nazism became the greatest mass movement in German history, including in its ranks members of all groups of German society, from hobos to members of the imperial family and the royal houses of the German states. By 1932, the Nazi vote had mounted to 14 million, and in March 1933, 17 million Germans (almost half the total vote) voted for Nazism; several more millions voted for nationalist and militarist parties that were Nazi in all but name. It is obvious that 17 million voters cannot consist exclusively of wealthy bankers and industrialists, and that only a party with a national, rather than class, appeal can obtain such high votes. In no other country has fascism ever been as widely popular as in Germany, but there has been no fascist regime anywhere without some popular support.

**PSYCHOLOGICAL
ROOTS OF
TOTALITARIANISM**

In countries like Germany and Japan, the clue to the understanding of fascist tendencies lies in broad social forces and traditions. In those countries, the authoritarian tradition is predominant and democracy is still a very frail plant. As a result, a German or Japanese with fascist tendencies is no outcast and may be considered perfectly well adjusted to his society. Even when his society explicitly condemns fascism, as it is likely to do each time it loses a war, much in the implicit habits and customs of German and Japanese life tends toward the authoritarian way of life, and from authoritarianism to fascism there is only a step. In democratic societies such as Britain or the United States, on the other hand, the appeal of fascism can be more fruitfully judged from the angle of individual psychology. Empirical studies in the United States have shown that 10 per cent of Americans are strongly authoritarian and about 20 per cent partly authoritarian. (T. W. Adorno and others, *The Authoritarian Personality,* 1950.)

The traditional analysis of political dictatorship has been centered on the motivations of dictatorial leaders, driven by lust for power and sadistic cravings for domination. The followers and subjects of a dictatorship are viewed exclusively as "victims" who just happen to fall into the misfortune of oppressive rule. Every insurance company knows that some persons are more accident-prone than others, and every policeman knows that some persons are more likely to attract criminals than others.

Similarly, it is not too farfetched to suggest that some people and some nations are more "dictatorship-prone" than others. Plato's psychological insight led him to suggest in his *Republic* that constitutions grow not "from stone to stone," but "from those characters of the men in the cities which preponderate and draw the rest of the city after them." The very existence of an authoritarian mass movement like fascism depends on the *desire* of many persons *to submit and obey.*

Rational democrats may not understand why anyone should prefer to obey rather than take the responsibility of making decisions for himself; they take it for granted that men *should* make their own decisions rather than have their actions dictated by others. But this democratic stereotype overlooks what are the *comforts of irresponsibility* to many persons. Children love the feeling of being sheltered and secure behind the benevolent power and authority of their parents. The mark of the mature adult is his willingness and capacity to stand on his own feet, to take responsibility, and be independent of others. Yet relatively few persons ever attain this sort of maturity; the process of growing up, as every adolescent knows, is painful, and many rebel against a cold world where they must struggle for themselves without the omnipotence and omniscience of parental love and security. In all human beings there is a *latent tendency toward dependence* based on the parent-child relationship, although some people manage to achieve a more self-reliant adulthood than others. The totalitarian system, whether communist or fascist, appeals to people who, for whatever personal reasons, look for the father-child relationship, for security in dependence.

What are some of the empirically ascertainable traits that characterize the authoritarian personality, particularly the personality attracted to the fascist type of authoritarianism? First, a tendency to conform compulsively to orthodox ideals and practices; emotional rigidity and limited imagination; excessive concern with problems of status and strength; strong loyalty to one's own group ("in-group") coupled with vehement dislike of outsiders ("out-group"); and stress on discipline and obedience rather than freedom and spontaneity in human relations (education, sex, family, religion, industry, government). The "herd-minded" (or "ethnocentric") element in the fascist personality is perhaps the single most important one, although no one element in itself conclusively defines a personality as authoritarian.

The key role of the *family* in the formation of basic attitudes seems to be brought out by all clinical and theoretical studies; but the family is not, after all, an isolated and independent agent. Rather it reflects the predominant social goals and values, and constitutes to the child the cultural and psychological representative of society at large.

No person is ever completely authoritarian or completely democratic, just as no human being is ever an utter devil or a perfect angel. In each case it is a question of quantity and degree, although differences of quantity eventually become differences of quality. Although there has been no major fascist mass movement in the United States so far, it is a matter of record that some Americans looked upon German and Italian fascism in the nineteen thirties as the "wave of the future" (as it was called in a book of that title) and that others sympathized with Argentine fascism in the nineteen forties and fifties.

Dependence and submission in a totalitarian society—fascist or communist—give a person the security for which he hungers, but deny him self-expression and self-assertion, the needs for which are as deeply embedded in human nature as the desire for security. Thus denied, these drives turn into repressed hostility and aggression, for the expression of which fascism provides two channels, one for the ruling class, one for the ruled. Within the apparatus of the dictatorial party and government, there is the pattern of the cyclist: crouching before the superior above, pressing down on the subordinate below. Only the leader need not crouch before anyone—he only presses down. Below the top leader—"Big Brother," as Orwell called him in *1984,* the classic fictional portrait of totalitarianism—although each member of the party and government hierarchy must kowtow to someone above him, in return he may tread on those below him.

Persons outside the ruling class, however, have no one to command; they can only obey. How can they express their hostility and aggressiveness? Since the vast majority of the people in a totalitarian state form the group of those who can only take, but not issue, commands, this is a serious problem for every dictatorship. Although officially the dictator claims that he is universally beloved, he knows that there is much repressed hatred and hostility directed (or capable of being directed) toward him and his regime.

The answer of totalitarian dictatorships is to *direct this latent hostility of the people against real or imaginary enemies.* For the communist, the enemy may be the bourgeois, Trotskyites, Titoites, or Wall Street. Hitler first chose the Jews as the target of German aggression; once given a direction for their savagery, the Germans were not satisfied until they had sent six million Jews from central and eastern Europe to the gas chambers. Later new enemies took the place of the Jews: Britain, the United States, Churchill, Roosevelt, Bolshevism, the churches. Finally, when they felt that the end was close, Hitler and his cohorts unleashed their vengeance on the Germans themselves; if they had to go down, the German people had to be destroyed with them. In a more recent fascist regime, peronist Argentina, American imperialism and international finance were the chief targets of fascist hate propaganda.

If men cannot be masters of their own lives, fascism promises mastery over other peoples; and if fascism cannot deliver the triumphs it promises, the hatred of the people may turn against their leaders, as it did against Mussolini, who was tried before a partisan committee in northern Italy in April 1945, executed, and then publicly hung from a lamp-post in Milan. Having taught his people violence and hatred, he reaped himself what he had sown.

The psychological interpretation of totalitarianism—fascist or communist—is of particular value where the prevailing cultural pattern is not authoritarian, where it takes some personal quirk to break with the democratic pattern of the environment. Thus, in societies like Britain or the United States, the psychological analysis of people who have embraced communism or fascism is of great value because there emerges from such an analysis a definite pattern of personality factors that is typical in many American fascists or communists.

Yet it would be futile to explain the strength of fascism in Germany or Japan, or of communism in China or Italy, by means of personal psychology. It may be argued that an American or Englishman who embraces communism or fascism is not well adjusted, comes from a broken home, or has had an unhappy childhood, but the same can hardly be said of 17 million Germans who voted for Hitler in 1933, or of the many millions of Frenchmen and Italians who have persistently voted communist since the end of World War II. Where totalitarianism assumes the proportions of a mass movement, the main avenue of analysis must be that of the great social, economic, and cultural forces and traditions of a nation.

Whereas the cure for an American fascist or communist may be found on the psychoanalyst's couch, the cure for five million Frenchmen who vote communist is more take-home pay every Saturday, and a more decent life all round. Similarly, the origins of fascist totalitarianism in Germany, Japan, and Argentina lie deeper in the collective lives of those nations than can be revealed from a study of individual personalities. There was plenty that was wrong in Hitler's personality as viewed through non-German eyes, but to the 17 million Germans who identified themselves with him in the election of March 1933 he must have been an admirably adjusted personality.

ELEMENTS OF FASCIST DOCTRINE AND POLICY

Although fascism, like communism, is a movement that exists everywhere, it has no such authoritative statement of principles as communism has; moreover, there is no one country, at present, directing a fascist world conspiracy. During the Nazi regime (1933-1945), Germany was the most powerful of the fascist states then in existence, and world fascism was very largely directed, financed, and inspired by German brains and money. Since the defeat of the fascist Axis (Germany, Japan, Italy) in World War II, however, there has been no really major fascist state; Argentina never possessed anything like the worldwide influence that Nazi Germany had until 1945.

The absence of a universally recognized authoritative statement of fascist principles is not total. Hitler has left in *Mein Kampf* (1925-1927) a trustworthy guide to his thought, and Mussolini's *The Doctrine of Fascism* (1932), a moderate statement of fascist principles, expresses the Italian brand of fascism. The latter has served as a model for most other fascist movements in the world because it is more universal in outlook; Nazism, a specifically German brand of fascism, has proved for that reason less suitable for export.

Although there is no *Fascist Manifesto* with undisputed authority among fascists, it is not too difficult to state the principal elements of the fascist outlook:

(1) Distrust of reason

(2) Denial of basic human equality

(3) Code of behavior based on lies and violence

(4) Government by elite

(5) Totalitarianism

(6) Racialism and imperialism

(7) Opposition to international law and order

(1) The *distrust of reason* is perhaps the most significant trait of fascism. The rational tradition of the West stems from Greece, and is one of the three basic components (the other two being Jewish monotheism and Christian love) that have given the West its characteristic culture and outlook. Fascism rejects this Greek root of Western civilization and is frankly *antirationalist,* distrusting reason in human affairs and stressing the irrational, sentimental, uncontrollable elements of man. Psychologically, fascism is *fanatical* rather than reflective, *dogmatic* rather than open-minded; as a result each fascist regime has its taboo issues such as race, empire, the leader, and it is the nature of a taboo issue that it must be accepted on faith and cannot be critically discussed. During the fascist regime in Italy (1922-1945), Mussolini's picture was shown in every classroom in the country over the caption "Mussolini is always right."

The communist states have the taboo issue of Marxism-Leninism, a set of final truths that must not be questioned. In addition, there are the more passing taboo subjects as defined by the top party leaders: Khrushchev in Russia, Mao in Red China, or Tito in Yugoslavia.

As a matter of basic principle, *democracy recognizes no taboo issue:* there is no subject that cannot be questioned or challenged, not even the validity of democracy itself. In practice, of course, democracies do not always live up to that ideal. Thus, it is argued by some that in the United States the question of the validity of democracy is on its way to becoming a taboo issue, especially since the Supreme Court's 1951 decision upholding the constitutionality of the Smith Act of 1940 (under which the advocacy of the duty, desirability, necessity, or propriety of revolution is a criminal offense).

The individual, too, may have taboo issues, dark corners in his heart or mind that must not be pulled out and subjected to rational examination. The mentally healthy individual has few or (ideally) no taboo issues because he is able to face reality as it is and does not insist on living in a dream world in defiance of reality. Psychologically, the existence of taboo issues in the individual or in a group, party, or nation is due to a sense of insecurity or guilt, or both.

Under conditions of stress and strain, the individual as well as the collective group may take refuge in the temporary shelter of the taboo, postponing the facing of reality, but unable to shut it out forever. Since totalitarian regimes permanently operate in a state of high tension and crisis, the taboo is part and parcel of their normal environment. Democracies succumb to the temptation of the taboo, and its false security, only in periods of exceptional strain; it is significant that the Supreme Court's decision on the Smith Act took place in 1951, at the height of the Korean war.

(2) The *denial of basic human equality* is a common denominator of fascist (as well as communist) movements and states. True enough, democratic societies do not always live up to the ideal of human equality, but they are subject to attacks of conscience if they fail, and they at least accept equality as the long-term goal of public policy. By contrast, fascist societies not only accept the *fact* of human inequality, but go further and affirm inequality as an *ideal*.

The concept of human equality goes back to the three roots of Western civilization. The Jewish idea of one God led to the idea of one mankind, since all men as children of God are brothers among themselves. The Christian notion of the inalienability and indestructibility of the human soul led to the ideal of basic *moral* equality of all men. Finally, the Greek-Stoic concept of reason led to the oneness of mankind on the basis of reason as the most truly human bond that all men have in common.

Fascism rejects this Jewish-Christian-Stoic concept of equality as soft and nonsensical, and opposes to it the concept of inequality, which can most simply be spelled out in the contrast of superiority and inferiority. Thus, in the fascist code, men are superior to women, soldiers to civilians, party members to nonparty members, one's own nation to others, the strong to the weak, and (perhaps most important in the fascist outlook) the victors in war to the vanquished. The chief criteria of equality in the Western tradition are man's mind and soul, whereas the fascist affirmation of inequality is based ultimately on *strength*.

(3) The fascist—like the communist—code of behavior stresses *violence and lies* in all human relations, within and between nations. From the democratic viewpoint, politics is the mechanism through which social conflicts of interest are peacefully adjusted. By contrast, the fascist view is that politics is characterized by the *friend-enemy* relation. Politics begins and ends, in this fascist way of thinking, with the possibility of an enemy—and his *total annihilation*. The democratic antithesis to the friend is the *opponent,* and in democratic na-

tions the opponent of today is considered the potential government of tomorrow. (The opposition in the British Parliament is officially called "Her Majesty's Loyal Opposition," and the leader of the Opposition receives a special salary to do his job well.) The fascist knows only enemies, not opponents, and since enemies represent evil incarnate, total annihilation is the only solution. This doctrine applies to domestic as well as to foreign enemies; thus, the Nazis first set up concentration camps and gas chambers for German citizens, and later used the same facilities on non-Germans.

Contrary to common opinion, *concentration camps* and *slave labor camps* are not incidental phenomena in totalitarian systems like fascism and communism, but are of their very core. It is in the concentration and slave labor camps that totalitarian regimes seek to destroy the legal and moral person in man, and to deprive him of the last residue of individuality. The technique of brainwashing used by fascists and communists deliberately seeks to break man's mind to the point where he will publicly confess to crimes he did not commit and perhaps could not have committed. After a period of brainwashing, the victim no longer has a mind of his own; he merely plays back, like a record, what is expected of him.

By institutionalizing organized mass murder in concentration and slave labor camps, totalitarian regimes demonstrate to the entire population what is in store for anyone in disfavor with the men in power, and at the same time they provide the shock troops of the regime with a peacetime outlet for savagery and fanaticism. Immediate death is often considered too humane a penalty by such regimes; moreover, the slow death of concentration or slave labor camps has a greater demonstration value than the clean, old-fashioned method of the execution squad or the gallows.

(4) *Government by elite* is a principle that fascists everywhere frankly oppose to the "democratic fallacy" that people are capable of governing themselves. The concept that only a small minority of the population, qualified by birth, education, or social standing, is capable of understanding what is best for the whole community, and of putting it into practice, is not an invention of twentieth-century fascism. Plato, one of the founders of Western political philosophy, strongly believed that only one class, the "philosopher-kings," are fit to rule society. The contrary belief, that the people as a whole are capable of self-rule, is of relatively recent origin, and has successfully worked only in limited areas of the globe.

The fascist idea of government by a self-appointed elite (a fascist government usually shoots its way into power) is undemocratic.

"God knows what we'd do if anything should ever happen to him!"

Such a government does not always lack popular approval; strange as it may seem to the democrat, who expects everybody to behave as he does, people throughout history have frequently approved of autocratic governments. Approval alone, however, is no evidence of democracy. What makes a government democratic is that it always depends on popular consent given in free elections. In fascist regimes, even when the government enjoys popular approval, it is carried on independent of popular consent, without free elections, a free press, or a freely functioning opposition.

The fascist *leadership principle* expresses the extreme form of the elite concept. It fully reflects the irrational nature of fascist politics; the leader is considered infallible, endowed with mystical gifts and insights. In a conflict between popular opinion and the fascist leader, the will of the latter prevails; the leader represents the public interest, the way all people would think if they knew what was best for the whole community (what Rousseau called the "General Will"), whereas the people express only individual whims and desires not necessarily in harmony with the public good (Rousseau's "Will of All").

The emphasis on leadership is contrary to the fascist enforcement of orthodoxy and conformity. Hitler, Mussolini, and Perón grew up in nonfascist societies with considerable free competition. So far it has been impossible to appraise the leadership qualities of a generation born and bred under fascism. The German, Italian, and Argentine brands of fascism did not last long enough (1933-45 in Germany; 1922-45 in Italy; and 1943-55 in Argentina) to supply conclusive evidence on the matter.

(5) *Totalitarianism* in all human relations characterizes fascism as a way of life rather than as a mere system of government. There are many dictatorships, particularly in Latin America, in which the authoritarian principle is applied only in government. If the people do not make any trouble politically, and do not interfere with the rule of the dictator and his henchmen, they can lead their own lives pretty freely. Education, religion, business, and agriculture are not touched very much by the political dictatorship. By contrast, fascism is totalitarian; it employs authority and violence in *all* kinds of social relations, whether political or not.

With regard to women, the largest discriminated-against minority of the world, fascism is antifeminist. Women should stay in their place, said the Nazis, and their concern should be the famous three K's—*Kinder, Küche, Kirche.* Since women are unable to bear arms, they are automatically second-class citizens according to the fascist view, and are excluded from leadership positions in government or party. They have the right to vote, but since this right in fascist countries means only the right to be enthusiastic about the leader and his party, it is not much of a practical asset. Within the family the father is the leader, and both his wife and his children get a strong taste of domestic authoritarian government, which has more effect on their everyday lives than the operations of the remote political government in the capital. In the extreme case of modern fascism, Nazi Germany, the contempt for women was finally demonstrated in the official ridicule of the institution of marriage as a false Jewish-Christian prejudice, and German women were encouraged to produce children for the fatherland outside of wedlock.

Fascist countries also make a point of refusing to employ women extensively in schools. From the fascist viewpoint, schools are to teach discipline and obedience, specifically to prepare the boys for military service and the girls for related domestic activities. In a program of such importance, fascist educators feel women teachers have no place.

Thus it can be seen that fascist totalitarianism, unlike the old-fashioned dictatorships of Latin America, is *totalitarian in its objective:* to control all phases of human life, political or not, from the cradle to the grave. It begins the control even before the cradle, by pushing definite population policies, and has been known to reach into the grave, so to speak, to decide whether a dead person should have a burial at all, and if so, in what form.

But fascism is also *totalitarian in its means*. It will use any form of coercion, from verbal threats to mass murder, in obtaining its ends. By contrast, the classical authoritarian dictatorship was, and is, more restrained in its means, and resorts to murder only on a limited scale. Thus, whenever a Latin American dictator is ousted, he is usually permitted by his opponents to assemble his family and peacefully depart to a foreign country.

(6) *Racialism and imperialism* express the two basic fascist principles of inequality and violence as applied to the society of nations. Within the nation, fascist doctrine holds, the elite is superior to the rest and may impose its will upon them by force. Similarly, between nations the *elite nation* is superior to others and is entitled to rule them. German fascism went furthest in its racialist and imperialist policies. A straight line led from the theories of the superiority of the German-Nordic "race" to the mass murder of millions of people. The German objective of world domination included the elimination of some nations through genocide and the enslavement of the rest. After the expected defeat of Britain and Russia, the United States was to be next on the list. The Japanese race theories found their practical imperialist expression in the concept of "co-prosperity," under which Japan would prosper by exploiting Asia and the Pacific.

Italian fascism was for a long time (from 1922 to 1938) remarkably free from exaggerated race theories; early Italian propaganda in this general field concentrated on the idea of reviving the old Roman empire. In 1938, however, Mussolini discovered that the Italians were a pure and superior race, and he became more closely tied to Hitler Germany.

In Argentina, the Perón government strongly emphasized the mission and destiny of Argentina, and accompanied this doctrine of Argentine superiority with a deliberate policy of imperialism. Peronist imperialism, probably out of respect for the tremendous power of the United States in the Western Hemisphere, which makes any fascist territorial ventures highly dangerous, limited itself to economic, political, and ideological expansion; but Argentina built up a vast armament industry, and her neighbors could not help wondering against whom this Argentine war potential was to be used. Only the overthrow of the Perón dictatorship in 1955 removed these fears of Argentine imperialism.

Racialism and imperialism are not an exclusive monopoly of fascism. Although communist theory rejects both, Russian communism is strongly imperialistic, and after World War II a Great Russian cult was built up, differing only in degree from the Great Russian superiority concept as it was officially held in pre-Bolshevik Russia. More recently, Red China has made use of the propaganda argument of race and color in her struggle with Russia for supremacy in the communist world and for leading the underdeveloped countries—mostly inhabited by nonwhites—toward communist revolution.

In the democracies, too, there is a tradition of racialism; in the United States, for example, racial discrimination has seriously corroded the vitality of democratic ideals. Called (by the Swedish social scientist Gunnar Myrdal) "the American dilemma," the race issue in the United States may ultimately decide the fate of the democratic way of life at home and abroad.

The communists have concentrated much of their propaganda in Asia and Africa on British imperialism and American racialism; both points have proved effective in many of the underdeveloped countries, and if the communists have frequently failed to make converts out of such propaganda, they have at least succeeded in paralyzing Anglo-American influence by fostering a position of neutralism, as in India and Latin America. Neutralist India is so haunted by the phantom of yesterday's British imperialism that she is unable to grasp fully the reality of today's communist imperialism.

(7) *Opposition to international law and order* is the logical outcome of the fascist belief in inequality, violence, racialism, imperialism, and war. Whereas nonfascists (with the exception of out-and-out non-resisting pacifists) accept war as a tragic fact, which should be abolished, fascists raise war to the level of an ideal, because, as Mussolini put it, "war alone brings up to their highest tension all human energies and puts the stamp of nobility upon the peoples who have the courage to meet it."

Any type of international organization assumes some form of government by consent, which is directly contradictory to the fascist principle of *government by force*. Also, equality of states before the law of nations is a basic principle of international order. The fascist concept of the elite leads, as we have seen, to the leadership of one nation over the society of nations as it does to the leadership of one man within the nation's government. Fascist states, therefore, shy away from international organizations in which they are expected to abide by majority decisions and in which government is carried on by methods of discussion rather than by force.

The fascist regimes of Italy and Germany had no use for the League of Nations; Germany withdrew at a very early date in 1933, and Italy in 1937. In the United Nations, peronist Argentina consistently played a lone wolf role. In the Organization of American States, she did all she could to prevent effective cooperation between the United States and the Latin American republics—a policy that was later faithfully copied by Cuba under Castro.

In sum, it can be seen that the fascist theory and practice of international politics are not so different from those of communism. Both accept force and war as the vehicles of resolving differences.

For the communist, the concept of *class* plays the dominant role in the struggle, whereas fascism sees in *race* and *nation* the key concepts in the dynamics of change.

In practice, both communism and fascism lead to the same thing in international relations, although their theoretical starting-points differ. When Germany and Russia finally clashed in 1941, the reason was not ideological but practical; they could not agree on the division of the spoils. Since Russia was not satisfied with German proposals for dividing up the world, Germany attacked Russia as an obstacle on its path to world dominion.

FASCIST ECONOMICS: THE CORPORATE STATE

The corporate state applies fascist principles of organization and control to the economy. The fascist economy is subdivided in state-controlled associations of capital and labor, and each association has a monopoly in its trade or occupation. *The one-party state is the ultimate arbiter of conflicts between capital and labor.*

The philosophy of the corporate state rests on two assumptions. First, man (except for the small ruling elite) should not be politically articulate as a citizen, but only as a worker, entrepreneur, farmer, doctor, or lawyer; general political problems are assumed to be too complicated for the mass of the people, who are only expected to understand issues that bear directly on their vocational or professional work. Second, members of the small ruling elite are supposed to understand broad problems that affect the whole society, and they alone are therefore qualified to govern the community. This conception is Platonic in origin, and in modern times antidemocratic thinkers like Burke and Hegel have supported it against the claims of the democratic theory.

The democratic conception rejects this corporate approach to economic and political organization for several reasons. In the first place, it is not always easy to separate economic from political aspects. Tariffs seem to be a purely economic issue, yet they directly affect political and diplomatic relations with other states. Immigration seems at first sight to be an economic problem, yet delicate psychological and diplomatic issues are involved in it. Economic aid to other nations, as the United States has learned in the last twenty years, has profound military and political aspects as well as economic effects.

Second, the democratic theory holds that only the man who wears the shoe knows where it pinches—the mystic knowledge and insight of the ruling elite are no substitute for the experience of the ruled—or, as Aristotle put it, the guest is a better judge of the meal than the cook. Fascists insist that the cook not only ought to be the final judge of his product but also should impose his judgment on the guests, by force if necessary.

Finally, the democratic theory rejects the fascist assumption that members of one particular class are superior in judgment to the rest of the people and are therefore the nation's natural rulers. Formal education can supply knowledge only, not judgment. Judgment is not something that can be learned in fascist schools for leaders; it is the result of character, intelligence, experience, and personal philosophy. Formal training and education in leadership, party doctrine, public administration, history, and politics do not necessarily add up to true leadership. Jesus did not obtain a Ph.D. in religion, Socrates did not attend a school of education, Lincoln did not major in political science, and Churchill never went to college at all.

The kind of wisdom and moral courage that make up the essence of leadership may be greatly aided by formal education, but the two should not be confused. The democratic theory thus rejects the assumption of fascist doctrine that only a small elite has insight into the public good. From the democratic viewpoint, only God has a perfect understanding of Truth with a capital T, but every man is capable, at least partially, of seeing truth with a small t.

What the one-party state with the secret police and concentration camps is to the political side of fascist regimes, corporatism is to fascism's social and economic aspects. Just as in the political sphere fascism replaces the pivotal concept of individual liberty with unlimited state authority, so in the economic sphere it rejects the conception of a free welfare economy—be it capitalist, socialist, or middle-of-the-road. The objective of the corporate state is the *power of the state* rather than the welfare of the individual. More specifically, the ultimate objective of the corporate organization of the economy is the preparation of a *permanent war economy,* because aggressive imperialism is the ultimate aim of fascist foreign policy.

The Italian fascist regime, installed in 1922, set up a corporate state that was to show to the Italians and the world that fascism was not mere reaction, directed against liberal capitalism and socialism, but a new creative principle of social and economic organization. The economy was divided into syndicates of workers, employers, and the professions. Only one syndicate was recognized in each branch of business or industry, and although membership in a syndicate was not obligatory, the payment of dues was. The officials of the syndicates were either fascist politicians or persons of reliable loyalty to the fascist regime. In effect, these associations of workers and employers were nothing but instruments of state policy, with no will or life of their own. Since each syndicate had a monopoly of organization in its field, state control was made that much easier.

To make this method of control more nearly complete, the fascist government established *corporations* which were administrative agencies in a given industry designed to unite and control the associations of *workers and employers* in that industry. According to law, the syndicates were autonomous; in fact, however, they were run by the state. The corporation, supreme instrument of fascist economic organization, made no pretense of autonomy, being as it was nothing but an administrative agency of the state and in no way different from the prisons and the other tools of fascist government by force and propaganda.

Despite the same name, the fascist corporation is, of course, not to be confused with the business corporation in the United States. They have nothing whatever in common. The fascist corporation is a government agency, whereas the American business corporation is a company of limited liability, owned by private citizens, and engaged in business.

In the final analysis, the much advertised corporate state was no new principle of social and economic organization, but merely a sign of the fact that in the totalitarian system of fascism economic relations, like all other aspects of society, could not be left to the free interplay of the competitive liberal society. In his speech of November 14, 1933, Mussolini stated that the essential bases of the corporate state were a *single party,* a *totalitarian government,* and an atmosphere of *strong ideal tension.* The Fascist Party provided the first two essentials of the corporate state, and the strong ideal tension was brought about by the ceaseless propaganda of expansionist imperialism.

The first real test for the corporate state in Italy, the best-developed historical example so far, came with that country's entry into World War II in June 1940. Fascist Italy revealed itself to be wholly unequal to the task of fighting a first-class war, not only from the military and political viewpoint, but also for the standpoint of economic efficiency. For twenty years the corporate state had sacrificed the welfare and happiness of a poor people to the dream of a powerful empire and the megalomania of a would-be conqueror of continents. Yet when the first real test of battle came, Italian fascism failed on the economic front even more than on the military front. The economic legacy of the corporate state was not wealth and empire, but the loss of the colonies, poverty, and destitution.

After the execution of Mussolini in the spring of 1945, the Italian people destroyed whatever vestiges were left of the corporate state and embarked upon a new chapter of economic rehabilitation, based on a mixture of economic liberalism and political democracy. In the last analysis, much of the economic ruination of Italy wrought by fascist corporatism was ultimately paid for by the American taxpayer, as the United States poured billions of dollars into Italy after World War II to help her stand on her own feet again.

In the Western Hemisphere, Colonel Perón, speaking for the fascist regime in Argentina just after the successful *coup* of June 1943, declared his admiration for the fundamental conceptions of the corporate state at the very moment when Italian fascism, the model and inspiration of Argentine fascism, had reduced Italy to ashes and ruins. To Argentina as to other nations, the corporate state under Perón brought inflation and meatless days—meatless days in a country that formerly had been the largest exporter of meat in the world. Above all, corporatism in Argentina (called *justicialismo*) meant the end of free labor unions and their replacement by government-sponsored puppets. The employing class, too, was put under the control of the government. Finally, the peronist regime followed the corporate systems of other fascist states by dedicating the economy to the hasty development of heavy industry and the manufacture of armaments. Thus, *justicialismo,* which set out to defend justice against both capitalism and socialism, ended up as the servant of an imperialistic dictator and his political machine, until both were overthrown in 1955.

PERONISM:

THE CASE

OF ARGENTINA

The defeat of the Axis in World War II has by no means removed the threat of fascism forever. In terms of military security, to be sure, the chief danger now confronting the free nations is the danger of communist aggression; there has been no major threat of fascist aggression after the defeat of the great fascist powers, Germany and Japan. As an attitude of mind, however, and as a reflection of social and political authoritarianism, fascism has shown that it can survive temporary defeats; only a few years after fascist regimes led Germany and Italy to disaster and humiliation, neo-fascist organizations in both countries brazenly resumed operations.

The case of Argentina is more complex, and it proves that the Western Hemisphere is not immune from the virus of fascism. In 1943, a group of discontented younger officers overthrew the existing democratic regime, which was far from being perfect, but which nevertheless was democratic. The officers were under the leadership of Colonel Juan Perón who in several years in Italy as a military attaché had become a fervent admirer of Mussolini and of fascist ideas. As soon as the peronist clique took over, Argentine foreign policy became openly hostile to the democratic nations in World War II, and friendly to the fascist powers. On March 27, 1945, when the war was practically over, Argentina, in order to be admitted to the San Francisco Conference under the terms of the Yalta agreement, declared war on Japan, as well as on Germany "in view of the character of the latter as an ally of Japan." Thus the pro-fascist and pro-Nazi sentiment of the peronist regime was manifested in the wording as well as the timing of its declaration of war.

Perón at first stayed in the background, but then took over the ministries of war and labor. The war ministry gave him control over the armed forces, with which he could supplement the deep affection in which the people allegedly held him. Control over labor removed, as in other fascist states, any threat of organized mass action. The radio was completely subordinated to the government, and the opposition was deprived of access to it. In the newspaper field, Perón leveled his sights at *La Prensa,* one of the five or six great newspapers in the world, having an old and revered tradition of independence. First the peronist government tried to cajole and harass *La Prensa* into submission by administrative subterfuges rather than by open action. When all pressures and threats failed, Perón seized *La Prensa* early in 1951 and converted it to the pro-government, fascist line. *La Prensa*'s owner, Dr. Ezequiel Paz, obliged to flee to the United States to save himself from prison, was the most famous Argentine refugee; but he was just one of the many who sought asylum in the other American republics and in France and England.

In most of its policies, the peronist regime followed the techniques and aims of Hitler and Mussolini. Yet in one respect—and a very important one—Perón showed intelligence considerably superior to that of his models and masters. Without exception, all the other fascist dictators—like all communist dictatorships—abolished political parties other than the ruling party; and since there could be no regular elections without opposition candidates, fascist elections became plebiscites, in which the voters were presented with a major issue and asked to vote yes or no. The votes in fascist elections were usually announced to be somewhere in the neighborhood of 99.6 per cent in favor of the dictator.

It is at this point that Perón improved on Hitler and Mussolini. Perón apparently had too much of a sense of humor to announce to the world that 99.6 per cent of his people insisted on his leadership. He was satisfied with considerably less. In the presidential elections of 1946 Perón was elected by a majority of only 55 per cent, a figure that gave the election the appearance of having been fought under conditions of free campaigning. Nothing was further from the facts, and early in 1944 all political parties had been abolished. This measure hurt the opposition parties more than the government, and it was only shortly before the elections, in late February of 1946, that political parties were reconstituted. Much of the election campaign was conducted in a state of siege, a favorite measure in Latin American dictatorships, under which the government can legally suspend all rights of individual civil liberty. The opposition parties and their leaders were subjected to physical terror from a mob that operated under government protection. In many cases, the police itself used violence against antiperonists, and there were numerous murders in the campaign.

In 1949, Perón had the Argentine Constitution of 1853 changed because under it immediate re-election of the President was illegal. A modest man, Perón claimed he did not wish to run for the presidency again, but as a patriotic Argentine he finally gave in to the mounting pressure from all sides and allowed himself to be drafted. The election of November 1951 gave Perón a victory of over 60 per cent, still way below the 99.6 per cent victories of the other fascist dictators.

In the 1951 election, terror against opposition parties was practiced even more openly than in 1946. Hundreds of candidates were jailed during the campaign for no worse crime than daring to run against the existing regime, and conditions were so chaotic that two presidential candidates were out of the race even before the campaign was over. The socialists withdrew from the campaign altogether when it became apparent that the whole thing was a farce. Their candidate for the presidency had been imprisoned, as were hundreds of leaders of other parties, six weeks before the election. In typically fascist fashion, the government declared that it had discovered a subversive plot, and a state of siege was once again proclaimed, so that ruthless terror could be legally employed. In the congressional elections of April 25, 1954, the peronist slate obtained two-thirds of the popular vote. Every radio station was compelled to broadcast Perón's speeches, and the opposition was unable to get any radio time for its candidates. This monopoly of the government was supplemented by many other forms of discrimination, and occasional terror, against the opposition. It was remarkable in the election of 1954, as in 1946 and 1951, that so many Argentines still dared to vote against the peronist regime.

Late in 1954 Perón started his campaign against the Roman Catholic Church; this was the beginning of his undoing. After persisting in that campaign for several months, he was excommunicated by the Vatican on June 16, 1955. On that same day, the Argentine air force and parts of the army staged an armed uprising, but it failed. Three months later, provincial units rebelled again, and this time Perón's fate was sealed when the entire navy went over to the rebels. Only four days after the outbreak of the revolution, on September 19, 1955, Perón quietly slipped away in a Paraguayan gunboat, fleeing eventually to Spain. Since there was virtually no resistance to the revolutionary forces, Perón had to escape in a hurry.

What he left behind came as a shock to the Argentine public. Many were aware that agriculture and industry were in a mess, that public finances were in chaos, that graft was widespread, that Perón's nearest relatives were among the leading grafters, and that honesty and integrity had just about disappeared from public life. But few people knew much about Perón the man, as distinct from Perón the dictator.

In his several homes were found stacks of Argentine currency, totaling millions of dollars; boxes of gold money and valuables made of gold and silver; fabulous jewels of his late wife, Eva Perón, and foreign bank books. It was estimated that his bank deposits in foreign banks must be worth many millions of dollars. Since Perón had always posed as an anticapitalist and friend of the poor, the extent of his private wealth and grafting came as a shock to many of his followers.

Since Perón's downfall, Argentina has steadily progressed toward constitutional government and a sane economy. Although direct experience with fascism has an immunizing effect, the transitional phase of recovery and recuperation may take some time. This was confirmed in 1962, when the peronists were able to show up as the largest single party in the elections, winning about one-third of the popular vote. President Frondizi, who had shown little ability in coping with the renewed pressure of peronism, was removed from office by the military. In 1963, presidential elections were held, in which the moderate elements won, while peronism suffered a sharp decline.

Argentina's relations with the democratic nations, particularly with the United States, have greatly improved since the elimination of peronism. During that dictatorship, opposition to the democratic cause became identified with hostility to the United States, and peronist economic policies, based on extreme nationalism and little respect for agreements, proved a source of anxiety and fear to foreign businessmen.

However, the legacy of peronism will not vanish overnight. Relapses into economic nationalism (as in the case of the expropriated U.S. oil companies in November 1963) show that Argentina still has far to go before she attains economic and political stability.

Like fascism elsewhere, fascism in Argentina would never have come into power if the democratic forces of the nation had been more alert to subversion. This was not the first time that Argentina was ruled by a dictatorial regime, but this was her first experience with fascism. Authoritarian political dictatorships have come and gone in Latin America, but the peronist regime was the first example in the Western Hemisphere of a full-fledged fascist state, totalitarian in objectives and totalitarian in means.

IS FASCISM STILL A THREAT?

Is fascism still a threat in the leading democratic nations? The tendency now is to say emphatically, no. On balance, this may be the right answer, but to say that fascism is unlikely to take over the government of the United States, for example, is not to say it may not be a serious menace. To the extent that an *anti-intellectual tendency* exists in this or any other democracy, it undermines the faith in rational processes; whereas such a tendency need not lead straight to fascism, it prepares the mentality without which there can be no effective fascist movement. *Racialism,* to the extent that it still exists, is another source that feeds the fascist potential in the United States, as in other democracies. Democracy as known before no longer exists in South Africa, for example: racialism and democracy just do not mix. The racialism that started out in South Africa to be directed solely against the Negroes later turned against the Indians, and finally took in the whole English-speaking part, nearly one-half, of the white population. Conversely, to the extent that there has been progress in race relations in the United States—and the progress in the last twenty years has been truly inspiring—the chances of fascism in the United States have decreased.

The *cold war* with world communism has been another contributing factor in the revival of fascism. Because fascism and democracy are both opposed to communism, some democrats have wrongly concluded that democracy and fascism are natural allies in the struggle against communism, overlooking this important distinction: the quarrel between communism and fascism results from the inability of burglars to agree over the division of the loot, whereas the quarrel between communism and democracy is that between the burglar and the law. The same quarrel exists between fascism and democracy.

Possibly the most dangerous softening up of democratic resistance to fascism is the destruction of democratic habits and institutions, not by outside attacks, but within the citadel of democracy itself. If there is any fascist threat to democracy today—and there is—it no longer comes from Berlin, Rome, and Tokyo. It derives its parasitic strength from the inertness and apathy of the citizens of a democracy, because without such civic diseases there can be no support for demagogues and fearmongers who seek to aggrandize themselves at the expense of the whole body politic.

It should be kept in mind that the practical alternative is not between 100 per cent virtue and 100 per cent sin, but always between mixtures with varying proportions of ingredients. The danger in a democracy like the United States is not outright fascism on the German, Italian, or Argentine patterns, but the insidious and unnoticed corroding of democratic habits and institutions by prefascist and profascist attitudes. Huey Long, who as governor of Louisiana in the early nineteen thirties set up the nearest thing to a fascist dictatorship in the United States, once jokingly said that if fascism ever came to the United States it would be under the slogan of 100 per cent Americanism.

Long was right. The open, self-confessed fascist will not get a sympathetic hearing in the United States because the verbal symbols of fascism are identified too profoundly with evil in the American mind; the fascist fellow traveler, the crypto-fascist, the proto-fascist, the prefascist, and the pro-fascist are more dangerous than the plain unhyphenated fascist. By publicly declaring himself to be what he is, the fascist cannot work under the mantle of respectability. A politician with fascist leanings who denies that he is a fascist and who emphasizes his patriotism can do much more harm than the admitted fascist who is not permitted to work within the institutional framework of public life. The danger of not recognizing this prefascist attitude is that, should it become full-fledged fascism (as it well might in an economic depression or in some other disaster of the sort that periodically shakes men's faith in democracy), recognition of it as a threat may come too late for those whose earlier judgment was too lenient.

FOR FURTHER READING

Adorno, T. W. and others, *The Authoritarian Personality.* New York: Harper & Bros., 1950.

Alexander, Robert J., *The Perón Era.* New York: Columbia University Press, 1951.

Arendt, Hannah, *The Origins of Totalitarianism,* 2nd ed. New York: Meridian Books, Inc., 1958.

Baumont, Maurice and others, *The Third Reich.* New York: Frederick A. Praeger, Inc., 1955.

Bettelheim, Bruno, *The Informed Heart: The Human Condition in Modern Mass Society.* 1960.

Blanksten, George I., *Perón's Argentina.* Chicago: University of Chicago Press, 1953.

Bullock, Alan, *Hitler: A Study in Tyranny.* New York: Bantam Books, 1955.

Cohen, Elie A., *Human Behavior in the Concentration Camp.* New York: W. W. Norton & Co., 1953.

Ebenstein, William, *Fascist Italy.* New York: American Book Company, 1939.

————, *The German Record.* New York: Rinehart & Company, Inc., 1945.

————, *The Nazi State.* New York: Rinehart & Company, Inc., 1943.

————, *Totalitarianism: New Perspectives.* New York: Holt, Rinehart and Winston, Inc., 1962.

Friedrich, Carl J. and Z. K. Brzezinski, *Totalitarian Dictatorships and Autocracy.* Cambridge, Mass.: Harvard University Press, 1956.

Fromm, Erich, *Escape from Freedom.* New York: Rinehart & Company, Inc., 1941.

Germino, Dante L., *The Italian Fascist Party in Power.* Minneapolis, Minn.: University of Minnesota Press, 1959.

Gilbert, G. M., *The Psychology of Dictatorship.* New York: Ronald Press, 1950.

Hilberg, Raul, *The Destruction of the European Jews.* Chicago: Quadrangle Books, 1961.

Hoess, Rudolf, *Commandant of Auschwitz.* New York: Popular Library, 1961.

Kogon, Eugen, *The Theory and Practice of Hell: The German Concentration Camps and the System Behind Them.* New York: Berkley Books, 1950.

Meinecke, Friedrich, *The German Catastrophe.* Cambridge, Mass.: Harvard University Press, 1950.

Nathan, Peter, *The Psychology of Fascism.* London: Faber, 1943.

Nyiszli, Miklos, *Auschwitz: A Doctor's Eyewitness Account.* New York: Crest Books, 1961.

Orwell, George, *1984.* New York: New American Library of World Literature (Signet Books), 1950.

Payne, Stanley G., *Falange: A History of Spanish Fascism.* Stanford: Stanford University Press, 1961.

Rauschning, Hermann, *The Revolution of Nihilism.* New York: Longmans, Green & Co., 1939.

Russell of Liverpool, Lord, *The Scourge of the Swastika.* New York: Ballantine Books, 1956.

Schapiro, J. Salwyn, *Liberalism and the Challenge of Fascism.* New York: McGraw-Hill Book Co., Inc., 1949.

Shirer, William L., *The Rise and Fall of the Third Reich.* New York: Crest Books, 1962.

Thyssen, Fritz, *I Paid Hitler.* New York: Farrar and Rinehart, Inc., 1941.

Viereck, Peter R. E., *Metapolitics: The Roots of the Nazi Mind.* New York: Capricorn Books, 1961.

Warren, Robert Penn, *All the King's Men.* New York: Random House (Modern Library), 1953.

Wheeler-Bennett, J. W., *The Nemesis of Power.* New York: St. Martin's Press, Inc., 1953.

Whitaker, Arthur P., *Argentine Upheaval.* New York: Frederick A. Praeger, Inc., 1956.

————, *Spain and the Defense of the West.* New York: Frederick A. Praeger, Inc. (Praeger Paperbacks), 1962.

PART **2**

The Democratic Way of Life

3

Democratic Capitalism

TWO
CONCEPTIONS
OF DEMOCRACY
In 1948, George Bernard Shaw proposed that, in order to eradicate misunderstanding and confusion about the meaning of democracy, the leading scholars and thinkers of the world be convened and the issue be settled once and for all. Unfortunately, the root of the trouble lies deeper. Disagreements about the concept of democracy are not semantic, but reflect differences of a more fundamental nature.

When a representative of the United States, Britain, or France talks about democracy, he frequently means the very opposite of what a Russian or Chinese communist has in mind when he uses the same term. Thus at the end of World War II, when the United States, Britain, France, and the Soviet Union occupied Germany, one of their chief objectives was the democratization of Germany. At first all four powers wholeheartedly agreed on the objective, but it soon became evident that the Russian concept was entirely different from the Anglo-American-French understanding of democracy.

The Western powers took the view that bringing democracy to Germany meant free elections; a free press; freedom of political association; freedom of religion, thought, and speech; equality before the law; the right to oppose the government; the right to choose one's job; the right to form free trade unions; the right to move freely within one's country, go abroad temporarily, or emigrate permanently; and—in a general way—the right of every person to develop his mental and moral faculties to the fullest possible extent.

Above all, *freedom from fear* is basic in the Western concept of democracy. No society can be called free unless its citizens feel safe from unwarranted intrusion into their affairs by governmental authorities.

This aspect of democracy has been most aptly described in this way: in a free country, a knock at the door early in the morning means the milkman is there; in a totalitarian country, the same knock might mean the secret police are there, come to snatch a man from his home and family and to jail, exile, or execute him without trial or due process of law.

The communist conception of democratizing Germany was entirely different from the Western. In the first place, when the communist speaks of democracy, he has in mind, not government *of* the people, nor government *by* the people, but, as a leading Soviet philosopher puts it, "whether this or that policy is carried out in the interests of the people, in the interests of its overwhelming majority, or in the interests of its minority." (G. F. Aleksandrov, *The Pattern of Soviet Democracy,* 1948.)

Which doctrine reveals whether government is carried out *in the interests of the people?* Marxist-Leninist doctrine. Who interprets this doctrine correctly? The Communist party. Who in the Communist party determines the party line? The Presidium, a group of a dozen men or so. Who in the Presidium determines its general policy? The communist dictator, Khrushchev in Russia, Mao in China, and whoever controls the army, the party, and the secret police in the lesser communist states.

In the elections of West Germany in 1953, only 2.2 per cent of the vote was for the Communist Party. After being outlawed in West Germany in 1956, the party remained legal in West Berlin. In the West Berlin city elections of 1958, the communists obtained 1.9 per cent of the vote, and in the city elections of 1963 only 1.3 per cent. Yet from the communist viewpoint, West Germany is a dictatorship because the *interests* of its population are not determined by the one party that knows what is best for the Germans, the Communist Party. In particular, as long as capitalism exists in Germany there can be no democracy there, the communists say, because capitalism is by definition a dictatorship of the wealthy over the poor, even though a majority of the latter may vote in its favor. From the communist viewpoint, West Germany today could be called a democracy only if the Communist Party, supported by 2.2 per cent of the popular vote, ruled Germany, because only the Communist Party could rule in the interests of the German people.

It is for this reason that the communists call the essentials of democracy—freedom of speech, press, and association, equality before the law, and all the other fundamental democratic rights and liberties —*formal* democracy, as compared with the *real* democracy of communism, in which the means of production are owned by the state. In this communist conception, the traditional democratic freedoms assume a new meaning.

Freedom of the press? By all means, provided the newspapers function "in conformity with the interests of the toilers." (Article 125 of the Constitution of the Soviet Union.) Freedom of speech? Completely and unqualifiedly, provided the speaker's words support the communist cause.

The Soviet Union therefore looks upon East Germany as a true democracy because the means of production have been transferred to public ownership and management. The fact that a communist one-party dictatorship rules East Germany, the fact that a network of concentration and slave labor camps has been set up through the area is irrelevant to the communist proof of democracy.

DEMOCRACY
AS A WAY
OF LIFE

From the above illustration, the principal characteristics of the Western concept of democracy as a way of life clearly emerge.

(1) Rational empiricism
(2) Emphasis on the individual
(3) Instrumental nature of the state
(4) Voluntarism
(5) The law behind the law
(6) Emphasis on means
(7) Discussion and consent in human relations
(8) Basic equality of all human beings

(1) *Rational empiricism* is perhaps the most important single element in the free way of life. It is based on confidence in reason, and in the applicability of reason, not only to physical nature, but also to human relations. Dogmatists—such as communists or fascists— *know* what the truth is; for communists the concept of class is the ultimate in truth, whereas to fascists race and nation are the last repositories of truth. Since the dogmatist is so sure that he knows, he need not inquire further; his aim is to strengthen what he knows

already, and he brands whoever questions his knowledge guilty of intellectual subversion. The psychological and historical relation between dogmatism in philosophy and authoritarianism in politics is clear: absolute certainty of knowledge leads to fanatic enthusiasm in sentiment, which in turn leads to intolerant repression in government.

In contrast, empiricism, first fully developed by John Locke (1632-1704), is based on the idea that *all our knowledge derives from experience.* In this conception, truth (with a small *t*) is tentative, changing, and subject to constant checking and verification.

Since the history of both physical science and social thought is full of truths that turned out to be wholly or partly untrue, the rational empiricist refuses to believe, as the dogmatist believes, that mankind has in any field finally arrived at the end of its quest for truth and knowledge. The rational empiricist views truth, in the study of nature as much as of man, as an endless process, and considers the knowledge or truth of today no more than a *probability,* to be changed if new facts are brought to light. Bertrand Russell writes in his *Philosophy and Politics* (1946) that the genuine liberal says not "This is true," but "I am inclined to think that under present circumstances this opinion is probably the best."

In science, opinions cannot be accepted as true simply on the basis of authority; they must be verified by rational methods of observation. Because the scientist is aware of the incompleteness and temporariness of his data, he bears no grudge against the person who disagrees with him, but expects that the stronger evidence will ultimately prevail. Because he knows he may be wrong, the scientist does not consider his opponent as an enemy or traitor, a moral derelict to be liquidated or otherwise silenced. In a sense, *liberal democracy seeks to apply this rational, empirical outlook to the field of politics.*

The democratic process, like the scientific process, prescribes *how* truth is to be ascertained, not *what* specific truth is going to be discovered. The Constitution of the United States does not primarily determine, as a dogma would, what laws of Congress are good or bad, but rather prescribes what methods are to be used in making, executing, and interpreting the laws. Just as the scientist seeks to discover all available evidence that bears upon a problem before he decides upon the probable solution to that problem, the democratic procedure requires that *all opinions be heard* before a decision is made. Since in a democracy no one can claim infallible *a priori* knowledge of the true answer to a social problem, the only way to find out is to get all the ascertainable evidence.

The English Parliament started out as a High Court, and to this day parliamentary procedure in all democracies follows the judicial method of gathering and weighing all available facts and opinions before the legislative judgment is rendered.

As in science, too, the democratic method in politics can never promise, nor deliver, final truths. Whereas dogmatists and totalitarians are never satisfied with anything that is not the final answer, rational empiricists and democrats tackle smaller issues that settle nothing definitively. The communist, in approaching the problem of economic organization, sees only the dilemma of complete capitalism versus complete collectivism. The democrat does not set out to abolish hell or bring heaven overnight; he is more interested in free school lunches or in increasing the income tax by two per cent than in providing the final answer to the problem of poverty and suffering.

Because the rational empiricist knows that his viewpoint cannot be perfect, he does not feel that criticizing it is a sign of moral delinquency on the part of the critic; in fact, he is anxious to have it criticized so that it can be improved. The dogmatist, by contrast, knows that his truth is final and perfect, and criticizing it is therefore a grave intellectual error at the very least, if not downright moral subversion.

It is probably no coincidence that rational empiricism and democracy have developed more or less simultaneously in England, France, and the United States. In England, for example, John Locke, the founder of empiricism, is still the most persuasive exponent of political liberalism. In the United States empiricism has been the dominant school of thought, culminating in John Dewey (1859-1952), whose application of rational empiricism to philosophy and politics has been a lasting contribution to the American liberal heritage.

(2) The *emphasis on the individual* sharply separates liberal democracy from both fascist and communist totalitarianism. In fascism, the emphasis is on nation, state, race, and empire. In communism, the emphasis is on the concept of class. By contrast, liberal democracy stresses the *individual* as the center of all doctrine and policy. In the eyes of the liberal democrat, no social or political institution, be it a local boy-scout group, a party precinct, or the state, has a purpose of its own other than to serve and aid the individual in living a fuller life.

In the totalitarian doctrine, the state is the master, the individual the servant. Hegel, the intellectual ancestor of both fascism and communism, says in his *Philosophy of Law* (1821) that the individual finds his liberty in obeying the state, and the fullest realization of his liberty in dying for the state. Only when the individual dies for the state does he lose the last trace of any personal whimsicality and uniqueness and become completely a part of the state.

By contrast, Locke sees the indestructible essence of man in resisting, rather than in blindly obeying, the state. The liberal principles of life, liberty, and the pursuit of happiness are thus the exact opposite of the authoritarian concept of citizenship as duty, discipline, and death for the state.

Thomas Jefferson, one of the greatest liberal individualists of all time, remarked in a letter to Colonel William Stephen Smith, dated November 13, 1787, that "the tree of liberty must be refreshed from time to time with the blood of patriots and tyrants." The Declaration of Independence, too, states that life, liberty, and the pursuit of happiness are among the unalienable rights of man, and that "whenever any form of government becomes destructive of these ends, it is the right of the people to alter or to abolish it, and to institute new government, laying its foundations on such principles, and organizing its powers in such form as to them shall seem most likely to effect their safety and happiness."

The historical roots of individualism are three: first, the Jewish concept of one God leads to the idea that all men, as children of God, are brothers to each other. Second, the Christian doctrine of the indestructibility of the human soul maintains that whatever social, economic, and political inequalities may exist, all men possess a spiritual equality and uniqueness that no earthly power can override. Third, in the Stoic view, the one principle of action that governs all things is *to be at one with oneself,* to know oneself, and to act in conformity with one's rational principles and purposes. The true self of man, according to the Stoics, is not his flesh or bones, but the faculty that uses them, his *reason,* the part of man that more than anything else characterizes him as human.

At no time, of course, has this individualism been fully accepted, and the counterforces of totalitarianism always threaten it. At the present time, in particular, the threat of all-destructive atom and hydrogen bomb war leads to a strengthening of anti-individualist attitudes, stressing the idea of "let's close ranks" rather than "let each man decide what is right or wrong and act accordingly."

(3) The *instrumental theory of the state* views the state as a mechanism, to be used for ends higher than itself. Both Plato and Aristotle, the founders of Western political theory, conceived of the state as an organic entity, with a life and purposes of its own, superior to the purposes of the individual. Plato and Aristotle thought of the state as the *highest moral good,* the source of moral values and spiritual enrichment for the individual.

From the Jewish-Christian viewpoint of religion, the instrumentalist theory of the state maintains that the highest values in man's life relate to God, and that no earthly law can claim to supersede God's. The function of the state is to maintain peace and order, so that men can pursue their activities devoted to higher ends. From the rational-humanist viewpoint, the instrumentalist theory of the state affirms that the ability of the individual to use his reason in discovering what is right and wrong is the ultimate test of political authority, and that the state therefore cannot turn evil into good or wrong into right solely because it possesses the means of physical coercion.

The liberal doctrine stresses society far more than the state; in the classical liberal doctrine—and to a considerable extent today—*society is considered basically self-sufficient,* and *the state is to step in only when the voluntary efforts of society fail.*

The instrumentalist theory of the state thus relegates the state to a supplementary position. As long as individuals can get along without the state, the liberal bias is against the state, even if the state could do the same thing a little better.

In the totalitarian state, the assumption is always in favor of the state, because it is credited with omniscience and omnipotence. Thus the totalitarian state organizes and controls, not only the sensitive areas of the economy, education, and religion, but even chess players and Sunday afternoon hikers, because the state does not wish to leave any activity to the free discretion of its citizens.

(4) By contrast, the democratic theory sees in the principle of *voluntarism* the very lifeblood of a free society. Fellowship can most deeply be experienced in small, voluntary groups. Such groups were first formed in seventeenth-century England on a religious basis, and to this day the English-speaking world abounds with thousands and thousands of religious sects that are small in size and entirely voluntary in nature.

Later, the principle of voluntary association was applied in the field of politics (parties), education (private schools), and economics (labor unions and employers' associations). In charity, the Red Cross and local community chests testify to the fact that there is still a strong sentiment for retaining voluntary activity. Even in England, which has national health and social security programs covering every person from the cradle to the grave, there has been a reassertion of the importance of voluntary organization in social welfare, supplementing the governmental programs.

(5) The concept of *the law behind the law* flows directly from the *federal* view of state and society in classical liberalism. Society is conceived as an aggregate of diverse voluntary associations, and the

state itself is looked upon as an essentially voluntary body because its authority is derived from the consent of the governed. Whenever authority is organized on a federal basis, there has to be a higher law defining the relationships of the parts among each other and of each part to the whole.

Classical liberalism, therefore, has always adhered to the idea that the relations between state and society, between government and individual, are ultimately defined by a law higher than that of the state. In fact, classical liberal thought in Britain and the United States assumes that the *law is not the product of the state, but precedes it.* The right to life, liberty, property, and the pursuit of happiness is not a gift of the state to the individual, but precedes the state. The function of the state in relation to man's basic rights is to protect and define such rights, not to create them.

In the United States, in particular, the concept of the law behind the law has never been challenged as the foundation of American political thought and experience. The Declaration of Independence specifically recognizes it, and the Constitution has also recognized that no legislative body can make laws without due process, or laws that otherwise violate basic principles of reason. The very existence of the United States is, of course, due to the insistence that above the law then ruling, the law of imperial Britain, there was a higher law to which the revolutionary colonists pledged allegiance.

Opponents of democratic government have charged that this concept of a higher law, making government dependent upon the consent of the governed, opens the door to rebellion and anarchy. In his *Two Treatises of Government* (1690), John Locke answers this charge with three counterarguments. First, Locke concedes that the democratic theory of government admits of the possibility of rebellion, but he denies that it does so more than any other theory. When the people are made miserable, they will rebel under any form of government; let the governors be "sacred and divine, descended or authorized from heaven, give them out for whom or what you please, the same will happen." Second, Locke says, men do not rebel "upon every little mismanagement in public affairs," or "for light and transient causes," as the Declaration of Independence puts it. Third, and here Locke moves from the defensive to the offensive, government by consent coupled with the right of the people to rebel is "the best fence against rebellion."

Locke could only guess in 1690 whether his arguments would be proved by experience, because democracy was then still a thing of the future. Yet experience has proved him perspicacious. The British

and American systems of government, based on the Lockean-Jefferso-
nian admission of the people's right to rebel against oppression, have
proved themselves the stablest and most successful political systems
the world has ever seen, and the same may be said of countries
(smaller in size but equally great in the glory of freedom) like Holland, Switzerland, and the Scandinavian nations. By contrast, where
the higher law has been rejected in the name of law and order, the
political results have been blood purges, conspiracies, plots and coun-
terplots, and violent swings from one extreme to another—the political
record, specifically, of communist and fascist dictatorships.

(6) The *emphasis on means* in democratic life is based on the realization that ends lead no existence apart from means, but are con-
tinually shaped by them. The totalitarian makes a clear-cut distinction
between means and ends. In his dogmatic way of thinking he is
absolutely certain of what the ends are, and possessing this certainty,
he pays little attention to the nature of the means. Thus, the communists believe in universal brotherhood and cooperation as their officially
professed end, yet they fail to realize that the means employed in
bringing about communism—secret police, slave labor camps, thought
control, denunciations, repression of dissent—increase hatred and
misery rather than diminish it.

One of the main difficulties in separating means from ends is the
fact that *in most practical situations a means is simultaneously an end.*
Thus, education is for some an end in itself; for others, it is but a
means to an end—to a degree, for example. Yet, a degree may again
be only a means to the end of a happier, fuller life, or a better job.
Again, a better job is not necessarily an end in itself; it is likely to be
a means to some higher end, such as expressing a sense of craftsman-
ship or serving society.

The central position of means in free societies is well entrenched
in their living experience. Magna Carta, Habeas Corpus, and jury
trial, to mention but a few roots of liberty in the English-speaking
world, are originally all procedural devices, means; and the history
of liberty may aptly be described as a history of procedure. In representative assemblies, too, it is not the legislative product that distinguishes a democratic body from a nondemocratic one, but the
difference of procedure. In the one case, procedure aims at the fullest
and fairest guarantee of the right of the minority to be heard; in the
other, procedure aims at silencing minorities and bringing about the
loudest possible volume of cheers for the dictator.

At present, the danger in democratic societies lies in the possible
waning of this awareness that differences over means are the heart

of the difference between democracy and totalitarianism. In fighting a totalitarian system like fascism or communism there is a natural tendency to imitate their means, and because the tendency is natural, special efforts must be made to guard against it. In defending democracy, some persons are willing to use means that are bound to destroy the very thing they seek to defend.

(7) *Discussion and consent* are the means by which a democratic society typically settles divergent viewpoints and interests. It is the democratic view that, since no one possesses absolute truth, both sides to an argument may make a contribution to the best possible answer, and that the only way to get that answer is to marshal all the available evidence.

The independent voter in a democracy typifies the person who is not willing to commit himself unconditionally to one party, either because he knows too little or (less often) too much about politics, or simply because—whatever his level of political information—he does not expect much from government in any case. In a totalitarian state there are no independent voters, only followers or enemies of the prevailing manner of thought. The importance of the independent voter can be clearly seen in many elections. Thus, in 1952 the Republican party selected General Eisenhower over Senator Taft as its presidential candidate, mainly for his wider appeal to independent voters. In contrast, Nixon's defeat in the presidential election of 1960 was attributed by many to his relatively weak appeal to independent voters.

In the theory of the democratic society, governments derive "their just powers from the consent of the governed" (Declaration of Independence), because the state has no reason for existence other than to serve the people. If the state becomes oppressive and unmindful of the rights of the people, then the democratic theory, as was pointed out earlier, upholds not only the right, but the duty to revolt against such government.

However, this right to rebel can be claimed only where the methods of discussion and consent are blocked by tyrannical despotism; where the channels of discussion are open, as in a democratic state and society, no democrat would claim the right of rebellion against the state.

The communist who today claims the right to revolution as a general democratic privilege utterly distorts this concept for his own purposes. From the democratic viewpoint, *the democrat has the moral right, and duty, to rebel against the totalitarian system, but the totalitarian possesses no such right against the democratic system.*

(8) The *basic equality of all human beings* is a point of democratic doctrine and policy that is frequently misunderstood. No democrat has ever said that all men are identical, but only that in basic respects they are equal. The very uniqueness of each and every person creates a kind of equality that is important in the democratic outlook. From the religious viewpoint of the Jewish-Christian tradition, all men are equal before God; God's challenge to every human being is the same, although men's response to it varies enormously. From the rationalist-humanistic viewpoint, all men share, over and above differences of race, sex, religion, nationality, and class, one common trait: the ability to reason. In this sense, all men are citizens of the world rather than of a particular, distinctive group, and their basic equality derives from what they have in common rather than from what separates them.

The Declaration of Independence makes it perfectly plain that all men are created equal, in the sense that they have certain unalienable rights, such as life, liberty, and the pursuit of happiness. The equality that men receive at birth, according to democratic theory, is thus not in the nature of an outright gift or grant, but a loan, as it were, an *opportunity,* a *challenge*. The Jeffersonian phrase, "pursuit of happiness," admirably expresses the thought that man does not have the right to happiness, in the sense that the state or his family or friends owe him happiness, but only in the sense that he has the right to *pursue* happiness, unhindered by unreasonable obstacles.

However, equality does not mean, as Plato charged it meant, "dispensing a kind of equality to equals and unequals alike." The contrary is true, of the ideal democracy at least. In practice it is not easy to ascertain when equals are still equal and when they become unequal. Thus, to take an illustration: the most common interpretation of democratic equality is "equality of opportunity." A grave difficulty arises immediately. If all men were endowed with the same talents and abilities, and were born into the same homes, and received the same schooling, giving all an equal opportunity would be a fair solution. Yet people differ in native talent, and even more in background and education.

Legislative action cannot equalize the I.Q. of the population, and there will always be differences of ability, drive, and motivation, but laws can make equality of opportunity more real by trying to equalize conditions before the race starts: increased inheritance taxes lessen the impact of inherited wealth, progressive income taxes favor the lower-income groups, and free education (from nursery school to university) benefits the indigent more than the affluent. In other words, equality of opportunity, if it allows ability alone to operate, quickly establishes and perpetuates inequality. *Need, too,* must be considered; it adds to the principle of efficiency that of happiness.

CONDITIONS OF POLITICAL DEMOCRACY

Of all the aspects of democracy, the political has top priority. Although political democracy is not identical with democracy as a way of life, the instinct of those who tend to identify the two is not unsound. Experience has shown that political democracy, if practiced over any length of time, leads to the extension of the democratic principle to social, economic, and international problems. So far, there is less evidence that social or economic democracy leads to political democracy. Precisely because political democracy merely defines "the rules of the game," it is more far-reaching than social or economic democracy, which is concerned with one particular substantive area of problems.

The first characteristic of democratic government is the maintenance of a political climate in which *political liberty* can thrive. In every society, those who uphold the orthodox views may freely express them. No one is hindered in Russia today from publicly proclaiming Nikita Khrushchev the greatest statesman of the present. In Yugoslavia, no one is jailed today for referring to President Tito as the greatest president in Yugoslav history. *Political liberty begins at the point where unorthodox opinions may be freely presented, without legal, social, or economic penalties.*

The political liberty of a society can best be measured by the *margin of unorthodoxy* that is *tolerated* in that society. This yardstick enables us to go beyond the crude classification of dictatorship and democracy, which is valid only on a general level. Examining first the totalitarian states by this criterion, we find the least margin of unorthodox opinion in Nazi Germany (1933-1945) and in communist states today, a much wider margin of unorthodoxy in fascist Italy (1922-1945) than in either Nazi Germany or Soviet Russia, and the relatively largest unorthodoxy in the present Portuguese and South American dictatorships.

Measuring the margin of unorthodoxy in democratic societies, we find Britain, France, Scandinavia, Holland, Australia, and New Zealand on the top of the list, while the United States trails somewhat behind. Needless to say, the positions are never fixed, and the range of unorthodoxy constantly changes; by general agreement there is

"I say he's a disturbing influence in this community."

more uniformity and conformity of thought in the United States today than thirty years ago, and there may be less again ten years hence.

The *common agreement on fundamentals* is a second condition indispensable to the successful working of political democracy. The most important agreement, and the one no written constitution can by itself guarantee, is the common desire to operate a democratic system. Where there is no written constitution, as in Great Britain, there is no protection of political minorities or individual nonconformists other than the decency and restraint of the majority. Legally, the British government could outlaw the opposition and introduce a totalitarian state overnight. But the government is not doing that because it is a party to an unwritten agreement to abide by democratic principles.

By the same token, written constitutions are not necessarily a protection. Fascism developed in Italy, Germany, Japan, and Argentina despite written constitutions, and the presence of a democratic constitution in Czechoslovakia after World War II did not restrain the communists from distorting and destroying it.

The lesson of all this historical experience is simple: *the strength of a democracy is never greater than the will of the people to uphold it.*

Where agreement on fundamentals is lacking, political democracy suffers from stresses and strains that may well become fatal. An irreconcilable division on fundamentals between major parties may lead to civil war or dictatorship. Such a situation existed in the United

States in 1860 when there was no agreement on the basic issue of slavery. In 1930, the German political system was a democracy as far as the paper constitution was concerned; but two-thirds of the electorate wanted to set up totalitarian dictatorships of either the communist or fascist type, and the fascists finally won out in 1933. Obviously, no constitution, however perfect on paper, can save a democracy if the antidemocrats outvote the democrats two to one. A democratic constitution *assumes,* but *cannot* in itself *create,* the will to maintain democratic institutions.

The Fourth Republic of France (1945-1958) provides another example. During its existence, the forces favoring or tolerating republican government based on an omnipotent parliament mustered just a little over one-half of the electorate. On the extreme Left, the communists, dedicated to the principle of totalitarian dictatorship, were supported by one-fourth of the electorate. On the extreme Right, supported by about one-fifth of the electorate, there were groups that either sought to set up a new republican regime based on a strong executive or that aimed at doing away with democracy altogether.

Such disagreement on fundamentals could not work, and it did not work. The Fourth Republic ended in May 1958, and the new Fifth Republic was centered on the personality of Charles de Gaulle. In the elections of September 1958 a new equilibrium of forces emerged; the communists, with 19 per cent of the popular vote, remained the only force opposed to any form of democratic government. Nearly 80 per cent of the popular votes were obtained by parties (Socialists, Catholic Democrats, Radicals, Gaullists, and Independents) that were united on the formula that French republicanism could only be saved by a strong executive as proposed by de Gaulle. Time will tell whether the Fifth Republic reflects a new French agreement on fundamentals or whether it is but another makeshift solution covering up the absence of such basic agreement.

Is agreement on economic policy a necessary condition of political democracy? A generation ago, this question was answered more often in the affirmative than today. Conservatives frequently expressed apprehension lest the new socialist principle of public ownership undermine the whole fabric of institutions. In contrast, socialists frequently expressed the fear that conservatives would be unwilling to adhere loyally to democratic principles if socialist parties were given a chance to change the economic organization of society by constitutional means and that the propertied classes would put property above constitutional democracy.

Experience has shown that both sides have been wrong. In theory, the disagreement on basic economic policy between conservatives and socialists looked bigger than it has worked out in practice. The conservatives have abandoned much of their old economic laissez-faire position, and the socialists, having considerably modified their economic philosophy, are now satisfied with a program consisting of welfare state legislation and the socialization of only a few basic industries.

In 1945, the British electorate was faced with a choice, not between socialism and capitalism, but between two programs not too different in nature. The socialists aimed at 20 per cent nationalization of the economy. The conservatives would have preferred 10 to 15 per cent. There was no question of zero versus 100 per cent that was presented in the past as a matter of theory.

The very nature of the democratic process makes the choice of zero versus 100 per cent virtually impossible. Since elections are generally decided by the floating independent vote, which by definition is middle-of-the-road, no extreme program has a chance of being accepted.

Government by more than one party expresses the democratic principle, borrowed from the law, that "the other side must also be heard" (*audiatur et altera pars*). The dogmatic, totalitarian viewpoint holds that there is only one Truth, and from that position to the one-party state there is a direct line. The democratic viewpoint holds that different men perceive different aspects of truth, mainly in the light of their lives and experiences, and that there will be at least two sides to any major question.

The communists say that the two-party system is a product of capitalism; that the opposing interests of capitalists and workers must be represented in opposing parties; and that, since capitalism has been abolished in the Soviet Union, there is no need for an opposition party to the Communist party.

This line of argument has serious flaws. In the first place, it wrongly assumes that property is the only line of political party. In Europe, party loyalties are frequently based on religious or ideological loyalties; in the United States the regional factor is often important. Also, the communist argument exaggerates the impact of property on party. Only about 60 per cent of the British working class vote Labor, and in the United States the correlation between income and vote is equally indecisive. If income were the only decisive factor, political prediction would be much easier than professional pollsters have found it to be.

Moreover, if inequalities of income are important politically, the need for a multi-party system is more urgent in the Soviet Union than in the capitalist countries, because the inequality between managers and workers, and between skilled and unskilled workers, is much greater in the Soviet Union than in capitalist countries. There is little doubt that if freedom of association were suddenly introduced in the Soviet Union, parties would be formed for the purpose of asserting the claims of peasants, the unskilled workers, and the various nationalities such as the Ukrainians and White Russians.

Even if capitalism could be abolished in the most democratic manner, there would still be need for more than one party. Assuming a classless society, in which all productive property is owned publicly, and in which incomes, too, are relatively equal, there would still be questions of vital concern to the community, questions admitting more than one answer. For example, every state, whether democratic, fascist, communist, socialist, or capitalist, has to decide each year what portion of its national product is to be consumed and what portion is to be saved and invested. Another typical question that every community has to face is how much to spend on social welfare, and which groups should be favored—the claims of the old compete with those of the young, education may compete with health. The answer to such questions cannot be found in the form of economic organization.

After all, even when there was no capitalism in the modern sense, there was a multitude of parties. When the suffrage was limited to the propertied classes, as it was in most countries until about one hundred years ago, the existing parties were divided not on the basis of rich and poor, but along other lines—town versus country, secularism versus clericalism, states' rights versus centralism, free trade versus protection, republicanism versus monarchism, slavery versus freedom, to name but a few.

PSYCHOLOGICAL ROOTS OF DEMOCRACY

Man has lived for about a quarter million years on this planet, yet he has had some knowledge of democratic ideas and practice for only about twenty-five hundred years. Even today, democracy as a way of life exists only in a relatively small portion of the world. Democracy, then, can scarcely be called "natural." On the contrary, the democratic way of life is the most difficult of all; it does not emerge spontaneously and by accident, but is the result of deliberate thought, seeking to correct what is natural, all too natural, in human behavior.

Just as the behavior of the child is more natural than that of the adult, the behavior of the authoritarian is more natural than that of the democratic personality. The process of growth and development from childhood to maturity is natural only in the biological and physiological sense, not in the social and cultural sense. Socially and culturally, the transformation of the child into the mature adult demands much forethought, planning, and hard work.

Politically, the authoritarian personality is fundamentally the grownup who has never become mature, the ostensible adult who still accepts the dependency and security characteristic of childhood. By contrast, the democratic personality is the emotionally and intellectually mature adult, the person able to stand on his own feet and shape his life for himself. The mature adult does not need security provided by an external authority; he possesses security within himself. The price of this emotional and intellectual independence is high, since to attain it a person must face responsibilities and make decisions by himself, without being able to blame anyone afterwards if his decisions are wrong.

There is no growing up without making mistakes, and the overprotected child *can* make no mistakes—his father will see to that! Similarly, in a dictatorship, the system prevents the individual from experimenting and acting on his own, so that (in theory, at least) he always does the right thing. By contrast, the process of growing up, of moving away from supervision to personal responsibility, implies the possibility of choosing the wrong thing, of making mistakes; in this sense, *democracy may be defined as the right to make mistakes.*

Implied in this concept is not the desirability of erring for the sake of erring, but the recognition that freedom implies choice between alternatives, and that no one can grow to maturity, no one can be truly democratic, without learning to make choices, and without occasionally making the wrong choice.

The 200 per cent American defenders of democracy who want to make it a crime for anyone ever to think or act wrongly are trying to have a democracy with authoritarian personalities, people who only think and do what authority has allowed them to think or do.

The attitude of the democratic personality toward the leader is markedly different from that of the authoritarian personality. The latter regards the leader of the nation with a mixture of loyalty and reverence resembling the emotions he first felt toward his parents, particularly his father. The traditional reference to a chief of the state as the "father of the country" is the linguistic expression of a profound psychological tie; the adult in such a society has really never outgrown the father-child relationship.

By contrast, *the democratic personality puts more emphasis on the group than on the leader.* This feeling goes back to that of the rebellious child, who joins with his brothers in a league of equals to destroy the authority of their father. "Liberty, equality, fraternity," the three ideals of the French revolution, express the attitude of the democratic personality against authority.

For this reason, democracies frequently act with deep suspicion whenever a great leader appears. Churchill was opposed in England before World War II because he was "too clever," not average enough, and therefore potentially dangerous. Clemenceau was removed from French public life after World War I because he was too much of a leader. Many American voters who cast their ballot against Franklin D. Roosevelt were motivated by the unconscious fear that he was not Mr. Average American. Lincoln attracted the same kind of hatred, although much of it was rationalized in political and ideological arguments.

It is for this reason, too, that impersonal factors like constitutions, charters, and congresses play such an important part in democratic states; leaders come and go, but the institutions continue unimpaired. In contrast, the authoritarian personality thinks in terms of allegiance to a particular person. In Spain and Latin America, for example, political loyalty revolves around the phenomenon of *personalismo;* the political attachment and allegiance are to one particular person, rather than to a party, program or constitution. Even democratic parties in such countries usually are split into various factions, each led by one man, to whom his group owes allegiance. But this is even more true, of course, of antidemocratic movements: thus we speak of Hitlerism, Peronism, Stalinism, but not of Churchillism, Eisenhowerism, or Johnsonism.

The formation of the democratic personality is first determined in the *family.* It was Sigmund Freud who emphasized that the first five years are probably the most decisive years of life as far as basic attitudes are concerned. In the early years of life, the home is school, church, and government all rolled into one. In some societies, parents are accorded absolute power over their children; in such societies the family resembles a miniature absolutist state, in which the fiat of the absolute ruler, the father, is the law.

In contrast, democratic family relations give the child the first experience of democracy. In the United States, the family unit resembles, in most cases, a small parliament in which every member feels free to have his say when family decisions are in the making. Children do not expect to be told what to do, what line of work to pick, or whom to marry. Far from being the absolute ruler of an authoritarian family, the American father has often learned to be satisfied if he has a chance to be heard. His hope is not of being obeyed *because* he is the father, but rather (if we can take the cartoonist's word for it, at least) of getting a fair hearing *although* he is the father.

One of Germany's leading child psychologists, Kurt Lewin, came to the United States in 1934 and stayed here until his death in 1945. In 1936 he wrote a paper on "Some Social-Psychological Differences between the United States and Germany" (reprinted in his *Resolving Social Conflicts,* 1948), in which he makes the following observations:

"To one who comes from Germany, the degree of freedom and independence of children and adolescents in the United States is very impressive. Especially the lack of servility of the young child toward adults or of the student toward his professor is striking. The adults, too, treat the child on a much more equal footing, whereas in Germany it seems to be the natural right of the adult to rule and the duty of the child to obey. The natural relation of adult and child in the United States is not considered that of a superior (*Herr*) to a subordinate (*Untergebener*) but that of two individuals with the same right in principle. The parents seem to treat the children with more respect. Generally they will be careful, when requesting the child to bring some object, to ask them in a polite way. They will let the child feel that he is doing them a favor in a situation in which the German parent is much more likely to give short orders. It is more common in the United States to hear a parent thank the child after such action. The parent may even do so after he has had to apply considerable pressure in order to make the child comply, whereas the same situation in Germany would probably lead to 'the next time you should do it right away.' In Germany the adult will tend to keep the child in a state of submission, while the American may want to put the child back on an equal footing as soon as possible."

The *school* is, next to the home, perhaps the most important single source of a child's basic psychological patterns. What children formally learn in school is much less important than what they pick up unconsciously from the way in which the school operates. Authoritarian societies consider the school as little more than a phase of premilitary training, in which the function of the teacher is to inculcate habits of order and discipline.

In a democratic school system, the main function of the teacher is to help the child develop his own personality, and to help him learn *how* to think rather than what to think. The permissive attitude of the democratic school is premised on the assumption that people will generally choose the right way if given the proper help and guidance, and that trust will beget trust.

Also, most democratic societies do not hesitate to run the schools on a coeducational basis and to employ women on a large scale. By contrast, authoritarian schools separate boys from girls to make sure that the boys grow into tough men rather than soft sissies; also, men are generally preferred as teachers, mainly because only men can play the necessary role of father-substitute.

The democratic nature of the school is also determined by the relation of teacher and parent, and that of teacher and political authority. In student government, the students are given the opportunity to learn formal self-government and to make their rules of self-government without interference from the outside. In many colleges, much of the discipline, from exams ("honor system") to staying-out hours, is regulated and enforced by the students themselves. This type of experience teaches a student more about democracy than a reading assignment about the theory and ideals of democracy.

Moreover, the existence of private schools in democracies is a further expression of freedom in education. In totalitarian societies, the state generally abolishes all private schools since there is only one pattern that is right and the state knows what it is and has the means to enforce it. In democratic societies, many important educational innovations have been given their first trial in small experimental schools; if successful, such advances then spread to the public school system.

The attitude toward women in society sharply differentiates the democratic from the authoritarian personality. The authoritarian generally desires to keep women in their place; his scale of values is oriented strongly toward masculine traits and preferences. Many legal codes officially recognize the superior position of the man by declaring him to be the head of the family, and by subordinating his wife to him in matters of property and other basic issues.

Feminism is not only the creed of rebellious women who wish to assert their equality, but also the feeling of democratically inclined men who resent the treatment of women as inferiors just as they resent the treatment of any other human being as an inferior on the

"I hate everybody, regardless of race, creed, or place of national origin!"

basis of race, for example, or religion, or nationality. As in other cases of intolerance and inequality, the democratic personality is keenly aware of the fact that *unfair and arrogant treatment is harmful not only to the person so treated, but also to the person who metes it out.* This aspect of racial segregation was recognized by the Supreme Court when it declared racial segregation in public schools unconstitutional in its historic decision of May 17, 1954.

The *range of affection* determines the degree to which a person matures, to which he can be called democratic. The child first knows only himself. Gradually he discovers a world outside of his own body and desires—his mother, father, brothers and sisters, neighbors, and classmates. The degree of his maturation and adulthood is in direct proportion to his capacity to enlarge his horizon and make friends with all kinds of persons.

The immature personality stops early in this process; he can only identify with his own group (the in-group), and considers others (the out-group) as dangerous and hostile. This group-egotism may include the family only, or it may extend to social class, political party, or nation. In all these cases, the attachment to the in-group is frequently more an *expression of hatred for the outsider than of affection for the insider*.

By contrast, the democratic personality is always aware of his own imperfections and those of his social class, party, or nation, and this realization makes him tolerant of different people, different races, different religions, different ideas. His capacity to cooperate and love is not a rigid fixation on one particular object, but the expression of a *general capacity to cooperate, to share, to love*.

Love that is exclusively directed at one person or group is usually not love, but either masochistic self-abasement or sadistic domination. Love and cooperation in the democratic sense imply freedom, equality, and integrity, not exclusiveness and domination. When St. Paul said that there was "neither Jew nor Greek, neither bond nor free," he gave expression to a conception of human relations in which there was no in-group and no out-group, but only one humanity.

The strength of the democratic personality is proportionate to the strength of democratic institutions and practices in the society in which he lives. To the extent that persons are given leeway to develop and to act freely and spontaneously, they will experience less frustration and hatred.

Aggression is generally the *result of frustration*, although the causal relationship does not always appear immediately. Many persons are able to repress temporarily their aggressive impulses following frustration; such delays and repressions do not destroy the aggressive reaction, but merely postpone, exaggerate, and distort it. The democratic society minimizes frustration by removing its sources as much as possible. Thus, in a democracy, everybody has the right to criticize any political leader, the government, or any idea.

This *freedom of expression serves as a safety valve*, preventing resentment and hostility from being repressed and transformed into aggression and hatred. As everybody knows from his own experience, once he has told somebody off he feels better. Freedom of expression is a psychological catharsis, in which the soul keeps itself from accumulating resentment and hostility.

In contrast, a totalitarian society seems to be happy and united, and apparently there is no dissent. Yet this artificial calm builds up tremendous resources of hatred, which can often be expressed only in gossip, jokes, and other informal channels of expression. But when the lid is off, the accumulated frustrations break out into open violence. Hitler at the end of his regime, obsessed with the idea that everybody was conspiring to kill him, finally issued arrests for such close intimates as Goering, his second in command.

The artificiality of the calm and uniformity in totalitarian regimes is best demonstrated by the periodic purges and blood baths that are characteristic of communist and fascist states. Thus, Lavrenti Beria, one of the top three rulers in Russia, was executed in December 1953 for a long assortment of crimes he allegedly committed or planned to commit. A regime in which treason can reach so high up that the man in charge of the nation's secret police and internal security is killed as a spy in the pay of Wall Street, is scarcely a model of internal strength.

Finally, totalitarians invariably misjudge the apparent dissensions and disagreements in a democratic society. It is precisely because such disagreements are openly expressed that there is so little smouldering hatred and hostility within a free society, and it can act unitedly and strongly in the hour of need.

It is generally agreed that the democratic personality is more tolerant, more cooperative, friendlier, and fairer than the authoritarian personality. But the question is often raised whether these human gains are not paid for by the loss of efficiency. Controlled experiments with children and adults have shown that the efficiency of a group can be raised by substituting a democratic group decision for a lecture, request, or command from the top. In industry, management is increasingly using democratic group discussions to raise efficiency. This is still a new field of experimentation, but there is certainly no evidence that the autocratically run group produces more efficient individuals.

In the field of education, too, schools and colleges are trying to get away from the lecture method, by which the teacher tells the student that such and such is so and so—period. The advantage of the discussion method over lecturing is that the teacher no longer functions as a little god issuing the law from Mount Sinai, but is more in the nature of an umpire who sees to it that the rules of debate are properly observed; the discussion itself has to be carried forward by the students, and whatever conclusions they arrive at are the product of their own group thinking, not of superior authority. Discussion, of course, assumes equality; superiors do not discuss with inferiors, but tell them what to do.

The *feeling of being wanted is one of the strongest driving forces of action and allegiance;* nothing can produce that feeling better than the democratic process of consultation, discussion, and free exchange of ideas. With love, greater things can be accomplished than with hatred. This old religious truth is also borne out by psychology, politics, and history.

In the last two hundred years, not a single major war has been won by the apostles of hatred and strife over the more democratic side, which would indicate that totalitarian efficiency fails even in the one field where it is supposed to be highest: war. The reason for such failure may be the tendency of the totalitarian personality to close his mind to new and changing circumstances, to adhere rigidly to fixed dogma, to aim at unrealistic objectives, or to pursue possible objectives with impossible means. Self-criticism is one of the most crucial correctives in doing any job; and although everybody is somewhat sensitive to criticism, the democratic personality can tolerate more of it than the totalitarian.

INDIVIDUAL FREEDOM AND NATIONAL SECURITY

The best introduction into the problem of individual liberty is still John Stuart Mill's essay *On Liberty* (1859). Mill wrote his essay at a comparatively civilized time, when there seemed to be little need for it. Yet he foresaw that illiberal forces would gain in influence, and he hoped that men would then turn to *On Liberty*. Though Mill modestly disclaimed originality other than that which "every thoughtful mind gives to its own mode of conceiving and expressing truths which are common property," the essay has grown in stature as time goes on, because many of Mill's predictions have come true, and much that he has to say is still valid today, a century later.

As Alexis de Tocqueville had done in his *Democracy in America* (1835-1840), Mill attacked the illusion that evolution of government from tyranny to democracy necessarily solves tthe problem of individual liberty. *Tyranny can be exercised by one, by a few, or by the majority,* and the latter is potentially the worst of all, since it commands the widest moral support, whereas oppression by one or a few is mainly physical. The power of public opinion in a democracy often exercises more restraint and repression against dissidents than a dictator exercises by physical means in a dictatorship. Protection against political tyranny is therefore not enough. It must be supplemented by protection against social tyranny, which leaves fewer means of escape, "penetrating much more deeply into the details of life, and enslaving the soul itself."

Mill sees that the natural tendency of man is not to be tolerant and open-minded, but to impose his views on others, and that lack of power is frequently the major cause of tolerating dissent. It makes little difference how numerous the dissenting minority is: "If all mankind minus one, were of one opinion, and only one person were of the contrary opinion, mankind would be no more justified in silencing that one person, than he, if he had the power, would be justified in silencing mankind."

Silencing an unorthodox opinion is not only wrong but harmful, because it robs others of an opportunity to get acquainted with ideas that may be true or partly true. "All silencing of discussion," Mill argues, "is an assumption of infallibility." Therefore Mill states that, unless *absolute freedom of opinion*—scientific, moral, political, and theological—is guaranteed, a society is not completely free.

No individual can grasp more than a fragment or portion of truth; no society can speak for all mankind; finally, whole eras are no more infallible than individuals. History is full of opinions held by one age as the last truth only to be considered false and absurd by subsequent ages.

Just as liberty is not complete unless it is absolute, so discussion must be completely unhampered, and free discussion must not be ruled out when "pushed to an extreme," because the arguments for a case are not good unless they are good for an extreme case. Mill is aware of the argument that some opinions are so useful and important to society that they must be excluded from public discussion and criticism, but he answers that the "usefulness of an opinion is itself a matter of opinion."

Mill does not accept the "pleasant falsehood" that truth inevitably triumphs over persecution; history "teems with instances of truth put down by persecution." In the history of religion in the West, for example, there are numerous sects and churches that have been successfully suppressed, and Mill therefore concludes that "persecution has always succeeded, save where the heretics were too strong a party to be effectually persecuted."

Moreover, *the greatest harm of persecution is inflicted not on those who dissent from established beliefs, but on those who do not,* because the mental development of the latter is stifled by the fear of expressing unorthodox or dissenting views. In an atmosphere of cowed uniformity there may be a few exceptional great thinkers, but not an intellectually active people. "No one can be a great thinker who does not recognize that as a thinker it is his first duty to follow his intellect to whatever conclusions it may lead."

Moreover, dogmatism robs truth of its vigor and vitality, and is more likely to destroy truth than keep it alive. For its own health, truth needs to be "fully, frequently, and fearlessly" discussed. If possible at all, the opposing opinion should be expressed by someone who really believes in it. Only in the constant process of being challenged can truth grow and remain healthy. "Both teachers and learners go to sleep at their posts, as soon as there is no enemy in the field."

The necessity of the fullest expression of opinion may be based on three grounds. First, the silenced opinion may be *wholly true,* in which case its suppression is wholly unjustified. Second, the silenced opinion may be *partly true and partly false,* as most opinions tend to be, in which case "it is only by the collision of adverse opinions that the remainder of the truth has any chance of being supplied." Third, even if the silenced opinion be *wholly erroneous,* it should not be suppressed, because its very challenge of truth prevents the latter from degenerating into dogma and prejudice.

The purpose of individual liberty is personal self-development. It is the privilege of every person to interpret experience in his own way, and his moral faculties can only be brought into play when he is obliged to choose between alternatives. A person who merely follows custom and tradition makes no choice, nor does he who lets others make his decisions for him. *Different persons should be permitted to lead different lives;* the principle of liberty thus inevitably implies that of variety and diversity.

It should be noted that the progress of industrial civilization does not make it easier for men and women to remain individual personalities, because increasingly "they now read the same things, listen to the same things, go to the same places, have their hopes and fears directed to the same objects, have the same rights and liberties, and the same means of asserting them." People who do the same things tend to think the same thoughts.

This standardization has progressed enormously in the last hundred years; the radio, television, and movie industries have added new dimensions of prefabricated opinion. The number of daily papers is steadily declining in Britain and the United States (there are hundreds of cities and towns with only one daily paper) and the number of newspaper readers is constantly increasing, so that more and more people are reading fewer and fewer papers. Moreover, standardization has now reached the point where not only is identical news coverage published in thousands of papers, but even editorials, purporting to present the viewpoint of the local paper's editor, are actually "canned," prepared in a New York or Washington agency and then "farmed out" all over the country.

Mill reminds those who are willing to repress individual liberty for the sake of a strong state that the worth of a state is no more than the worth of its individual citizens. When the state "dwarfs" its men, and reduces them to docile instruments, it will find that "with small men no great things can really be accomplished."

Mill is still the best guide to liberty based on reason. Yet *On Liberty* is a century old, and it cannot be expected to give clear-cut answers to the problems that baffle us today. In particular, Mill did not deal with two problems that did not exist in his day but are of paramount importance today.

First, Mill always assumed that in every debate both sides were after the truth and were honestly searching for it. Today we face a situation where totalitarian movements like fascism or communism disseminate statements which not only are false, but which the communist or fascist propagandists *know to be false*—for example, the communist stories of American germ warfare in Korea.

The second problem that did not exist in Mill's day and that has tremendous practical importance today is the phenomenon of a *revolutionary, subversive party directed from abroad*. In Mill's day, apart from a few mild anarchists or theoretical revolutionaries whom no one took seriously, there was no organized movement of a revolutionary, subversive nature. Today, revolutionary subversion is organized in powerful movements, movements that are particularly difficult to cope with because they are not homegrown but instruments of a foreign power, whose purposes alone they serve.

In the United States, the curbing of revolutionary movements by legal means is based on the Smith Act of 1940, Section 2 of which makes it unlawful for any person knowingly or willfully to "advocate, abet, advise, or teach the duty, necessity, desirability, or propriety of overthrowing or destroying any government in the United States by force or violence, or by the assassination of any officer of such government." In 1948, eleven top communist leaders were indicted for violation of the Smith Act. The trial, one of the most important political trials in American history, lasted over nine months and required almost 16,000 pages to record. Finally, the Supreme Court took up the case and decided against the communist leaders on June 4, 1951.

The main constitutional issue involved was *whether the Smith Act violated the First and Fifth Amendments.* The First Amendment provides that Congress shall make no law "abridging the freedom of speech, or of the press; or the right of the people peaceably to assemble, and to petition the government for a redress of grievances." Under the Fifth Amendment, no person "shall be deprived of life, liberty, or property, without due process of law." By a majority of six to two, the Supreme Court held the Smith Act constitutional.

A central concept in the conflicting opinions of the Court was the *clear and present danger* doctrine, as expressed by Mr. Justice Holmes in 1919: "The question in every case," Holmes wrote, "is whether the words used are used in such circumstances and are of such a nature as to create a clear and present danger that they will bring about the substantive evils that Congress has a right to prevent. It is a question of proximity and degree."

Writing for the majority in the case of the communists, Chief Justice Vinson declared that the communists *did* create a clear and present danger in recommending the overthrow of the government by force and violence. Chief Justice Vinson even went beyond the "clear and present danger" doctrine by accepting a narrower concept of *probable danger:* "In each case [courts] must ask whether the gravity of the 'evil,' discounted by its improbability, justifies such invasion of free speech as is necessary to avoid the danger." In a concurring opinion, Mr. Justice Jackson denied that the clear-and-present-danger doctrine could properly be applied to the case; otherwise communists plotting a revolutionary conspiracy would be protected during its period of incubation, and the Government could move "only after imminent action is manifest, when it would, of course, be too late."

In his dissenting opinion, Mr. Justice Black emphasized that the communist leaders were not charged with any nonverbal acts designed to overthrow the government, and that the outlawry of verbal expressions of revolution constitutes a drastic qualification or complete repudiation of the clear-and-present-danger doctrine. Mr. Justice Douglas, in his dissenting opinion, concedes that "the freedom to speak is not absolute," and accepts, in general, the Holmesian principle. However, whereas Holmes left the meaning of his principle rather vague, Douglas quotes approvingly Mr. Justice Brandeis in *Whitney v. California* (1927) that "no danger flowing from speech can be deemed clear and present, unless the incidence of the evil apprehended is so imminent that it may befall before there is opportunity for full discussion." Following Brandeis, Douglas argues that free speech *has* destroyed communism in the United States, and that it is "inconceivable" that advocates of communist revolution in the United States would have any success.

Under the Brandeis doctrine, it might be one thing to preach publicly against conscription when there is ample opportunity to rebut pacifism in public debate, and quite another thing to preach pacifist doctrine outside a draft board, when such opportunity to rebut does not exist. Similarly, a person may publicly attack income taxes as harmful to liberty and full personal development, but such propaganda would hardly be tolerable outside an office of the Bureau of Internal Revenue, because there would be no opportunity to debate the issue, and the harm of such antitax propaganda might be done before the other side of the debate could be presented.

The Brandeis doctrine was expressed much earlier by Thomas Jefferson, who was willing to "tolerate error so long as reason is left free to combat it." In his first inaugural address Jefferson said that "having banished from our land that religious intolerance under which mankind so long bled and suffered, we have yet gained little if we countenance a political intolerance as despotic, as wicked, and capable of as bitter and bloody persecutions." Going into the fundamental question of how to deal with those who advocate basic change, Jefferson had this to say: "If there be any among us who would wish to dissolve this Union or to change its republican form, let them stand undisturbed as monuments of the safety with which error of opinion may be tolerated where reason is left free to combat it."

Jefferson was willing to allow even antirepublican (or antidemocratic, as we would say today) doctrines, not only on the basis of rational argument, but also because he had tremendous faith in a free America, "the strongest government on earth." It is possible that our present wavering with regard to the Jeffersonian doctrine coincides with something deeper: a loss of self-confidence in the strength of liberty, and the growing fear that antidemocratic propaganda, if unchecked, might gain too many converts.

There are indications that a return to more traditional American concepts is under way. Virtually reversing its position of 1951, the Supreme Court ruled on June 17, 1957, in the case against fourteen West Coast communist leaders that a distinction must be made "between advocacy of forcible overthrow as an abstract doctrine and advocacy of action to that end," and that "mere membership or the holding of office in the Communist Party" did not constitute sufficient evidence of the intent to overthrow the government by force. While this decision did not explicitly invalidate the constitutionality of the Smith Act, it marked, at least, a return to the clear-and-present-danger doctrine that had been strongly modified, if not abandoned, in 1951. In any case, the 1957 decision of the Supreme Court re-established the traditional democratic (and American) concept under which all doctrines, including revolutionary ones, may be lawfully advocated and propagated. In other words, the validity of democracy is no longer a taboo issue that must not be challenged.

It is noteworthy that this new approach of the Supreme Court to the issue of individual political liberty and freedom of expression occurred four years after the end of the Korean war, nearly three years after the Senate's censure of the late Senator McCarthy, and a month after the latter's death. However, as tensions between the United States and the Soviet Union mounted, the Supreme Court moved again in the direction of putting national security above individual liberty. On June 5, 1961, the Supreme Court ruled, first, that the Communist party of the United States must register with the Department of Justice as an agent of a foreign power (the Soviet Union), as prescribed by the Internal Security Act of 1950. Second, the Supreme Court also ruled that a member of the Communist party incurs the penalties of the Smith Act, provided his membership is "active" rather than "passive" or "nominal," and provided the member has a "specific intent to bring about the violent overthrow" of the government. The Communist party of the United States is not a mass party with many nominal or passive members, but a small, tightly knit organization of a few thousand dedicated activists. Thus the government will not find it too difficult to prove in most cases the required "activism" and "intent" of Communist party members, as required by the Court's ruling of 1961, since few (if any) persons join the Communist party in order to spread abstract revolutionary doctrine. It seemed to many that the Supreme Court's interpretation of the Smith Act in 1961 was closer to the position the Court had taken in 1951 than in 1957. The hesitancy of the Court in abandoning, or at least substantially modifying, the relatively liberal position of 1957 for a more stringent interpretation in 1961 was expressed in the 5-4 division of the Court.

In the protection of traditional liberties, the judiciary has held up best in the contemporary crisis; and the executive branch also has at least made an honest effort to administer a complex program fairly and equitably.

Several judicial decisions deserve particular attention. On June 23, 1955, the United States Court of Appeals upheld the "natural right" of American citizens to travel abroad, thus denying the Department of State the authority to decide arbitrarily who may travel abroad. Since that decision, the government can deny the issuance of a passport only after due process of law, whereas until that time it could, and did, make such vital decisions on its own discretion.

An even more important decision was that of the Supreme Court on July 11, 1956, when it ruled that the security program for federal employees could be applied only to "sensitive" jobs, that is, jobs concerned with "the nation's safety" (such as in national defense, intelligence, secret scientific research, and similar activities). Since half the number of persons dismissed under the security program had held nonsensitive jobs, this decision of the Supreme Court had immediate practical results; more importantly from an over-all viewpoint, it helped to create a new, and more rational, climate of opinion in matters relating to loyalty and security in the government.

On June 17, 1957, a day on which it made history in several issues affecting individual liberty, the Supreme Court also dealt with the scope and authority of legislative investigatory committees. The first case was that of John Thomas Watkins, a labor organizer in the automobile industry. Watkins appeared before a subcommittee of the Committee on Un-American Activities of the House of Representatives in 1954, where he candidly told about his own past political activities, but refused to talk about persons who years ago may have been communists but were so no longer. As a result, he was fined and sentenced for contempt of Congress to one year in prison. The Supreme Court reversed the decision of the lower court, arguing that the purpose of a legislative inquiry must be explicitly stated and that the questions asked of witnesses must be pertinent to a legitimate legislative purpose. While conceding that Congress must have the authority to conduct investigations, and that such investigative powers are broad, the Supreme Court also emphasized that such powers are "not unlimited," that Congress is not a "law enforcement or trial agency," and that it has no power "to expose for the sake of exposure." Indirectly referring to the use by some legislators of investigative publicity as a principal means of political fame and advancement, the Supreme Court finally issued this weighty reminder: "Investigations conducted solely for the personal aggrandizement of the investigators or to 'punish' those investigated are indefensible." Although the Supreme Court later weakened its stand with respect to the authority of legislative investigatory committees (in the *Baren-*

blatt case in 1959 and in the *Wilkinson* case in 1961), the decision of the *Watkins* case has had its salutary effect on subsequent practices of Congressional and state investigatory bodies. In general, such bodies have shown a more sober and dignified attitude in their investigation than before 1957.

Another important case, also passed on by the Supreme Court on June 17, 1957, dealt with the issue of academic freedom. Professor Paul Sweezey, after lecturing at the University of New Hampshire on economics, was questioned by the state's attorney general about his political activities and beliefs. He denied the charge that he had ever been a member of the Communist party, but refused to give any information about his teaching or his political opinions and associations. As a result, he was held to be in contempt by the New Hamp-

TORCH OF LIBERTY

Herblock in the *Washington Post*

1949   1957

shire Supreme Court. The United States Supreme Court decided that Professor Sweezey's conviction was invalid, and added the warning that government should be "extremely reticent" to tread in the areas of academic freedom and political expression: "No one should underestimate the vital role in a democracy that is played by those who guide and train our youth. To impose any strait-jacket upon the intellectual leaders in our colleges and universities would imperil the future of our nation."

	Capitalism developed historically as
CLASSICAL	part of the great movement of *ration-*
CAPITALISM	*alist individualism.* In religion, that
	movement produced the Reformation;

in learning, the growth of the physical sciences; in human relations, the social sciences; in politics, democratic government; and in economics, the capitalist system. The concept of *capitalist civilization* is therefore a legitimate one; it suggests that capitalism is more than an economic system, that it reflects a way of life. It first developed in eighteenth-century Britain; later it was transplanted to northwestern Europe and North America. A few basic traits have characterized capitalism from the beginning.

In the capitalist system, *ownership of the means of production* (land, factories, machinery, natural resources) *is held by individuals, not by the state.* This does not exclude public ownership of natural monopolies or basic public services (post office, atomic arms), but such cases are considered the exception rather than the rule.

The bias of the capitalist civilization in favor of private ownership of the means of the production is based on two considerations. First, ownership of productive property means power over the lives of other people; it is preferable that such *power* be *diffused among many property owners* rather than held by one owner, the state. Moreover, the economic power of private property owners can be curbed by the popularly elected government; were the state to own all productive property, economic and political power would coincide, and the outlook for personal economic liberty would be dim. Second, the assumption of capitalist thinking is that *technological progress* is more easily attained when each person minds his own business, and has a personal incentive to do so.

The second principle of the capitalist system is that of the *market economy.* In the precapitalist era, the economy was generally local and self-sufficient; each family produced just about what it needed, supplementing its simple needs with some barter or exchange operations in a primitive local market. *Division of labor* was barely known, and each family had to do many jobs that nowadays are spread among hundreds of various crafts and specialties. Also, the type of occupation a person was in and the price he could charge for his goods and services were largely predetermined for him by custom and usage. In contrast, the market economy of the capitalist system is based on specialization of labor. Each person supplies only a very small part of his needs through his own skills and labors. The products or services are designed not for the producer's own household, but for the market.

Neither custom and usage nor the commands of a political authority determine the price in the market; this function is fulfilled by supply and demand. If prices are high, the market provides a signal that the supply of certain goods or services would be profitable; if prices are low, the market seems to say, "Try your luck in something else."

In the totalitarian economy (fascist or communist) the state, in trying to plan the whole economy, runs up against the difficulty of the limitations of the span of control. No human being can anticipate all the possible developments in an intricate economic system, encompassing many millions of persons and operated by economic decisions running daily into tens of millions.

In the capitalist market economy, each decision-maker has to watch over a much smaller area, and his span of attention and control is more limited and manageable.

The market economy is the touchstone of all economic systems. Neither communism nor fascism believes in it; in fascism, ownership of the means of production is formally still in the hands of private individuals, but this is not too important, because fascism does away with the market economy, and substitutes for it the *command economy*. The state tells the individuals where to work, what jobs to choose, what to eat, what to produce, what prices to charge, and how to invest savings and profits. Communism abolishes private ownership of the means of production and the market economy. The communist economy, too, is a totalitarian command economy, in which economic decisions are made by a totalitarian state. In contrast, the market economy is an economy in which free individuals make their own economic decisions in the light of their interest, experience, and intelligence.

The tremendous political implications of the market economy have finally been recognized by socialist economists. W. Arthur Lewis, a British economist, examines this question in a book written for the Fabian Society, *The Principles of Economic Planning* (1949). As a socialist, Lewis is opposed to the orthodox concepts of laissez faire (as are most nonsocialist economists today).

The real issue, Lewis argues, is not between planning and no planning, but between *planning by direction* and *planning by inducement*. In the former, the government (as under fascism or communism) tries to get the right things done by direct control and regulation of output, prices, and wages. A government agent watches every step in the plan, and those workers or managers who fail to fulfill their quota are punished as traitors and saboteurs, although neglect or incapacity rather than willful disregard may have been the cause of their failure. The key mechanism in such a command economy is terror, specifically the fear of the prison or the slave labor camp.

In a democratic state, the government indirectly stimulates certain economic activities through the budget, taxation, interest rates, and other policies of planning by inducement, thus avoiding the two main defects of planning by direction: bureaucratic centralization and economic inefficiency. Far from rejecting the free market as the normal mechanism of economic adjustment, Lewis holds that "our aim should be to preserve free markets wherever possible." It is also of no little interest that Lewis, in accepting the principle of the market economy, is driven to the conclusion that the nationalization of all industry is undesirable because of the usual reasons against monopoly: inefficiency, lack of initiative, and concentration of power.

Thus, the *function of the free market as a mechanism of political liberty* is now increasingly being recognized by socialists, and it gradually dawns on them that the question of ownership is less important than the question of whether economic decisions are made by free, independent individuals or corporations on the one hand, or by the state on the other.

The distinction between the command economy and the market economy thus reflects in the economic field the more basic political distinction between totalitarianism (fascism and communism) and liberalism (socialism and capitalism).

The most important specific liberties of the free market economy are the following: for the *worker,* to choose his line of work and his particular job; for the *businessman,* to choose his type of business, and set it up at the place of his choice; for the investor, to invest his capital in whatever enterprise he chooses; finally, for the *consumer,* to buy the product he prefers.

This last freedom ("consumer sovereignty") is, in many respects, the most important of all, because it is the preference of the consumer that ultimately decides in a free market what is to be produced, at what quality, and in what quantities. In totalitarian economies, fascist or communist, consumer sovereignty is seriously curtailed. In the totalitarian economy, the state decides what is to be produced for consumption purposes, and how it is to be distributed.

Thus, a person with a high income in Russia may be unable to buy an automobile, because the government has decided that only a small number shall be produced, and that that small number shall be rationed among a small group of meritorious persons—who also, generally, happen to be high government officials. Consumer sovereignty is thus replaced by that of the commissar.

Another essential characteristic of the capitalist economy is *competition*. In the precapitalist economy, custom and usage dictated what goods and services were worth, and there were many persons who could not compete at all because they were excluded from certain occupations. In the capitalist economy, everybody is free to choose whatever line of work he prefers ("freedom of occupation"), and there is to be no artificial restriction or exclusion (such as on the basis of racial or religious prejudice) from any occupation or profession. Similarly, the capitalist market provides the place where goods and services are offered for sale, the quantity and quality of which are regulated by free competition. The basic assumption of the classical capitalist economy is that there is relative equality of bargaining power within, and between, buyers and sellers.

The freedom to compete in the market results from four basic capitalist freedoms: freedom of trade and occupation, freedom of contract, freedom of property, and freedom of profit-making. To the extent that any of these four freedoms is curbed, free competition is reduced.

The alternative to competition is either private monopoly or the omnipotent state. In both cases, the arbitrary determination of the prices of goods and services by a *de facto* authority (as in the case of private monopoly) or a legal authority (as in that of the state) takes the place of the free interplay of buyers and sellers, following their own choice.

The economic justification of competition is that it keeps everybody—worker, businessman, investor—on his toes, constantly alert to changes in the market, and constantly on the lookout for ways to increase his efficiency and thereby improve his chances in the market. By increasing his own efficiency, the individual worker or entrepreneur proportionately increases the efficiency and productivity of the whole market. Better products, lower prices, better services, and ultimately higher living standards for all result from the constant incentive to keep up with, and if possible to outdo, one's competitors.

In industry, *research* has become one of the keenest areas of competition. Research today means cheaper and better products tomorrow, and the vitality of competition is seen in the fact that companies are spending an increasingly larger share of their budget on research. In 1930, research expenditures in the United States amounted to 160 million dollars; in 1963, they exceeded 15 billion dollars. About two-thirds of this outlay is financed by the federal government, most of the rest by private industry. Research, by accelerating the rate of change in the economy, promotes competition at an early stage, long before the product of service reaches the market.

The *profit* principle is another basic principle that characterizes the capitalist system. So far, no historian has been able to show that before capitalism the profit principle was absent—the merchant in ancient Greece, for example, did not stay in business for his health.

Yet there is one tremendous difference between capitalism and pre-capitalist systems: the capitalist economy provides more opportunity for profit than any previous economy because it guarantees three freedoms that were not commonly found in precapitalist systems: freedom of trade and occupation, freedom of property, and freedom of contract. Obviously, where the institution of slavery exists, the slaves cannot enter the profit system. Their economic fate is determined by their social position; not possessing any of the other three basic economic freedoms, they have no access to the profit system.

In the Middle Ages, products were made by guilds and sold at prescribed prices. The profit system was thus doubly limited. Only a member of the guild could enter the process of production; furthermore, prices were defined not by freedom of contract between buyer and seller, but by the authority of custom, the church, or the state.

Even in modern states like Germany and Japan, the American occupation authorities after World War II were amazed to find how many professions and trades were virtually closed to outsiders, and they found it no easy task to induce the German and Japanese lawmakers to allow more freedom of trade and occupation.

The expansion of the profit system under capitalism thus does not necessarily show that the greater chance of profit makes capitalism more unethical; rather, it shows that capitalism is more democratic in opening profit opportunities for persons and classes which traditionally have been excluded from them. The profit concept goes beyond the entrepreneur, of course; the worker who takes a job at the place of his choice, for example, has an access to profit that he would not have had in a precapitalist society.

Moreover, whenever the capitalist system is described as a profit system, it is frequently forgotten that the other side of the medal is equally important—capitalism is also a *loss* system. Although it is true to say that never have so many made so much profit as under capitalism, it is equally true that in no other system have so many lost so much as under capitalism. In American economic development, losses, bankruptcies, and failures were very heavy in the early mining, railroading, and automotive industries. In the more recent field of television, a pioneering company like the Radio Corporation of America lost many millions of dollars when it first introduced color television; the initial stages of black and white television were also loss operations.

These are not isolated instances. In 1960, a typical business year, about four out of ten corporations reported net losses. Out of 1,140,000 corporations, 670,000 showed net profits amounting to 50 billion dollars; the other 470,000 corporations reported losses amounting to nearly 7 billion dollars.

The unparalleled opportunities of profit and loss in capitalism have one thing in common: *personal risk-taking*. Capitalism does not order anybody to take risks; it merely holds out the promise of profit to the person who is willing to take risks. Where the spirit of risk-taking is weak, investors prefer secure investments in bonds, which offer a guaranteed (and lower) return. Where the spirit of risk-taking is strong, investors prefer the common stock of corporations, which in the long run usually yield higher returns than bonds.

However, if the quest for security is so strong that many investors shy away from risk investments, as so often happens in underdeveloped countries, economic stagnation is inevitable. The sudden and phenomenal growth of the air-conditioning industry in the United States is due to the fact that enough investors were willing to take a chance on an unknown industry rather than invest their capital in a sure thing.

**STRESSES AND
STRAINS IN
MODERN CAPITALISM**

The theory of capitalism approximated reality most closely in its classical period, roughly from the middle of the eighteenth to the end of the nineteenth century. In the twentieth century, capitalism has had to face stresses and strains, some internal, such as technological developments of industry itself, others external, such as wars.

The separation of ownership from management and financial control was made legally possible by the invention of the *corporate form of business:* each shareholder in a corporation is liable only to the extent of the shares he owns, no more and no less. In the precapitalist economy, a partnership involved full personal responsibility of each partner for the operations of the business. Partnerships tended to be relatively small, and each partner had a sense of personal involvement, financial and moral, in the business. In a big modern corporation, where fifty million or one hundred million shares are owned by more than half a million shareholders, the link between the individual shareholder and the corporation, of which he is part owner, is very tenuous. The corporation may be located thousands of miles away from most of the shareholders, and in most corporations only a small fraction of shareholders, generally less than one per cent, attend the annual meetings in which officers are elected and other important business is transacted.

Management draws up the list of officers to be elected, management presides over the elections, management explains why its proposed policy decisions should be adopted, management decides the salaries of management, management finally submits all its proposals to a vote: the vote is normally between 95 and 99 per cent in favor of management. This is a comfortable majority, as compared with average majorities of 52 to 55 per cent in political elections. "Like a stockholders' meeting" is a common phrase used to describe any perfunctorily run meeting.

In fact, whenever there is a real fight between management and a strong opposition, as there was over the New York Central Railroad in 1954, the controversy makes the front page. Of course, when the unusual happens and the opposition manages to acquire control, a new cycle of one-party rule starts again, until after several more decades there is some new revolt.

The essence of the problem is simple. In government, democracy has established the principle that *those who wield power must be accountable to the public.* The people are the boss, the government their agent. Political power in a democracy must not be held for the benefit of the rulers; it is a trust, the purpose of which is to protect the interests of the people.

In the economic realm, on the other hand, a constitutional situation prevails that runs counter to the basic concept of democracy: corporation managers wield far-reaching power over stockholders and employees, and they constantly make decisions affecting the public interest, without any clearly defined responsibility to the public. Whereas in a capitalist democracy political policies are arrived at through processes of consent that begin at the bottom and end at the

"The motion has been made and seconded that we give ourselves a raise in salary. All those in favor say 'Aye.'"

top, in corporate business economic policies are made from the top and passed on to the bottom. The character of modern industrial organization is hierarchical, founded on discipline and obedience.

More recently, however, the traditional pattern in industry has been considerably modified and made more democratic, mainly by organized labor, legislation, public opinion, and the growth in the business class of a sense of responsibility toward the community.

The more capitalism succeeds, the more it destroys—paradoxically enough—its original institutional and ideological character by collectivizing and socializing the framework of business. The first collectivists in the capitalistic era were not its critics, but the most successful capitalistic entrepreneurs, men like Andrew Carnegie, John D. Rockefeller, and Henry Ford who created vast industrial empires.

Like other empires, industrial empires tend to become bureaucratic and conformity-minded, to follow routine and precedent, and, above all, to transform personal initiative and enterprise into impersonal rules of administrative routine. Whereas the original individual capitalists were men of bold, daring adventurousness, the bureaucratic administrators of the new, vast industrial empires tend to put security above everything else. If risk-taking was one of the most characteristic traits of original capitalists, large corporate business has tended to shy away from risk-taking investments, and stick to "safe bets."

The danger is that, as business becomes bigger, the free-enterprise system may gradually become a "safe-enterprise" system.

Psychologically, there is *less difference between large-scale capitalist enterprise and large-scale socialized enterprise on the one hand than between small-scale capitalist enterprise and large-scale capitalist enterprise on the other.* It is for this reason that such defenders of capitalism as Justice Brandeis and President Wilson were afraid that the "curse of bigness" might eventually destroy not only big private enterprise, but private enterprise itself. Again, this problem of bigness is not peculiar to the economic institutions of liberal capitalism; in politics, too, there is the threat of "big government" destroying the very elements that give life and color to democracy.

Who owns American business? Until recently, there were only guesses on this question, but now the facts begin to come to light. About 60 per cent of all corporate stock is owned by individuals, the rest by investment companies, insurance companies, foundations, and institutions. On the positive side, there has been a substantial growth of the number of families owning stock: 8 per cent in 1952, 10 per cent in 1955, and 14 per cent in 1960. On the negative side, there is the fact that in 1963 fewer than 0.1 per cent of the taxpayers owned 19.5 per cent of all individually held stock, and those with incomes over $25,000 (about 1 per cent of all taxpayers) owned 48 per cent of all individually held stock. While concentration of stock ownership has been slightly declining in recent years, the present degree of concentration is high enough to suggest that the American economic system still has a long way to go before it can rightfully be called "people's capitalism."

To get some idea of the role of big business in the American economy: the 200 largest nonfinancial corporations hold 40 per cent of all corporate wealth, and employ about one-fifth of the nonagricultural private labor force. In manufacturing, with a total labor force of 17 million, 40 per cent of the employees are employed by 360 corporations, and 15 per cent are employed by the 23 giant corporations with 50,000 or more employees. Analyzing the broader category of manufacturing, mining, retail and wholesale trade, and certain service industries, we find that out of a total labor force of about 30 million persons, one-tenth (about 3 million) are employed by the top 28 giant corporations, and that 28 per cent (nearly 8.5 million) are employed by the top 438 companies.

Examining research and development as the key to industrial progress and competition, we find that concentration is even heavier. The 7 largest corporations engaged in research and development employ 20 per cent of the total research and technical personnel; the largest 44 companies alone employ 45 per cent of the total technical and scientific personnel, and account for over half of the total expenditure on research and development.

The phenomenon of concentration can best be illustrated by a giant corporation like General Motors. In 1962, its assets in the United States were over $9 billion, or about 1 per cent of all corporate assets. It employed in the United States alone 464,000 persons (or 1 per cent of all employees in private, nonagricultural establishments, or nearly 3 per cent of all employees in manufacturing); its payroll of over $3 billion was about 1.5 per cent of all wages and salaries paid in private business. Its tax bill (federal, state, local, sales, and excise taxes) was nearly $3 billion, equal to 2.5 per cent of all receipts of the United States government, or to 7 per cent of all corporate income and excise taxes combined. Its federal income tax alone was nearly $1.4 billion, equal to the income taxes paid by 85 per cent of all corporations. Its net profit after taxes was about $1.4 billion, or over 5 per cent of all corporate profits. In its own industry, General Motors produces around one-half of all cars; the Big Three—General Motors, Ford, and Chrysler—account for over 90 per cent of all passenger cars. In 1921, there were 87 manufacturers of cars; in 1964, only 4.

Yet there is another side to the picture. In the first place, it is not known whether concentration is increasing, decreasing, or standing still. In "The Measurement of Industrial Concentration" (in *The Review of Economics and Statistics,* November 1951), M. A. Adelman argues that in 1901 nearly one-third of manufacturing was produced in industries of high concentration, whereas by 1947 only about one-fourth of value added by manufacturing was produced in highly con-centrated industry. Adelman realizes the difficulty of considering such figures as final, but he concludes as follows: "The odds are better than even that there has actually been *some* decline in concentration. It is a good bet that there has at least been no actual increase; and the odds do seem high against any substantial increase."

Moreover, it is argued, though a high proportion of American industry is dominated by big business, its composition constantly changes. There is *no hereditary aristocracy in big business*. Taking the 100 largest corporations of 1909 as a starting point, we find that 64 had lost their top ranking by 1948, giving place to newcomers. The competition is not only between individual firms in this top group; changing conditions of the economy entail keen *competition between whole industry groups*. Thus, steel, coal mining, and textiles were relatively much more important in 1909 than in 1948, whereas the petroleum, chemical, and electrical equipment industries rose sharply in their relative importance in the top 100 corporations. This rapid change in the composition of the top group during four decades further illustrates the point that bigness is not to be identified with monopoly.

Defenders of big business maintain that a big country and a big market need big business. The very survival of the United States may depend on the productivity of big business, not only in turning out the necessary armaments and civilian goods and services, but also in giving economic and military assistance to the free nations whose freedom and security are linked with those of the United States.

Individual security, too, has a better chance in big business than in small enterprises, because the former can do a better job in long-term planning of production, stability of employment, and the provi-sion of services like pension and sickness benefits. In the field of labor-management relations, the greatest progress has been made in the mass production industries, like steel and automobiles, in which big business predominates; by contrast, labor unions have made little progress in agriculture and retailing, where the small unit prevails.

In research, too, as has been pointed out above, big business carries most of the work and responsibility. Occasionally, important inven-tions are still made in small laboratories; then it takes the resources and organization of larger corporations to translate the inventions into economic realities. More and more, however, industrial research is carried out by big corporations because it requires large financial resources and many years of waiting. Thus, du Pont spent $27 million and thirteen years of research before nylon could be marketed com-

mercially. In large companies, this situation is routine, not exceptional.
In 1959, du Pont started production of a new plastic, *Delrin,* on which
it had spent $42 million and eleven years of research.

Concerning the impact of big business on competition, it is argued
that the two are not incompatible. Big business produces a new kind
of competition—internal competition. Thus, not only is there competition between General Motors and Ford, but within General Motors
itself the Chevrolet competes with the Pontiac, the Oldsmobile with
the Buick. Moreover, there is competition in passenger transportation
between the automobile and the railroad.

The problem of competition in the changing American economy
is the key issue in *American Capitalism: The Concept of Countervailing Power* (1952), by John Kenneth Galbraith. In classical economics, competition was conceived in terms of many sellers, each with
a small share of the market, and restraint of excessive private economic power was provided by competing firms on the same side of
the market. Galbraith concedes that this classical model of competition has largely disappeared, since many markets have become dominated by a few firms, and since there is frequently tacit collusion
among these firms on major policy decisions. The most famous recent
case of such collusion was revealed in 1961 in the successful prosecu-
tion for price-fixing of the major companies in the electrical industry.

Yet Galbraith does not conclude from the widespread disappearance
of traditional competition that there is no longer any restraint of
private economic power left. In fact, new restraints have taken the
place of the old competitive mechanism, and these restraints—termed
by Galbraith "countervailing power"—are the very product of concentration and bigness.

These new factors of restraint appear not on the same side of the
market but on the opposite side, not with competitors but with customers and suppliers. The concentration of industrial enterprises not
only has led to a relatively small number of sellers, but also has
brought about the predominant position of a few buyers. Galbraith
explains the growth and expansion of retailers like Sears, Roebuck or
the A&P in terms of countervailing power; by contrast, the absence
of a few large firms in the housing industry has meant more traditional
competition and less efficiency, since the many small enterprises in
the housing industry are unable to use countervailing pressure against
labor unions and suppliers of materials.

In the field of labor, too, Galbraith is impressed by the fact that
strong unions have developed mainly when faced by strong corporations, as in the steel, automobile, and electrical industries. In contrast,

there is no major union of any consequence in the retail business or in agriculture, the closest approaches in the United States to pure competition. Galbraith concedes that countervailing power is not universally effective as a restraint on private economic power, and that it fails to operate in inflation when relative scarcity of demand disappears and too many buyers compete for available goods and services. If supply is small in relation to demand, the seller need not surrender to the bargaining power of the buyer, who thus loses his capacity to function as a countervailing power.

The weakness of the concept of countervailing power lies in the fact that, though the power of the large seller may be checked by that of the large buyer, the resulting benefit need not be passed on to the consumer. Monopoly benefits may be amicably split between the large buyer and the large seller at the expense of the consumer.

In substituting the few giant competitive units of the twentieth century for the many small ones of the eighteenth, the theory of countervailing power still assumes that a socially fair market equilibrium may be obtained without the intervention of the community in defense of the public interest. In a sense, therefore, the concept of countervailing power, illuminating and provocative as it is, is essentially a sophisticated restatement of the doctrine of the self-regulating market of classical economics, imaginatively adapted to the economic facts of today.

This reasoning was adopted by the Supreme Court in the du Pont case (June 3, 1957), the most important antitrust decision in over forty years. In 1917, du Pont acquired 23 per cent of the stock of General Motors and consistently supplied the bulk of that company's needs in automotive fabrics and paints. Since General Motors produces about one-half of all automobiles, the question arose whether du Pont's part ownership of General Motors was a violation of the Clayton (antitrust) Act.

Until 1957, the courts took the view that only "horizontal" acquisitions (that is, acquisitions of corporations in the same industry) constituted a possible violation of competition; since du Pont and General Motors are in different industries, the large share of General Motors owned by du Pont was not considered a violation of the Clayton Act. But in the du Pont case of June 3, 1957, the Supreme Court abandoned the theory of countervailing power between buyer and seller, and ruled that acquisition of the stock of a customer corporation, or "vertical" acquisition, also constituted a violation of the antitrust laws if competition was thereby likely to be diminished. In the specific instance of du Pont's owning 23 per cent of General Motors and supplying it with the bulk of its paints and fabrics, the Supreme Court found that "the inference is overwhelming that du Pont's commanding position was promoted by its stock interest and was not gained solely on competitive merit."

SOURCES OF STRENGTH OF CAPITALIST DEMOCRACY

Capitalism, it has been said by a close student of the subject,

. . . during its rule of scarce one hundred years, has created more massive and more colossal productive forces than have all preceding generations together. Subjection of nature's forces to man, machinery, application of chemistry to industry and agriculture, steam-navigation, railways, electric telegraphs, clearing of whole continents for cultivation, canalization of rivers, whole populations conjured out of the ground—what earlier century had even a presentiment that such productive forces slumbered in the lap of social labor?

The author goes on to say that capitalism "has accomplished wonders far surpassing Egyptian pyramids, Roman aqueducts, and Gothic cathedrals; it has conducted expeditions that put in the shade all former migrations of nations and crusades." This eulogy of capitalism was written, not by the research director of the National Association of Manufacturers or of the United States Chamber of Commerce, but by Karl Marx, in the *Communist Manifesto.* Few students of capitalism have been as aware as Marx of the fact that capitalism is a *revolutionary way of life,* creating a new material world as well as new intellectual and ethical values. To put the strength of capitalist democracy in one brief sentence: never before have so many had it so good. The population of the United States increased eight times between 1850 and 1960, yet its national income increased forty times (in constant dollars, to allow for changes in purchasing power). At the same time, the suffrage has been steadily broadened; education has been made available to more persons than ever before, work hours are shorter than ever before, and there is more leisure than man has known hitherto. Above all, *never before has there been so much concern with the welfare of the underprivileged classes in society.*

The abolition of slavery, education for all, health facilities on an unprecedented level, social security for everybody, the doubling of longevity within a century, the highest increase of population on record—all coincide with the development of capitalism. None of these could have been accomplished in a civilization motivated primarily by greed. Looking at precapitalist civilizations today, one is impressed by the survival of social inequalities (the caste system in India, the peon class in Latin America) that reflect a profound disregard of human dignity, an attitude that is no longer feasible in most capitalist societies.

In the fields of education, health, and welfare, more has been accomplished in capitalist societies in a spirit of service and disinterestedness than ever before in history. In the world today, the great charitable foundations are to be found primarily in the capitalist nations, particularly in the English-speaking world, not because there are no wealthy people in Asia or Latin America, but because wealthy persons in precapitalist societies rarely believe in the capitalist concept that *wealth can ultimately be justified only through service to the community.*

In the United States, there are over 7,000 private charitable foundations, with total assets of over $12 billion. The Ford Foundation alone, the largest of them all, has assets in excess of $3 billion. In 1956, it spent, in the United States and abroad, over $600 million on education, human welfare, and international aid. Yet philanthropy in the United States is not predominantly based on a few wealthy individuals or foundations. In 1963, Americans spent about $10 billion on philanthropic purposes; the bulk of this sum, about $8 billion, was contributed by individuals, the rest by philanthropic foundations and business corporations.

While some Indian statesmen, for example, lecture the United States on capitalist greed and imperialism, as contrasted with Indian spirituality and love of mankind, the United States Government and private American foundations gave India, in the years 1952-1963, 5 billion dollars. About one-third of this sum was donated as an outright gift, and the other two-thirds loaned. This program substantially aided India in such major areas as farming, industry, community development, education, and health. The progress in health, largely due to American assistance, has perhaps been the most dramatic. In 1953, for example, India had 75 million malaria cases, of which 1 million died. In 1962, fewer than 2,000 malaria cases were reported.

Yet this attitude is not new and is not a product of the cold war; it was practiced on a large scale long before communism existed, and long before it became a world menace. The Rockefeller Foundation, set up in 1913, spent over $500 million in the first forty years of its existence; most of this money was spent on education, much of it abroad. The Carnegie group (Carnegie Corporation, Carnegie Endowment, and Carnegie Foundation) has been active in the field of educa-

"Sure, Russia is always right there with military commissions, technical advisers, and all that, but Uncle Sam gets up the moola."

tion and international cooperation. None of these major charitable foundations confines its benefits to American institutions or individuals; they all had their own "foreign aid" programs long before the government stepped into the picture after World War II.

Moreover, *never before has a ruling class been willing, as under capitalism, to finance the very people who seek to change the existing social system.* Reform economics need not hide, in the United States, in secret, illegal sheets, but may be taught at private and public colleges and universities endowed by large capitalist fortunes or maintained by state legislatures.

Conservatives' suspicion of social science is well founded; their frequent confusion of social science with socialism is not quite as obtuse as it may appear to the reformer, since social science, by digging up the facts, may well lead to the very social changes the conservatives fear most.

The political implications of capitalism can now be clearly seen: first, *individual risk-taking,* the desire and capacity to make decisions, to assume responsibility, to determine one's own life. Without this kind of motivation, there can be no democracy, and historically there has been no democracy without it.

Logically, it is conceivable that democracy may develop in the future without this economic background, but so far it has not happened that way. Capitalist economy developed before democratic government, but the one was bound to lead to the other. Persons who constantly faced danger, risk, and responsibility in their economic affairs were ultimately unwilling to accept authoritarian government from kings and aristocracies, and when the capitalist middle classes could not obtain their objectives peacefully, they resorted to revolution: the English civil war in the seventeenth century, and the American and French revolutions in the eighteenth century.

In fighting for itself, the capitalist middle class appealed to the principles of universal human liberty, the rights of man, and natural law. It is for this reason that democracy became an intrinsic part of capitalist civilization, and for this reason also that the greatest advances in democratic government and human liberty have so far been made in capitalist societies.

The second principle of capitalism that directly affects government is the *diffusion of decision and power.* Instead of one central authority's laying down the law of the market, thousands of little decisions hold each other in balance. Many of these decisions are based on erroneous facts and bad judgment, but such defects are preferable to the big errors made by a central authority, particularly if the central authority is subject to no political checks. Every type of democracy seeks to diffuse power by various devices in order to avoid the abuse and corruption that follow the concentration of power. By strengthening the diffusion of power in the economic area, capitalism thus supports one of the key principles of democracy.

Taking a larger, world-wide view, it should be remembered that capitalist civilization, as represented primarily by Britain in the nineteenth and the United States in the twentieth century, revolutionized the underdeveloped continents. The masses of Asia, Africa, and Latin America learned from their contact with capitalism the appreciation of more and better material things. What is less often understood is that the West also taught the underdeveloped continents the principles of the dignity of man, the right of national self-determination, and the evil of racial superiority. Gandhi, Nehru, and the other leaders of the Indian independence movement were educated in England, and it was the ideas of John Locke that taught them individual and national liberty.

Asian communism, distorted and perverted as it may appear in the light of Western democracy, owes its existence partly to Western ideas and promises that Western capitalism made but failed to carry out. Marx gathered his ideas, not in the steppes of Central Asia or Siberia, but from German philosophy, English political economy, and French revolutionary politics. The communist promise of a happier, better life for all people regardless of class or race is the original promise of capitalism; to the extent that capitalism lives up to it, communism loses its appeal. If offered a fair choice, mankind will prefer economic welfare and political freedom to economic warfare and political slavery.

WHY SOCIALISM HAS NOT SPREAD IN THE UNITED STATES

The question is often asked why socialism has never been able to gain a strong foothold in the United States. According to socialist writers, the United States as the leading capitalist country in the world was bound to develop the "inner contradictions" out of which socialist mass movements would develop. Yet nothing of the sort has happened. Is it because socialism is European? There are strong socialist parties in Canada, Australia, New Zealand, Chile, Brazil, Japan, and other countries outside of Europe. Why the failure in the United States?

The basic reason probably lies in the fact that American capitalism —more than any other economic system in the world—has given to the people *now* much of what socialism promises them for the future. Specifically, socialism bases its appeal on two basic promises: (1) *social equality* and (2) the *abolition of poverty*. Although no one will argue that American capitalism has lived up 100 per cent to these two principles, it must have done so to a very large extent, since socialist propaganda so far has had little effect.

As to the principle of equality, the Constitution of the United States and the reality of economic life keep opportunity open to anyone who looks for it. Since in public opinion polls over 80 per cent of the American people describe themselves as "middle class," it is clear that psychologically, at least, there is little class-consciousness in the United States. Social mobility is very great, mainly because higher education is available to more persons than anywhere else in

Automation has helped to increase purchasing power of consumers.

Number of weeks average wage earner had to work to buy an auto:

1947 — 31.2

1962 — 24.5

Number of hours average wage-earner had to work to buy a refrigerator:

1947 — 180

1962 — 83

Number of hours average wage-earner had to work to buy a vacuum cleaner:

1947 — 39

1962 — 20

Number of hours average wage-earner had to work to buy a washing machine:

1947 — 95

1962 — 86

the world (there are, for example, about three times more college teachers in the United States than college students in Britain, although the American population is only about three and a half times the British).

As to the second basic promise of socialism, the abolition of poverty, American capitalism has had its serious flaws, crises, and depressions. Yet when all is said and done, and although things could be better still, living standards in the United States are by far the highest in the world, and they are constantly rising. Vast resources, a single national market, and huge government spending have all contributed to the success of the American economy, quite apart from its spirit of dynamic enterprise and technological progressiveness. In contrast, where capitalism has shown itself restrictionist, timid, inefficient, and tied to a rigid class system, as in many other countries, socialism has grown up in the shadow of capitalist inefficiency and inequality.

Intelligent foreign socialists are beginning to realize that the socialist-capitalist controversy does not make much sense in the United States. Thus a leading British socialist economist, C. A. R. Crosland, writes in *The Future of Socialism* (1957), the most searching analysis of socialism in the last twenty years, that in Britain a Leftist would be a socialist, whereas in the United States he would be much less concerned "to promote social equality or material welfare, of which plenty exists already, than with reforms lying outside the field of socialist-capitalist controversy" (p. 521), such as civil liberties, racial equality, juvenile delinquency, and foreign policy. With respect to inequality of wealth—a key theme in traditional socialist argumentation—Crosland points out that "in the United States, property is more equally distributed than in Britain" (*The Conservative Enemy,* 1962, p. 39). In Britain in 1953, the top 3 per cent owned 49 per cent of all wealth, and the top 10 per cent owned 76 per cent; in the United States, the top 3 per cent owned 33 per cent of all wealth, and the top 10 per cent owned 56 per cent. In both top groups of wealth-holders, the figures are considerably lower in the United States than in Britain. (Robert J. Lampman, *The Share of Top Wealth-Holders in National Wealth, 1922-1956,* 1962, p. 215.)

Hugh Gaitskell, the late Leader of the British Labor Party who died in 1963, was very close to Crosland's viewpoint. In analyzing the causes of Labor's defeat in the general elections of 1955, Gaitskell argued that improved living conditions had changed many people's ideas: "Call it if you like a growing Americanization of outlook." (*Socialist Commentary,* July 1955, p. 205.)

For generations, European socialists assumed that the absence of a strong socialist movement in the United States proved its reactionary, or at least conservative, political orientation. Now, there is a growing realization in Europe that the two primary problems that socialism seeks to solve—material welfare and social equality—have been largely solved in the United States by the capitalist system, and that therefore the major issues of American public life—such as civil liberties, racial equality, or foreign policy—have no relation whatsoever to the issue of socialism versus capitalism. That issue may, in fact, die out in European and other nations, too, once they manage to abolish poverty and social inequality.

THE WELFARE STATE

The main principles of the welfare state are relatively simple: first, the recognition that every member of the community is entitled, solely because he is a human being, to a *minimum standard of living;* second, the welfare state is committed to putting *full employment* at the top of social goals to be supported by public policy.

The Great Depression of 1929-1939 showed not only the economic ravages of unemployment, but also the human degradation imposed upon those who are able and anxious to work but cannot find a job for reasons over which they have no control.

Particularly in the United States, the adherents of the welfare state believe that free enterprise can be preserved and strengthened by full employment measures without having recourse to nationalization. Taxation properly adjusted to periods of prosperity and depression, interest rates determined by governmental decision according to economic needs, fiscal policies designed to redistribute purchasing power in harmony with the best interests of the nation, investment incentives in times of contracting business, public works for direct unemployment relief, government credits to builders or buyers of homes—these are but a few of the measures the government can adopt in stabilizing the economy without changing its foundations.

Social security, protection against the worst dangers of want, sickness, and old age, not only indicates humanitarian considerations, but also has important economic effects, since such measures of social security provide people with a minimum purchasing power indispensable to the functioning of industry in prosperity and depression.

Collective bargaining between labor and capital is another basic contribution toward a more stable and prosperous economy because higher wages—if based on higher productivity—create a bigger market for the products of industry and agriculture. Similarly, an active support program for agriculture, guaranteeing the farmer a minimum price level for his products, is of benefit not only to the farmer but also to the worker and the industrialist, since a prosperous industry depends upon a prosperous agriculture.

In the United States, the Great Depression undermined faith in the orthodox philosophy of laissez faire, according to which the disequilibrium of the market would eventually be restored to a new equilibrium without any interference from the outside. When the

American economy reached the stage in which one out of every four employable persons found himself out of work, in which the farmer could not sell his products at reasonable prices, in which more and more business enterprises went bankrupt or were unable to pay wages to their employees or earn profits for their shareholders, something had to be done. The New Deal, starting with the first term of President Franklin D. Roosevelt in 1933, was not so much a set of premeditated philosophical principles to be superimposed upon the American people as a series of emergency measures in response to urgent practical problems.

The Agricultural Adjustment Act (May 12, 1933) attempted to help the farmer by raising farm prices to a level that would enable farmers to buy industrial products as they had been able to do in the years 1909-1914. In order to make such "parity" possible, farmers were to reduce production, in return for which they would receive higher prices (as a result of decreased supply) from the consumer and subsidies from the government. The Act was declared unconstitutional by the Supreme Court in 1936, but Congress enacted subsequently the Soil Conservation Act, the Domestic Allotment Act, and, in 1938, a new Agricultural Adjustment Act. Traditionally opposed, in theory at least, to government interference, the farmers have been very content with that part of the welfare state which directly protects their interests.

Whereas in most countries relief to the unemployed was paid out in cash as a "dole," the American method of relief showed more understanding of the human problems involved. The federal government set up the Works Progress Administration in 1935 (renamed the Works Projects Administration in 1939) in order to provide work relief rather than cash doles. Though some of the projects were properly criticized for being excursions into boondoggling, the total impact of the program was highly beneficial, not only for providing financial help to those who needed it, but—and above all—for preserving a sense of self-respect in those who were employed by it. The peak of employment by WPA was reached in November 1938, when 3.3 million persons were on its payrolls. All in all, 8.5 million persons were employed at some time on WPA projects during the eight years of the agency's existence, and nearly $11 billion was spent.

The National Labor Relations Act (July 5, 1935), commonly known as the Wagner Act, established for the first time full statutory regulation of labor-management relations in the United States. In the preceding half century, the employer in the United States was free to recognize or not to recognize labor unions, and to deal or not to deal with them. Employers frequently discharged employees for union activities, and if unions became too strong, employers would use various means to break them—company unions, private police, labor spies, lockouts, and professional strikebreakers. In the absence of statutory regulation, court rulings were frequently sought to protect the interest of management, particularly during strikes. The Norris-LaGuardia Act of 1932 was the first major step in creating a more equitable balance between labor and capital, by limiting the use of court injunctions against labor unions; but since this act failed to establish an administrative agency to enforce its provisions, much of its original intent did not materialize.

The Wagner Act is the Magna Carta of American labor. Its main purpose was to encourage collective bargaining between labor and management, thus substituting peaceful discussion for violence. Just as the Constitution of the United States does not prescribe the contents of statutes to be passed by Congress, but merely sets down the rules and procedures of the legislative process, the Wagner Act, too, merely created a set of rules and an atmosphere in which labor and management could talk to each other. Although the law did not, and could not, compel both sides to agree, and strikes and lockouts still remained legal, the experience of collective bargaining quickly proved that the application of democratic methods of negotiation usually leads to results beneficial to both parties.

Dissatisfaction of management with some provisions of the Wagner Act led to its replacement in 1947 by the Labor-Management Relations Act, commonly known as the Taft-Hartley Act. Though spokesmen for labor voiced deep dissatisfaction with the Taft-Hartley Act, it left the basic principle of the Wagner Act—collective bargaining—substantially unchanged.

The issue of public policy is no longer the principle of collective bargaining itself, but the establishment of the proper balance between labor and management. It is to be expected that each side will have its own ideas on what constitutes the proper balance of forces. However, it is the function of the state, not to give any one side an *a priori* superiority over the other, but to see to it that democratic procedures are observed in the settling of industrial disputes.

The Social Security Act (August 14, 1935) marked another milestone in the movement for social reform in the United States. In modern industry the individual is frequently at the mercy of large impersonal forces over which he has no control. The efforts of the family, private charity, and the local community have all too frequently proved insufficient to protect the individual against the hazards of old age, sickness, or unemployment. The passage of the Social Security Act marked the recognition that the community, on the local, state, and federal levels, is partly responsible for assuring its citizens of some protection against want and insecurity.

The program is financed mainly by contributions of workers and employers; since the state can only give what it takes, citizens are reminded that if they want higher social security benefits, the only way to get them is to work harder, produce more, and pay for them before the need arises. In 1961, out of a civilian labor force of 65 million, 61 million and their families were covered by old-age and survivor insurance. Interestingly enough, private pension funds have grown faster than public pension funds. Assets of public (federal, state, and local) pension funds rose from $33 billion in 1953 to $61 billion in 1963; the assets of private pension funds during the same decade increased from $17 billion to $61 billion. Far from weakening private effort, public welfare—in the area of old-age pensions, at least—has greatly stimulated private pension funds.

In the field of health, it has been argued that existing conditions and facilities are inadequate in relation to needs. In 1949, President Truman urged the creation of a comprehensive national health program based on a prepaid compulsory insurance scheme, but administered primarily by state and local authorities. So far, such a program has been rejected on the grounds that it would lower standards of medical service, that it would cost too much, and that it would subject the medical profession to centralized bureaucratic direction.

The main positive effect of the debate on a national health service has been a greater public awareness of the problem and an increase of privately financed insurance schemes to provide medical and hospital facilities. At present, about 25 million persons, slightly less than one-seventh of the population, receive some form of federal medical care. The principal categories covered by federal medical care are veterans, members of the armed forces and the Coast Guard, Indians, and inmates of federal prisons.

In 1960 Congress opened the door to a more general health program by committing the federal government to medical aid for the aged. Low-income persons of over 65 years of age—about 12 million—are eligible. Each state sets up its own standards of need that a person must meet if he is to qualify, and each state determines what medical bills it will pay. The federal government is pledged to pay 50-80 per cent of the cost of the program—more for low-income states. The program has been attacked by its supporters on two main grounds: first, the "means test" required for eligibility, and, second, the administrative complexity of fifty separate state programs instead of one uniform federal program, attached to the federal social security system. Opponents of the program have attacked it because they see in it the first step toward a broader national health program for all citizens ("socialized medicine").

The welfare state has grown in scope and cost under both Democratic and Republican national administrations. In Eisenhower's first budget year (1953), the federal government paid out $7 billion in welfare activities, or nine cents of every dollar spent; in his last budget year (1960), the federal government spent over $20 billion on welfare, or about twenty-one cents of every federal dollar spent. Over

"It might not be such a bad life, security-wise."

20 million people in 1960 were recipients of social welfare benefits from the federal government: 15 million retired workers and dependents received pensions; 2.4 million elderly persons were on relief; 1.1 million disabled persons received pensions or were on relief; 1.9 million veterans (including families of deceased veterans) and 0.6 million retired civil servants received pensions; and about 100,000 students financed their college education through federally supported loans. This figure does not include 13.5 million school children, whose

lunches are partly financed by federal funds, nor does it include 2.5 million unemployed persons receiving benefits from state insurance programs, partly financed by federal aid. Omitting these last two categories, about one out of every eight Americans receives financial help from one of the many federal welfare activities.

Yet, although the total cost of public welfare programs (federal, state, and local) has risen from $7 billion in 1935 to over $50 billion in 1960, *the share of the national product spent on welfare has remained at the same level, about 10 per cent.* The cost of social welfare in proportion to all government expenditures (federal, state, and local) in 1935 was slightly under 50 per cent; in 1960, only about 37 per cent. Thus, while there has been an expansion of social welfare in terms of absolute cost, the relative cost of social welfare as a share of the national product has remained stable, and it has even declined as a share of all government expenditures in the period 1935-1960. Finally, the growth of the welfare state has not led to the feared shrinkage of local government at the expense of a monstrously swollen central government in Washington. In 1935, state and local government accounted for 55 per cent of all public expenditures on welfare; in 1960, the percentage was the same.

In Great Britain, the impact of the welfare state on the *redistribution of income* has been measured fairly accurately. In the lower-income group of the population, in which earnings are under £500 per annum (£1 = $2.80), each person receives annually about £18 more in social welfare benefits than he has paid in. Since the lower-income group of under £500 per annum includes nearly 40 million persons, or 80 per cent of the British population, it can be seen that the effects of redistribution through welfare state policies are not insubstantial. However, this picture is changed somewhat by the fact that redistribution cuts across class lines; for example, persons who smoke and drink pay a proportionately higher share of taxes than those who do not.

In the United States, it has been estimated that the lowest third of income recipients, having annual incomes of under $2,000 in 1950, comprised about 17 million spending units. The original income of this lowest third of the nation was $24.79 billion, and the redistributed income rose to $27.584 billion. Assuming about 2.5 persons per spending unit, the average gain of the 42 million persons in the lowest income groups amount to about $64 per person. (A. T. Peacock, ed., *Income Redistribution and Social Policy,* 1954.)

According to this estimate, only one-third of income recipients gain from redistribution in the United States, as contrasted with about four-fifths in Britain. The reason for this difference is simple: there is more poverty in Britain. The per capita income is less than one-half of that in the United States; as a result there is more need for redistribution. Moreover, *high social mobility in the United States* is, in a sense, a *permanent mechanism of redistribution;* with less social mobility in Britain, there is more need for monetary redistribution. Finally, since the British conception of the welfare state goes further than the American, Britons are willing to push redistribution further than the American public has been willing to do so far.

The main mechanism for bringing about redistribution is *taxation.* Thus in 1961 the top 20 per cent of consumer units in the United States received 45 per cent of the national income, but paid 61 per cent of all income taxes. The top 5 per cent received 20 per cent of the national income, but paid 36 per cent of income taxes. By contrast, the lowest 20 per cent received 5 per cent of the national income, but paid only 1.5 per cent of taxes. The proportionate share of the top 1 per cent of income receivers has suffered the most drastic decline. In 1929, the top 1 per cent received 14.5 per cent of total personal income, and in 1948, 8.4 per cent. In the same period, the share of the top 5 per cent dropped from 26.1 per cent of total personal income to 17.6 per cent.

Yet taxation cannot produce wealth; it can merely transfer property from one group to another. The improved material well-being of the American people in the last generation is due to increased production. At the same time, a heightened sense of equity underlying the philosophy of the welfare state has brought about more equality in the distribution of incomes than used to prevail in the United States. Incomes have improved both absolutely (in terms of actual size) and relatively (in terms of the distribution among various groups of the population).

The income revolution is illustrated by the accompanying chart. In it, American families are divided (in terms of 1957 dollars) into three main groups: low-income, under $4,000 per year; middle-income, from $4,000-$10,000; and high-income, over $10,000. In 1929, 73 per cent of families were low income; in 1957, only 36 per cent, a reduction by one-half. The percentage of families in the middle-income groups more than doubled, increasing from 22 per cent in 1929 to 52 per cent in 1957. The proportion of high-income families increased from 5 per cent of all families in 1929 to 12 per cent in 1957, or by nearly two-and-a-half times. *Whereas in 1929 low-income families outnumbered middle-income and high-income families combined by nearly three to one, in 1957 middle-income and high-income families combined outnumbered low-income families by almost two to one.* This absolute and relative improvement of the economic status of American families has been accomplished through a process of leveling up rather than leveling down. The proportion of high-income families rose from 5 per cent in 1929 to 12 per cent in 1957, or by nearly two-and-a-half times.

INCOME DISTRIBUTION IN THE UNITED STATES, 1929-1957

Family personal income in 1957 dollars (before taxes)	Per cent of families and unattached individuals		Per cent of total family income	
	1929	1957	1929	1957
Under $4,000	73	36	38	14
$4,000-$10,000	22	52	33	54
Over $10,000	5	12	29	32
Total	100	100	100	100

U.S. Department of Commerce, *U.S. Income and Output* (1958).

The trend toward greater equality in the distribution of income can be seen in the case of both the middle-income and high-income families with respect to their relative shares of total family income. In 1929, 22 per cent of all families were middle-income, and they took 33 per cent of total family income (or about one-half more than their share in terms of absolute equality). In 1957, 52 per cent of all families were middle-income, but they took only 54 per cent of total family income (or nearly their exact share in terms of absolute equality). In the case of high-income families the trend toward greater relative equality can be seen even more clearly. In 1929, 5 per cent of all families were high-income, and they took 29 per cent of total family income (or nearly 6 times their share in terms of absolute equality). In 1957, 12 per cent of families were high-income, and they took 32 per cent of all family income (or less than three times their share in terms of absolute equality).

Another aspect of the income revolution can be seen in the relative speed by which incomes of different groups have risen in the two decades of 1941-1961:

PER CENT INCREASE IN AVERAGE INCOME
(1950 DOLLARS)

Rank by size of income	1941 to 1961
Total	52
Lowest fifth	73
Second fifth	77
Third fifth	63
Fourth fifth	55
Highest fifth	41
Top 5 per cent	24

Source: *Statistical Abstract of the United States, 1963.*

We thus see that the average income in the United States rose by 52 per cent in the period of 1941-1961 (calculated in 1950 dollars). The lowest and second fifths of income receivers did considerably better than the national average; the third and fourth fifths did slightly better; the highest fifth advanced considerably less. Most striking is the relatively slow advance of the top 5 per cent of income receivers: their increase was only 24 per cent, or less than half of the national average of 52 per cent.

The income revolution can also be studied in the changing proportions of different sources of income. In 1929, 59 per cent of all personal income was derived from wages and salaries; in 1962 the percentage rose to 67. By contrast, income derived from dividends, interest, and rentals dropped from 22 per cent in 1929 to 13 per cent in 1962. This sharp drop is significant since income from dividends, interest, and rentals is primarily important to high-income groups. Income from transfer payments (public and private pensions, unemployment relief, veterans' benefits, and other types of assistance) rose from 1.6 per cent of all personal income in 1929 to 8 per cent in 1962. This item is mainly beneficial to the lower-income groups, and further illustrates their relative advance. Taking wages, salaries, and transfer payments as one combined major category of income, we find that this item accounted for 61 per cent of all personal income in 1929, whereas the percentage rose to 75 in 1962.

Inequality within the United States is much smaller than between the United States and the rest of the world. Thus, the top 6 per cent of income receivers in the United States receive about 22 per cent of the national income. The whole population of the United States is about 6 per cent of the world's population, yet it annually produces about 33 per cent of the world's goods and services.

Just as redistribution is a way of achieving internal peace and stability within the United States, our foreign aid programs apply the same principle to the community of nations, particularly the under-developed countries. If the welfare state at home is cheaper than un-rest and revolution, international welfare policies are cheaper than war and communist expansion.

As time goes on, the realization grows that *the welfare state is not a way of getting something for nothing,* that *every piece of welfare has to be paid for.* Since taxation in countries like England and the United States is reaching a level where there is not much left that can be obtained by soaking the rich, every increased social benefit must be paid for by increased taxation of the lower-income groups. The problem of the welfare state is less and less one of which philosophical principle one advocates or opposes, and more and more one of actu-arial calculation and specific taxation.

In the welfare state, the people agree that a high portion of their income should be spent by the government in a certain way. Experi-ence shows that people tend to save more easily if they have com-mitted themselves to an insurance policy or a mortgage with monthly payments, than if they rely on irregular voluntary deposits in a savings account.

In the welfare state the situation is similar. The individual hands over to the state the job of saving for him in case of an emergency such as sickness, old age, or death. If people themselves could save for all such emergencies, much of the welfare state would be un-necessary. But the average person finds it easier to pay higher taxes every month or every year, out of which his social security is ulti-mately to be paid for, than to save for such eventualities in a personal savings account.

There is nothing wrong in admitting this human weakness and en-trusting the state with the efficient administration of a comprehensive insurance system, as long as it is understood that the costs of such a system have to be borne largely by taxation, and that therefore the financial principle behind the welfare state is *forced personal and com-munal saving today for the needs of tomorrow* rather than a simple method of transferring property from the rich to the poor.

Is the welfare state compatible with capitalism? When the first basic measures of the welfare state were introduced thirty years ago, the dire prediction was made that the welfare state was the first step to communism, or at least to creeping socialism. Events have disproved

Drawing by Mulligan; © 1963 The New Yorker Magazine, Inc.

"Your management is proud and happy to announce that for the tenth consecutive year, despite oppressive government controls and taxation, the continuing cost-price squeeze, and unending and unreasonable wage demands, our net earnings have again topped all previous records."

that fear; after three decades of the welfare state, the American economy prospers more than ever before, living standards have reached an all-time high, productivity is higher than ever, people live longer and better, and there is more economic equality between the various income groups than in the past. Above all, the welfare state has in no way sapped the spirit of incentive and effort in the American economy; the whip of want and insecurity is not the best guide to progress, and in providing a minimum of social and economic security the welfare state has strengthened the economy as a whole. The performance of the American economy in World War II astounded the world; far from being coddled into softness and stagnation by the welfare state, it showed enormous dynamism, drive, and initiative. Since the end of World War II, the American economy has continued to grow vigorously, although not vigorously enough, some argue, because of the economic and military threat posed by world communism.

After Roosevelt's death in 1945, President Truman's Fair Deal continued and expanded the policies of the New Deal. When the Republican Party won the presidential election of 1952 it was feared by some that there would be a roll-back of welfare state policies. Yet, during both its terms the Eisenhower Administration vigorously broadened the scope and range of social welfare, covering more people than ever before, and increasing benefits to a record level. When President Eisenhower was re-elected in 1956, his victory was attributed, among other reasons, to the fact that he had convinced the American public, particularly the lower-income groups, that he was sincerely committed to the principle of public responsibility for social and economic welfare for all. In the presidential election of 1960, the major issue was foreign policy and the relative position of the United States in the world, and not the welfare state.

The welfare state—accepted in substance by both the Democratic and Republican Parties—has thus ceased to be the political football it used to be in the 1930's, and has become part of American life, an issue of efficient administration rather than high policy. Whatever the economic and social aspects of the welfare state, its political consequences are even more important. Without changing the basic form of government or way of life, the welfare state has strengthened democracy by strengthening the security, self-respect, and freedom of democracy's citizens.

FOR FURTHER READING

Barth, Alan, *The Loyalty of Free Men.* New York: Pocket Books, Inc., 1952.

Barzelon, David T., *The Paper Economy.* New York: Random House, 1963.

Bell, Daniel, *The End of Ideology.* New York: Collier Books, 1963.

Berle, A. A., *The American Economic Republic.* New York: Harcourt, Brace & World, Inc., 1963.

Berlin, Isaiah, *Two Concepts of Liberty.* New York: Oxford University Press, Inc., 1959.

Beveridge, William, *Full Employment in a Free Society.* New York: W. W. Norton & Co., 1945.

Cahn, Edmond (ed.), *The Great Rights.* New York: The Macmillan Company, 1963.

Cantril, Hadley, *Human Nature and Political Systems.* New Brunswick: Rutgers University Press, 1961.

Chafee, Zechariah, *The Blessings of Liberty.* Philadelphia: J. B. Lippincott Co., 1956.

Cochran, Thomas C., *The American Business System.* New York: Harper & Row (Harper Torchbooks), 1962.

De Grazia, Alfred, ed., *Grass Roots Private Welfare.* New York: New York University Press, 1957.

Dollard, John and others, *Frustration and Aggression.* New Haven: Yale University Press (Yale Paperbacks), 1960.

Ebenstein, William, *Modern Political Thought,* 2nd ed., chaps. 2, 3, 10, 13. New York: Holt, Rinehart & Winston, Inc., 1960.

Friedman, Milton, *Capitalism and Freedom.* Chicago: University of Chicago Press (Phoenix Books), 1963.

Fromm, Erich, *The Sane Society.* New York: Holt, Rinehart & Winston, Inc., 1955.

Galbraith, John K., *American Capitalism.* Boston: Houghton Mifflin Co. (Sentry Editions), 1961.

————, *The Affluent Society.* Boston: Houghton Mifflin Company, 1958.

Gellhorn, Walter, *American Rights.* New York: The Macmillan Co., 1960.

Hacker, Louis M., *American Capitalism.* Princeton, N.J.: D. Van Nostrand Co., Inc. (Anvil Books), 1957.

Hayek, Friedrich A., *The Constitution of Liberty.* Chicago: University of Chicago Press, 1960.

Hook, Sidney, *Political Power and Personal Freedom.* New York: Collier Books, 1962.

Jessup, John K. and others, *The National Purpose.* New York: Holt, Rinehart & Winston, 1960.

Karr, David, *Fight for Control.* New York: Ballantine Books, Inc., 1956.

Kuznets, Simon, *Shares of Upper Income Groups in Income and Savings.* New York: National Bureau of Economic Research, 1953.

Lampman, Robert J., *The Share of Top Wealth-Holders in National Wealth, 1922-1956.* Princeton, N.J.: Princeton University Press (for the National Bureau of Economic Research), 1962.

Lerner, Max, *America as a Civilization.* New York: Simon and Schuster, Inc., 1957.

Lilienthal, David E., *Big Business: A New Era.* New York: Harper & Row, 1953.

Mason, Edward S., ed., *The Corporation in Modern Society.* Cambridge, Mass.: Harvard University Press, 1959.

Maurer, Herrymon, *Great Enterprise: Growth and Behavior of the Big Corporation.* New York: The Macmillan Co., 1955.

Means, Gardiner C., *The Corporate Revolution in America: Economic Reality vs. Economic Theory.* New York: The Crowell-Collier Press, Inc., 1962.

Meiklejohn, Alexander, *Political Freedom.* New York: Harper & Row, 1960.

Moore, Wilbert E., *The Conduct of the Corporation*. New York: Random House, 1962.

Morgan, James N. and others, *Income and Welfare in the United States*. New York: McGraw-Hill Book Co., 1962.

Myrdal, Gunnar, *Beyond the Welfare State*. New Haven, Conn.: Yale University Press (Yale Paperbacks), 1962.

Peacock, Alan T., ed., *Income Redistribution and Social Policy*. New York: The Macmillan Co., 1954.

Prospect for America: The Rockefeller Panel Reports. Garden City, N.Y.: Doubleday & Co., 1961.

Robbins, Lord, *Politics and Economics*. New York: St. Martin's Press, Inc., 1963.

Rostow, Eugene V., *Planning for Freedom: The Public Law of American Capitalism*. New Haven: Yale University Press (Yale Paperbacks), 1962.

Stouffer, Samuel A., *Communism, Conformity, and Civil Liberties*. Garden City, N.Y.: Doubleday & Co., Inc., 1955.

Sutton, Francis K. and others, *The American Business Creed*. New York: Schocken Books, Inc. (Schocken Paperbacks), 1962.

Titmuss, Richard M., *Essays on the Welfare State*. London: Allen & Unwin, 1958.

Wallich, Henry C., *The Cost of Freedom: Conservatism and Modern Capitalism*. New York: Collier Books, 1962.

Ward, Barbara, *The Rich Nations and the Poor Nations*. New York: W. W. Norton & Co., 1962.

Warner, W. Lloyd and James Abegglen, *Big Business Leaders in America*. New York: Atheneum Paperbacks, 1963.

Whyte, William H., *The Organization Man*. Garden City, N.Y.: Doubleday & Co., Inc. (Anchor Books), 1957.

Wright, David McCord, *Capitalism*. New York: McGraw-Hill Book Co., Inc., 1951.

4

Democratic Socialism

It is not easy to state when socialism first appears. Some have asserted that the ideal commonwealth in Plato's *Republic* is socialist, inasmuch as its ruling class has no property of its own and shares all things in common. Others have claimed that the Bible, particularly the Old Testament, constitutes the first socialist code, covering as it does the protection of workers, women, and the weak. The early Christians rejected the concept of "mine and thine," and practiced socialism in their everyday lives; and in the Middle Ages numerous sects and movements, mostly religious, attacked wealth and commerce as wicked and incompatible with the Christian life. Such sects frequently withdrew into isolation, living an austere existence, and sharing poverty in brotherly love as a protest against the prevalent greed in the world around them.

During the Renaissance and the Reformation, there was a revival of protest against inequality based on wealth. The new arguments increasingly combined the older faith with the newer rationalism, as evidenced, for example, in Thomas More's *Utopia* (1516). In the Puritan revolution of the seventeenth century, there arose, side by side with the main movement of middle-class origin, a more radical group—called Diggers or True Levelers—that sought to attain communal ownership of land not currently in use. The movement was short-lived, but its radical protest against private landed property was not to be entirely forgotten.

Yet despite all such illustrations from earlier times, *socialism* as a major political force can properly be said to have originated as the *result of modern industrial capitalism*. To the extent that socialism contains within itself an element of protest against social inequality—and no movement can call itself socialist unless it expresses that kind of protest—it is as old as Western civilization itself. Both Greek and Jewish-Christian thought categorically reject the conception of wealth as the basis of the good life.

Another feature of socialism, the protest against money as the chief tie between human beings, is also not confined to the socialist tradition; many nonsocialists have voiced their disapproval of the "cash nexus." If we thus look to something more specific and historically more concrete than a vague protest against social injustice, we find that socialism as an effective, organized political movement is the product of the Industrial Revolution.

Just as communism has happened—and is likely to happen—only in countries *before* they have undergone the full impact of the Industrial Revolution, democratic socialism develops only in societies *after* they have experienced considerable industrialization.

Wherever industrialization has taken place in societies without deeply rooted liberal institutions, the political adjustment to the resulting tensions is likely to be either some sort of fascism (as in modern Germany, Italy, Japan, and Argentina) or communism (as in Russia and China). Because industrialization in these societies is promoted and controlled by an authoritarian state, its purpose is the power of the state, not the welfare of the individual.

In contrast, *where industrialization has occurred in relatively liberal societies* (as in northwestern Europe, North America, Australia, and New Zealand), the purpose of the economy is the welfare of the individual, and the adjustment to the inevitable tensions and conflicts of industrial capitalism assumes some form of democratic socialism or social democracy, rather than fascism or communism.

This basic distinction between the authoritarian and the liberal society can cut away a lot of confusion. Thus, the question is frequently debated whether a fascist economy is socialistic (because of the complete regulation of economic activity by the state) or capitalistic (because the means of production are left in private hands).

Such discussions are endless and insoluble because they are based on a false premise: that the basic distinction in the world's economic systems is between socialism and capitalism. In actuality, the line of division runs differently: between *free market* or *welfare economies* (which operate democratically and aim at freedom, welfare, and happiness) and *coercive* or *command economies* (which operate by command and coercion, and aim at the power of the state through military expansion). Both capitalism and socialism fall into the group that is dominated by the concept of welfare economics, whereas fascism and communism fall into the second group, the command economy.

Differences among the species within each major group are important, but they are not crucial. Thus, capitalism and socialism disagree on the best method of how to bring the maximum welfare to all the people; the former stresses individual property and effort, the latter puts its faith in collective productive property and effort.

Fascism and communism do not see eye to eye in every detail on how best to operate an economy in the service of the state. Differences between fascism and communism, however, tend to fade into insignificance if it is recalled that the objective—the power of the state to wage aggressive war—is the same, and that the means—ranging from friendly pressure to slave labor and the concentration camp—are amazingly similar and frequently identical.

In some ways, of course, socialism opposes capitalism, but such opposition is the rebellion of the child against the father, not the total war of stranger against stranger. Just as the rebellious child uses arguments he has learned from his own father, socialism employs, in the controversy with its progenitor, a whole arsenal of capitalist values and attitudes, especially critical rationalism and pragmatic utilitarianism.

As to the specific problem of property, socialism inherits from capitalism one basic goal: *to preserve the unity of work and ownership.* In the seventeenth and eighteenth centuries, the early phase of modern capitalism, that unity was a reality. In the England of John Locke, or in the America of Thomas Jefferson, the average farm, store, or workshop was generally small enough to be owned and operated by one person or family. *Work and ownership coincided.* The chief threat to this unity came from the state, which sought to prescribe, to regulate, to snoop, in short, to play the role of an omniscient busybody in economic matters. This attitude was resented by the individual entrepreneur because he knew that he could run his own business without any unsolicited advice from pompous and self-confident state officials.

As the capitalist economy progressed, however, the individual (or single-family) form of ownership and work was gradually replaced, owing primarily to technological progress, by an economic system in which large-scale enterprise swallowed up the original capitalist-owner-manager. *As the size of industrial enterprise grew larger and larger, work became more and more socialized, collective, whereas ownership remained private.*

In seeking to restore the classical harmony between work and property, the reformer faces two alternatives—(1) the division of large-scale enterprises into small units, so that both work and ownership can coincide again in one person or family, or (2) collective ownership.

The former method is feasible in agriculture, where large landed estates can be physically broken up and divided among landless farm workers, as was done in France during her Revolution in the eighteenth century, in Mexico and Guatemala during this century, and—on a smaller scale—in Italy after World War II. Whether such a breakup of large landed estates is economically sound or not is highly debatable. In many cases the productivity of dwarf farms following agrarian reform is lower than it was before on large farm units. A reform government, however, may be willing to pay the price of lower productivity for the greater social benefit of having an independent farm class. In any case, the technology of agriculture is still simple enough so that large units can be broken up, and small units can be operated with relative efficiency.

In industry, this solution is physically out of the question. An automobile or aircraft factory cannot be divided up into 10,000 portions, each to be operated by one worker as his personal piece of property. The technological nature of modern industrial enterprise is such that there is no alternative to collective work and operation. Thus, in facing the task of reuniting work and ownership in industry, collective ownership seems to socialists the logical answer, just as the classical liberal deduced the right to individual ownership from the fact of individual work. In both systems—classical liberal capitalism and democratic socialism—there is the underlying assumption that the *right to property ultimately rests on work, effort, and industry, rather than on formal law, custom, or birth.*

John Locke, the founder of modern political and economic liberalism, based the right to property on human labor, and the value of property on the amount of labor "admixed" to nature's resources. The socialists have accepted the Lockean and capitalist rationale of labor. What has changed since Locke is simply the technological character of labor, not its ethical implications. If the logic of capitalism demands individual property for individual work, the logic of socialism demands *collective ownership* for collective work—*provided collective work is the only possible form of managerial organization.*

Where small property has survived as a technologically efficient unit, as in agriculture, the professions, the arts, and some areas of retailing, servicing, and manufacturing, socialists generally agree with adherents of capitalism that private ownership should be kept and strengthened. Thus, socialist governments have enjoyed long tenure in predominantly agrarian countries like Denmark and New Zealand because farmers in those countries have been sympathetic to the socialist program of maintaining their economic integrity and individualism by cheap credits, guaranteed parity prices, and other policies designed to protect the small farmer against the threat of domination by banks, insurance companies, and wholesalers.

ROBERT OWEN: CAPITALIST-SOCIALIST

The filial link between socialism and capitalism can be illustrated by the fact that the first modern socialist was a wealthy and successful capitalist. Robert Owen (1771-1858), generally regarded as the founder of British socialism, was the first to use the term "socialism." A self-made capitalist, he had made a fortune by the age of forty. He was a man of sound, practical judgment, and he easily could meet one test of experience frequently described by conservatives as essential whenever a reformer comes forth with some new scheme: "Have you ever met a payroll in your life?" Owen had. In his *A New View of Society* (1813), he describes himself as a "manufacturer for pecuniary profit."

His views were the result, not (like Marx's) of study in the British Museum, but of experience in his own industrial enterprises. Owen dedicated his book to His Royal Highness, the Prince Regent of the British Empire; he was no refugee from his own society, as were Marx and Lenin later, but a respectable, wealthy man, as English as mutton or tea. He considered drink as an incentive to crime and a main source of misery, and his list of virtues and vices would have appealed to Benjamin Franklin.

Far from looking upon capitalist Britain as a dungeon of inhumanity, he described the British constitution as being "among the best devised and most enlightened that have hitherto been established." Refusing to believe that evil can be transformed into good in a day, he advocated "progressive repeal and modification" of unjust laws and conditions; strongly rejecting the alleged blessings of revolutionary change, he felt that "the British constitution, in its present outline, is admirably adapted to effect these changes, without the evils which always accompany a coerced or ill-prepared change."

Realizing that love and fellowship cannot be conceived in hatred and born in strife, Owen appealed to "every rational man, every true friend of humanity," and he hoped for cordial cooperation and unity of action between the Government, Parliament, the Church, and the People.

Owen's rationalism also emerges from the fact that *A New View of Society* discusses one subject more than any other: *education.* Owen believed that the evils of his society were due to circumstances rather than to the depravity of man, and he was convinced that, just as crime and degradation were the result of specific social and economic conditions, education in a new environment could produce human beings endowed with rationality, habits of order, regularity, temperance, and industry.

In his own time, children of six and seven years of age were employed in factories for twelve hours a day and more, and Owen makes the suggestion, bold and radical for the capitalist conscience of 1813, that a regular workday of thirteen hours from six in the morning to seven in the evening should not be imposed upon *children under twelve;* after that age "their education might be finished, and their bodies would be more competent to undergo the fatigue and exertions required of them." Human nature, Owen says, is "universally plastic," and if education is the key to make men more rational and cooperative, "the best governed state will be that which shall possess the best national system of education."

Owen in the true liberal-capitalist tradition looked to society rather than to the state for important change. A century before Keynes and Beveridge, Owen understood the crucial importance of full employment for the maintenance of a civilized society. Yet he was opposed to the dole, cash relief to the unemployed, on the ground that the "industrious, temperate, and comparatively virtuous" should not be compelled to support the "ignorant, idle, and comparatively vicious." Owen clearly saw the human aspects of unemployment; yet he wished the state not to dispense employment, but to provide an educational system good enough to equip every person with the skills wherewith to find employment in the open market.

A believer in the individualist principle of *self-help,* Owen started the cooperative movement and supported the incipient trade union organizations springing up throughout England and Scotland. For Owen, cooperation was more than selling milk to housewives; he believed that *producers' cooperatives* rather than consumers' cooperatives would establish a new social order. He sank much of his fortune in producers' cooperatives in England, and he also spent several years and the better part of his wealth in a cooperative venture in the United States. His best-known experiment, the settlement of New Harmony in Indiana, did not succeed, but his ideas are today more important than ever.

The British experiment of nationalizing selected basic industries and services has raised the fundamental question whether the Owenite method of cooperation outside of the formal machinery of the national government is not preferable to nationalization as effected in Britain since 1945. In the British trade union movement, too, the Owenite bias against the state has strongly survived; if the trade unions have never been overly enthusiastic over nationalization schemes, it is because they dread the growth of the state machinery and the transformation of free trade union officials, responsible to their members, into semi-government officials, responsible to the state.

SOCIALISM AND DEMOCRACY

The link between democracy and socialism is the most important single element in socialist thought and policy. Looking at the history of socialism, it can be quickly seen that *successful socialist movements have grown up only in nations with strong democratic traditions,* such as Great Britain, Scandinavia, Holland, Belgium, Switzerland, Australia, New Zealand and, more recently, Israel.

The reason for this parallelism is simple. Where democratic, constitutional government is generally accepted, socialists can concentrate on their specific program, overambitious as that program may seem, namely: to create more opportunity for the underprivileged classes; to end inequality based on birth rather than service; to open the horizons of education to all the people; to eliminate discriminatory practices based on sex, religion, race, or social class; to regulate and reorganize the economy for the benefit of the whole community; to maintain full employment; to provide adequate social security for the sick, unemployed, and aged; to re-plan the layout of towns and cities; to tear down the slums and build new houses; to provide medical facilities for everybody, irrespective of the size of his purse; and finally, to rebuild society on the foundation of cooperation in lieu of competition, incentive, and profit.

All these goals of democratic socialism have one thing in common: *to make democracy more real by broadening the application of democratic principles from the political to the nonpolitical areas of society.*

Freedom of worship and freedom of political association, historically the first liberties to be conquered, are still the most essential foundations of democracy today. Where these foundations exist, therefore, and where democratic principles are firmly rooted in the hearts and minds of the people, socialists can concentrate on the "finer points" of democracy.

In contrast, socialist parties have fought an uphill and generally losing struggle in nations in which democracy is not a living thing, but an aspiration, a hope, an idea yet to be realized. For example, the Social Democratic Party in Germany always worked under one heavy handicap. In the Second Reich (1870-1918), political autocracy was a reality, and parliamentary institutions were a cover for the virtual dictatorship, first of Bismarck, and then of Kaiser William II. In the eighteen seventies, Bismarck outlawed the Social Democrats as "enemies of the state," and the party leaders who escaped being jailed fled to England, other free nations in Europe, or America.

During the Weimar Republic (1919-1933), the German Social Democratic Party was paralyzed again by the insecurity of democratic institutions; the main issue of the Weimar Republic was not this or that social reform in which the socialists could take a special interest, but something much bigger: the issue of democratic government itself. Whereas, in nations with long-established democratic habits, socialists could argue over issues *within democracy,* taking the existence of democracy for granted, German socialists constantly had to argue and fight over the *issue of democracy itself.* As fascism grew in the Weimar Republic, the German socialists became increasingly concerned with the defense of republican and democratic institutions rather than with problems of economic reform.

In Russia before 1917, the situation was even simpler. The despotic tsarist regime did not make even the pretense of democracy or self-government; social and economic reform by peaceful means was thus made virtually impossible, and the door for communism was opened.

World War II provides further illustrations of this point. In France, for example, the Socialist Party had become the strongest political party by 1936, far stronger than the Communist Party. During World War II, however, under the German occupation, the communists found the political environment of underground and illegal activity much more congenial to them than to the socialists. Democratic socialists in a country like France function best when they can carry membership cards rather than high explosives. The type of person who joins such a party is well-meaning and stable, probably a family man, in any event a skilled worker or civil servant with a steady job. People of this kind do not readily engage in illegal, terroristic activities such as were necessary in France under German occupation in World War II.

The communists, on the other hand, attract an entirely different type of person, more fanatical, more devoted to his cause, and used to illegality and semi-illegality even in so-called normal times. What the Third French Republic (1870-1940) could never accomplish, four years of German occupation managed to do; at the end of World War II, the communists, polling about twice as many votes as the democratic socialists, emerged as the strongest single party of France. The communists remained the strongest party until the elections of November 18 and 25, 1962, in which the Gaullist party (Union for the New Republic) heavily defeated them.

In contrast, the socialist vote in *the British general election of 1959 was 360 times larger than the communist vote.* The evidence (not only from Great Britain, but also from other democratic countries with strong socialist movements) indicates that fullest civil liberty for all ideas and parties, including subversive, revolutionary organizations, seems to be the best antidote against fascism and communism, and that repression is the natural soil for the growth of revolutionary movements.

If one were to rank democratic nations today primarily in the light of their respect for civil liberty, Great Britain, Norway, Denmark, Sweden, Holland, Belgium, Australia, New Zealand, and Israel would be at the top of the list; all these countries are, or recently have been, governed by socialist administrations or by coalition cabinets with strong socialist participation.

The reasons for this parallelism are not too complex. Democratic socialists are keenly aware of the fact that without the opportunities provided by liberal, constitutional government they could not get to first base. Once in control of the government, socialists still maintain the psychology of the opposition, because they know that the possession of political power does not automatically solve the problems of social and economic organization. In other words, before socialists take over the government, they are in opposition to the government *and* to the wealthy classes; after they gain control of the government, the oppositionist psychology, directed as it is against the economic status quo, necessarily persists.

Moreover, even in the purely governmental realm, socialists tend to preserve a certain degree of caution and suspicion after they get into office, because they realize that, though they can gain control of the legislature in an election, the other sources of political power, the civil service and the judiciary, may be hostile to them.

Another factor essential to this discussion is all too frequently neglected. Examining the remarkably high state of civil liberty in nations with strong socialist movements, one tends to overlook *the high respect for civil liberty demonstrated by the opponents of socialism.* After all, if the conservative and propertied classes had shown less respect for the letter and spirit of constitutional government, the chances of socialist growth would have been very slim. From the viewpoint of dollars and cents, the conservatives' genuine acquiescence in socialism meant that they valued their faith in democracy higher than their pocketbooks, and were willing to be heavily taxed even for programs they considered undesirable or unreasonable.

It can thus be seen that both groups took a gamble: the socialists trusted their opponents not to destroy the processes of democratic government in order to protect their financial interests; the propertied classes trusted the socialists not to abuse electoral victories, and to act reasonably and moderately when in office.

Where the propertied classes were unconvinced by the Biblical admonition that it is more blessed to give than to receive, and were unwilling to pay an occasionally higher income tax as an insurance premium for the maintenance and stability of the social order, the natural response to distrust was more distrust. It is in this kind of political atmosphere that democratic socialism has been pushed back in Italy and France, giving way to the more radical demands of communism.

SOCIALISM VERSUS COMMUNISM

Socialism and communism are not two of a kind, but represent two incompatible ways of thought and life, as incompatible as liberalism and totalitarianism.

There are several factors of irreconcilable antagonism between socialists and communists. First, *communists* seek to bring about the end of capitalism by a single act of *revolutionary upheaval and civil war. Socialists,* on the other hand, adhere to *strict constitutional procedures;* they seek power by ballots, rather than bullets, and once in office they know they are not in for keeps, but are subject to be voted out in the next election.

The British labor movement has at no time approved of any co-operation with communists. In the middle nineteen thirties, when the communists in many countries sponsored Popular Fronts and United Fronts of all antifascist forces against the Berlin-Rome-Tokyo Axis, the British labor movement forbade its members to have anything to do with such efforts, on the grounds that its integrity would be jeopardized by association with communist aims. Members of the Labor Party who violated the ban by cooperating with communists in front organizations or appearing with communist speakers on the same platform were ousted from the party. Among those expelled were such well-known men as Sir Stafford Cripps and Aneurin Bevan. At the time, the Labor Party's policy of not getting tangled up with communists was markedly different from that of antifascist parties, both socialist and nonsocialist, in other countries, and the Labor Party was attacked for being hypocritical, sanctimonious, intransigent, and dogmatic. The passage of time, however, would seem to have vindicated fully the consistent policy of British socialism to have no dealings whatsoever with communism.

In 1945, the Labor government surprised many people by allowing the fascists in Britain to reorganize as a political movement, although a number of fascists had committed treason during the war. One of the top fascists, William Joyce (popularly known as Lord Haw-Haw), had spent the war years broadcasting for the Nazis in Berlin, for which offense he was executed as a traitor after World War II. The socialists in Britain took the view that the fascists had a right to engage in political propaganda as long as they did not violate any laws; further, they felt that the effectiveness of fascist propaganda depended rather on the common sense of the people than on pro-hibitory laws. Above all, British socialist leaders saw that if fascism lacks the protective coddling of extreme right-wingers and conservatives, it has no way of permeating larger groups of people.

In most other nations, the political Left fought fascism, whereas the Right concentrated on communism; the division of labor was exactly the opposite in Britain. *Fascism was destroyed by the Conservative Party,* and *communism by the Labor Party.* Both major parties clearly understood that the issue of democracy versus totalitarianism must not be poisoned by partisan arguments, and that it is too big an issue to be dragged into the mud of election campaigns. As a result, there are few (if any) countries in the world in which both fascism and communism are as dead and ineffectual as in Britain.

Moreover, this fight against totalitarianism was primarily carried on by the British people through their party organizations rather than through the strong arm of the government. In the United States, the House Committee on Un-American Activities and the Attorney General of the United States periodically publish lists of subversive organizations and publications for the information of law-enforcement officers as well as interested citizens. In Britain, the Labor Party issues from time to time lists of communist or communist-dominated organizations which no member of the Labor Party is permitted to join. This policing of the communist movement and its network of front-organizations by the Labor Party is probably more effective than if the same job were done by the government because it uses publicity, a weapon the communists do not like, rather than the authority of the state. Communists thrive better under persecution than under the full exposure of truth and publicity.

Above all, the British Labor Party has successfully eliminated communism from its main position of influence—labor unions. *If communists are a negligible factor in Britain today, the main credit goes to the organized labor movement.* It has steadily and quietly fought them whenever and wherever they have tried to gain influence. In open elections, the communists are no menace in most democratic nations, but in labor unions the communist technique of infiltration has often been extremely effective. Because of the communist goal of revolution, it is understandable that socialist parties look upon communists as a group of troublemakers who must be kept out of unions or any other organized working-class activity. And because trade unionists have had the most intimate knowledge of communism— based on everyday contacts rather than on a study of ideology—they have generally proved themselves to be the staunchest opponents of communism in the labor movements. The purely political elements of the socialist parties have not always shown the same steadiness and vigor.

It is understandable why the communists work with such desperate energy for the control of organized labor: they know that no amount of propaganda will convert the middle and wealthier classes to communism. In contrast, the socialists have learned from elementary electoral statistics that parliamentary majorities cannot be obtained by appealing to one class only; a considerable proportion of the working class (in England about 40 per cent) does not vote Labor, and if the Labor Party is to obtain a majority, it must appeal to other groups. The communists, prisoners of their dogmas, can only think in terms of class and class antagonisms; the socialists have learned to think in terms of parliamentary majorities.

RELATIVE VOTING STRENGTH OF SOCIALIST
AND COMMUNIST PARTIES *
(as of January 1, 1964)

Country	A: Socialist % of total vote	B: Communist % of total vote	C: Relation of A to B
Australia	55.2	0.5	110 times
Austria	44	3	14.7
Belgium	35.8	1.9	19
Canada	13.5	0.18	75
Denmark	42.1	1.1	38
Finland	24.1	22.1	1.1
France	15.2	21.3	0.71
Germany (West)	28.8	2.2	13
Great Britain	43.8	0.12	360
India	10.7	10	1.1
Israel	50	2.8	18
Italy	6.1	25.3	0.24
Netherlands	30	2.4	12
New Zealand	43.6	0.22	200
Norway	48	3	16
Sweden	50.9	3.8	13.4
Switzerland	26.7	2.6	10

* In the period 1946-1963, socialist voting strength generally remained stable. As to communist voting strength, the only major increase was in India (from 3.3% to 10%). Major declines in communist voting strength occurred in Austria (from 5.4% to 3%), Belgium (from 12.7% to 1.9%), Denmark (from 12.5% to 1.1%), France (from 28.6% to 21.3%), West Germany (from 8.4% to 2.2%), Great Britain (from 0.41% to 0.12%), Netherlands (from 10.6% to 2.4%), and Norway (from 11.9% to 3%). The figures for Italian socialists refer to the Democratic Socialists under the leadership of Sarragat, but do not include the party under the leadership of Nenni (13.8%), since that group has often collaborated with the communists and has frequently been ambiguous on the issue of political democracy. In West Germany, the Communist Party was outlawed in 1956; the figures in the table refer to the election of 1953, the last in which communists participated.

In the crucial issue of public ownership, the gap that separates socialists from communists is unbridgeable. Communists visualize the transition from capitalist enterprise to public ownership as sudden and complete. There is no payment for expropriated property, because communists consider capitalist ownership of property no better than theft. In contrast, socialists do not believe that the transition from capitalism to public ownership of the means of production can be either sudden or complete. Most socialists believe in the instalment plan. Public ownership of the means of production is to be built up gradually, by instalments; if one phase works, then the next will be tackled. Responsible socialists feel that they must prove pragmatically, through actual accomplishments, the usefulness and practicality of public ownership in particular industries or services.

Concerning compensation, socialists tend to share the general democratic conviction that no citizen may be deprived of his property without due process and compensation. Important as public ownership of the basic industries is to their plans, socialists consider public ownership not as an end, but as a means to an end, and a means that does not justify the violation of property rights.

There is another vital difference with regard to public ownership. Communists seek to transfer all means of production, distribution, and exchange to the state, leaving to the individual only the free discretion over consumer goods. Communists insist on *total nationalization,* because their dogma tells them that publicly owned property is always preferable to private enterprise.

By contrast, socialists seek to work out a set of empirical principles that will indicate in a *particular* instance whether a specific *industry or service* is to be transferred to public ownership and control. The socialists' criterion may be that the industry under examination is a monopoly (such as gas and light, telephone, and other utilities tend to become); or that the industry is sick (as the British coal industry was before its nationalization); or that the industry, although neither inefficient nor monopolistic, is of such vital importance to the national economy in peace and war that it seems socially undesirable to leave its operation in private hands (the British iron and steel industry was nationalized on these grounds).

The British Conservatives are in substantial agreement with Labor on the first two criteria; on the third the two parties are in partial disagreement. Clearly, the irreconcilable difference of viewpoint with regard to private property is not between conservatives and socialists, but between democrats (conservatives, liberals, or socialists) and totalitarians (fascists or communists).

Philosophically and politically, the difference between communists and socialists goes to the root of things. As we saw earlier, Lenin's theory of the professional revolutionary is based on the assumption that the majority of the people (or the working class) are unable to think for themselves; that a minority, the Communist party, has the job of leading the proletariat; and that within the minority a small group of men, the professional revolutionaries, are to formulate policies and assume leadership. Thus, in Leninist theory (and in communist practice), a small minority within a minority is to be the ruling elite.

This elite concept is totally rejected by socialists, who believe in democracy and majority rule within their own party as much as in their own nation. Clement Attlee, British Prime Minister from 1945-1951 and leader of the Labor Party from 1935 to 1955, writes in his book *The Labour Party in Perspective* (1937) that his party's strength depends, "not on the brilliance of individuals, but on the quality of the rank and file." Attlee's own career confirms this diagnosis; brilliance was not his *forte,* and he lacked the dynamic leadership qualities of a Churchill or a Roosevelt.

Contrary to the communists, socialists believe in peaceful persuasion as the only method of promoting their program. Communists feel that it is useless to seek change by persuasion because all means of communication, education, and propaganda are biased in favor of the capitalist status quo, and that freedom of the press amounts to little if one lacks the necessary funds to start a newspaper. For this reason the communists were stunned when the British Labor Party polled its electoral victory in 1945 and again in 1950.

According to orthodox Marxism-Leninism, such victories were impossible. Since the British press was overwhelmingly in favor of the Conservative Party, how could the voters, who presumably had been reading the pro-conservative papers daily for years, vote Labor? According to Lenin, workers under capitalism are mentally enslaved to capitalist ideology, and cannot therefore be peacefully converted to socialist thinking until there has been a change in the economic structure of society. Only *after* capitalism has been destroyed, Lenin argues, will the workers be able to think along anticapitalist lines, because (as Marx said) it is the conditions of man's life that determine his thinking.

To the communist, every capitalist system, whether democratic, authoritarian, or fascist, is a bourgeois dictatorship; specifically, democratic institutions in a capitalist system are considered as so much façade and hypocrisy, which do not make the capitalist system any less dictatorial. Once capitalism—even liberal capitalism—is identified with dictatorship, the communist insistence on violence as the sole means of change is a logical conclusion.

Socialists, on the other hand, draw a fundamental distinction between two types of capitalist system, the political dictatorship and the liberal democracy. In a liberal democracy socialists believe in playing according to the rules of the game—provided, of course, the other side does the same.

Finally, *socialists reject the communist thesis that the choice in a democracy is between full capitalism and full collectivism.* Democratic parties do not concern themselves with bringing about the millennium as of a certain date, but seek to tackle issues that are comparatively manageable and to avoid definitive solutions that are irrevocable.

Socialists therefore envisage the transition from a predominantly capitalist economy (a purely capitalist economy exists and has existed only in the minds of the extreme Right and the extreme Left) to a predominantly socialist economy, not as a result of a sudden revolutionary *coup* that makes the return to private enterprise impossible, but as the result of gradual measures, none of which by itself irrevocably alters the nature of the whole economy.

Whereas the communists think in terms of three absolutes—capitalism, revolution, communist dictatorship—socialists think in terms of three *relative* concepts: a predominantly capitalist economy as the starting point, a long period of gradual change, and finally a predominantly socialized economy.

ELEMENTS OF SOCIALIST THOUGHT AND POLICY

The totalitarians of all shades have authoritative statements of doctrine, such as the *Communist Manifesto* or Hitler's *Mein Kampf*. Socialism, on the other hand, like many other liberal movements and ideas, has no bible, probably because liberals generally cannot agree on their beliefs and doctrines and are better at criticizing bibles than at writing them. Moreover, socialism has developed in different countries in accordance with different national traditions, and there has never been any central authority, such as world communism possesses in Moscow, to lay down a socialist party line.

Yet despite the absence of such authoritative statements of socialist doctrine, it is not too difficult to cull from socialist writings, and from the policies of socialist parties, the outlines of socialist thought and policy. What emerges, however, is not a consistent body of ideas and policies. It has been the main strength, and weakness, of socialism that it has had no clear-cut body of doctrine and that it has fed on contradictory sources, sources that reflect the contradictions of the societies in which socialism has developed.

The complex, and frequently self-contradictory, elements of socialist thought and policy can best be illustrated from the British socialist movement, the most influential in the world. The elements that stand out in the British movement are:

(1) religion
(2) ethical and esthetic idealism
(3) Fabian empiricism
(4) Liberalism

(1) In *The Labour Party in Perspective,* Attlee writes that "the first place in the influences that built up the Socialist movement must be given to religion. England in the nineteenth century was still a nation of Bible readers. To put the Bible into the hands of an Englishman is to do a very dangerous thing. He will find there material which may send him out as a preacher of some religious, social, or economic doctrine. The large number of religious sects in this country, and the various tenets that many of them hold, illustrates this."

The *Christian Socialist movement,* headed by two clergymen, Frederick Maurice and Charles Kingsley, reached its peak in the middle of the nineteenth century, and was an important source for the later development of working-class and socialist organizations. The Christian Socialists had as their guiding principle the concept that *socialism must be Christianized, and Christianity socialized.*

George Lansbury, Attlee's predecessor as the leader of the Labor Party, writes in *My England* (1934) as follows: "Socialism, which means love, cooperation, and brotherhood in every department of human affairs, is the only outward expression of a Christian's faith. I am firmly convinced that whether they know it or not, all who approve and accept competition and struggle against each other as the means whereby we gain our daily bread, do indeed betray and make of no effect the 'will of God.' " The late Archbishop of Canterbury, William Temple, came very close to socialism in his *Christianity and the Social Order* (1942). Temple holds that every economic system is, for good or ill, an immense educative influence, and that therefore the church must be concerned with it. The church is thus bound to ask "whether that influence is one tending to develop Christian character, and if the answer is partly or wholly negative the church must do its utmost to secure a change in the economic system so that it may find in that system an ally and not an enemy."

This practical concern of Christianity was particularly strong in Victorian England, throughout the whole second half of the nineteenth century. A sense of moral seriousness and dedicated disinterestedness characterized the Victorian period, and Victorian religion, while conceding that grace and faith were essential to salvation, nevertheless emphasized conduct and *salvation by works.* Many socialist leaders of the older generation who (like Attlee and Cripps) came from upper-class homes were steeped in an atmosphere in which religion was taken seriously.

Another religious influence of profound influence in Britain was the tradition of religious dissent, of *nonconformity*. In other European states, Protestantism had resulted in freedom *of* the church in relation to Rome, but not necessarily in freedom *within* the church in matters of doctrine and church government. To the nonconformist, Protestantism meant freedom of individual conscience and the freedom to organize voluntarily in associations of like-minded believers. This principle of *voluntary association* was later translated from religion into politics, where it became the life principle of the free, democratic society.

It was in the village chapels of the eighteenth and nineteenth centuries that many local leaders of working-class organizations learned to think for themselves, as well as to conduct public meetings and administer finances. *Wherever nonconformity was strong, labor unions and cooperatives were strong;* in fact, the trade unions have been aptly called the present-day descendants of the earlier nonconformist congregations. Nonconformity supplied more than a particular religious outlook: it was also the source, in the labor movement, of the idealism, the moral dedication, and of the seriousness that have characterized the movement and its leaders.

If one studies the internal organization of some nonconformist churches, one is struck by its similarity with the organization of trade unions: both are loosely federated unions of voluntary bodies freely associating with each other. The Labor Party today is also a federal union, made up of three main bodies—trade unions, cooperatives, and local constituency organizations—each of which is in turn made up of loosely federated organizations. Because the Labor Party has this federal character, its internal structure resembles more the American federal system than the much simpler and more streamlined political system of Britain itself.

The complexity of the religious root of modern socialism becomes apparent in the fact that *nonreligious, rational humanism* has also played a vital role in the evolution of socialist thought and action. Robert Owen was a rationalist and, among more modern socialist leaders in Britain, Sidney and Beatrice Webb, Harold J. Laski, G. D. H. Cole, Hugh Gaitskell, and Harold Wilson, to mention but a few, have not been much inspired by formal religious beliefs. It remains, however, of some interest that the political leaders of the labor movement, men like George Lansbury, Clement Attlee, and

Sir Stafford Cripps, have more often been profoundly religious, whereas the principal intellectual figures, the men who formulate ideas rather than policies, tend to represent the *rationalist* root of socialism.

In the United States, too, religion has played an important part in the cooperative and communal settlements established in the eighteenth and nineteenth centuries as well as in the more recent socialist activities of a political and propagandistic nature. In the twentieth century, democratic socialism in the United States has been symbolized above all by Norman Thomas, who was a minister of religion before he took up the cause of socialism as his life's mission.

In contrast, religion has played a much smaller part in continental European and Latin American socialism. In England religious dissent was the bridge between religious and political unorthodoxy; in the virtual absence of nonconformity outside of the English-speaking world, however, dissent from the established social and political order has generally also included dissent from the established church, or from religion itself.

Before World War II, there were small groups of religious socialists in countries such as France and Germany, but, on the whole, socialists tended to be anticlerical or at least indifferent toward religion since most churches in Continental Europe openly supported the political and economic status quo. During World War II, the heroic struggle of many priests and ministers against Nazi-fascist oppression brought about a closer understanding between churches and most socialist parties. Since then, the churches have become less committed to one particular set of social and economic theories, and the socialists have abandoned much of their earlier agnosticism and anticlericalism. Also, British socialism has proved to many socialists in other lands that socialism and religion do mix, provided the mixture is accomplished in the right spirit.

(2) *Ethical and esthetic idealism* is another important source of British socialism, although its impact cannot be measured in votes and membership cards. Expressed by poets like John Ruskin and William Morris, ethical idealism was not a political or economic program, but a revolt against the squalor, drabness, and poverty of life under industrial capitalism. Developing first in England, capitalism probably produced more ugliness there than anywhere else, because English industrialists had no way of imagining what the new way of life would do to the beauty of the English countryside, no way of foreseeing the rapid disfigurement of lovely old towns and villages by slums and factory centers.

Whereas Marx approached industrial capitalism in terms of cosmic laws—the development of world history according to inevitable social laws, philosophical materialism, the law of the falling profit rate, to name but a few—Morris kept his gaze closer to the ground. He saw around him ugly household goods and furnishings, and men and women who lacked joy and beauty in their daily lives. When once asked in a public meeting what he thought of Marx, Morris said: "I am asked if I believe in Marx's theory of value. To speak quite frankly, I do not know what Marx's theory of value is, and I'm damned if I want to know." What Morris cared about was human beings, not this or that "system." He felt intensely that the arts must be brought back again into everyday life, and that people's creative impulses should be given expression in their daily life and work.

The influence of Ruskin and Morris was more negative than positive. They showed what was wrong with a civilization—physically and morally—that was built on strife and squalor, but they did not formulate any specific program to improve the specific conditions to which they objected. Nevertheless, this esthetic and ethical revolt was important in preparing the intellectual environment in which socialism could later find a sympathetic response.

Ruskin and Morris were mainly read by the more educated class, which absorbed from them, as well as from Charles Dickens, Thomas Carlyle, and other writers, a groping understanding of what industrial civilization does to man, not only as a worker, but as a human being. The esthetic and ethical rebels of Victorian England undermined the self-confidence that then prevailed and fostered self-criticism; out of that doubt and self-criticism more positive socialist ideas could later be developed step by step.

In one particular field—town and country planning—the Labor Party reflects directly and explicitly the message of Ruskin and Morris. The whole concept of community planning—which is more than tearing down slums and building neat little row houses of uniform size and style—owes much to the outlook of the early pioneers of socialist thought, for whom problems of industry merged with more general problems of creating a community in which each member would have access to the means of civilized enjoyment.

(3) *Fabian empiricism* is perhaps the most characteristically *British* aspect of the British labor movement. The Fabian Society, founded in 1884, was named after a Roman general, Quintus Fabius Maximus Cunctator—the "delayer." The early motto of the society was: "For the right moment you must wait, as Fabius did; but when the right

moment comes you must strike hard, or your waiting will have been
vain and fruitless."

The founders and early members of the Fabian Society included
George Bernard Shaw, Sidney and Beatrice Webb, H. G. Wells, and
Graham Wallas. It was noteworthy that none of them came from
the poorer classes, and that there was a sizable proportion of writers
in the group.

In Sidney Webb's historical survey of the basis of socialism, included in the *Fabian Essays* (1889), we find what is still the basic
philosophy of Fabianism, and, more generally, of British socialism.
Webb looked upon socialism (eleven years before the foundation of
the Labor Party) as an inevitable outcome of the full fruition of
democracy, but he insisted that his "inevitability of gradualness" was
sharply different from the Marxian inevitability of revolutionary,
catastrophic change.

Webb emphasized in the *Fabian Essays* that social organization
can only come bit by bit, and that important "organic changes" can
only take place, in England at least, under four conditions: first, such
changes must be *democratic,* acceptable to a popular majority, and
"prepared for in the minds of all"; second, they must be *gradual,*
causing no dislocation; third, they must *not* be regarded as *immoral*
by the people; fourth, they must be *constitutional and peaceful.*

Marxians on the Continent and elsewhere aimed their propaganda
at the proletariat. As to the middle and upper classes, the job at hand
was to liquidate them, not to convert them to socialism. Because the
propaganda was thus exclusively aimed at the proletariat, it tended
to be highly emotional and sloganized, taking into consideration not
only the low educational level of the workers, but also the fact that
they were expected to be half converted before they were ever exposed to communist agitation.

The Fabian Society started from the assumption that there could
be *no progress toward a just social order in Britain unless the middle
and upper classes could be shown the reasonableness and equity of
the basic claims of socialist thought and policy.* Since government
in Britain was government by persuasion and consent, and since the
governing classes of Britain were largely recruited from the middle
and upper classes, there could be no change of policy in Britain without the preliminary consent of those classes. It was fortunate for the
Fabians in a country like England that they spoke the same language
—literally and metaphorically—as did the governing classes, and
knew how to *permeate* the latter in ways which would have been

closed to formal propaganda from persons outside of the same class.

The Fabian technique of permeation was based on the premise that you do not change a reasonable person through a one-time brilliant argument, lecture, or emotional appeal. It was the Fabian policy to work on the minds and feelings of their hearers in a slow, gradual process rather than in one sudden act of conversion, and preferably on social, informal occasions rather than on formal, official ones.

An emotional appeal to a high British civil servant, telling him that according to the Marxian dialectic the capitalist system is doomed, and that such doom will be followed by the classless proletarian society, was likely to have less effect than a casual reference at luncheon to a new government report, written by a fellow bureaucrat, on the incidence of disease and crime in slum areas. Similarly, serious discussion of a recent book by a scholarly economist of good repute on changes in the distribution of income among various social and economic groups was likely to have more effect on a conservative political leader than the shorter appeals of "Down with Capitalism" and "Long Live Proletarian Solidarity."

Permeation had also another side. The Fabians did not consider it their job to pass resolutions, make appeals to kings and parliaments, or address themselves to the masses of the people. They were interested in convincing a small group of persons, regardless of party affiliation as long as they had two qualifications: first, they had to be persons of *continuous* influence in public life, so that the long process of permeation, if successful, would pay off; second, such persons would have to be *reasonable,* by which the Fabians meant not partisan extremists. Since such persons could be found in all political parties, the Fabians cultivated conservatives who met their qualifications as well as liberals.

This sort of Fabianism assumes a *Fabianism in reverse,* or else it would not stand a chance of success. For example, Fabians and other socialists in England religiously read *The Times,* not because they agree with its editorial viewpoint (generally conservative), but because it is "a good paper." In most other countries socialists consider the local substitute for *The Times* a source of bourgeois contamination, from which they should steer clear.

The difference between the Fabian and Marxian-communist approach can best be seen by contrasting the writings of the two groups. Marx was little interested in the minutiae of life; his *magnum opus, Das Kapital,* is an attempt to give meaning to history as a whole, and much of his thought was devoted to fundamentals of philosophy. Lenin wrote volumes and volumes on such subjects as *Materialism and Empirio-Criticism.* In contrast, over 95 per cent of all Fabian publications have been pamphlets rather than heavy tomes, and pamphlets lend themselves more to small subjects like *Municipal Milk and Public Health* (Fabian Tract No. 122) than to the future of Western civilization. The Fabian Society is rarely to be found in high intellectual altitudes, sniffing the thin air surrounding the metaphysical peaks; it is more often found "nosing about in the drains," seeking to remedy some immediate and *specific* condition.

Early in the history of the Fabian Society, Fabian Tract No. 70 (written by George Bernard Shaw) made it plain that Fabianism was no rival to existing philosophies trying to explain the whole cosmos, and that it had "no distinctive opinion on the Marriage Question, Religion, Art, abstract Economics, historic Evolution, Currency, or any other subject than its own special business of practical Democracy and Socialism." This sense of practicality and concreteness is indicated by typical titles of Fabian Tracts and other pamphlets: *Liquor Licensing at Home and Abroad; Life in the Laundry; Public Control of Electrical Power and Transit; The Case for School Nurseries; The Endowment of Motherhood; The Reform of the House of Lords;* and *The British Cabinet: A Study of Its Personnel, 1901-1924.*

Two Fabian pamphlets, *Metropolitan Borough Councils: Their Constitution, Powers, and Duties,* and *Borough Councils: Their Constitution, Powers, and Duties,* were written by Clement R. Attlee in the spring of 1920, when Lenin was busy, not with the reform of borough councils, but with the destruction of states and empires.

The Fabian approach can perhaps best be shown in a simple illustration: if a slum clearance project is debated in terms of fundamental issues—such as socialism versus capitalism—agreement between advocates of the project and their opponents is unlikely. However, if the pertinent facts can be clearly brought out—the cost (in dollars and cents) of a slum area in terms of disease, crime protection, fire hazards, compared with the cost of building new houses with public assistance —the original gap has been considerably narrowed, and agreement will be likelier than it was when the argument centered on issues of apparently irreconcilable ultimate values.

The successes of Fabianism have probably stemmed chiefly from this concern with *reducing questions of principle to questions of fact.* Fabians gambled on the notion that facts do matter and that the impact of facts ultimately determines how people will think and act.

In his autobiography, *Power and Influence* (1953), Lord Beveridge has an interesting sidelight on the Fabian faith in facts. One of the greatest contributions of Sidney and Beatrice Webb was the creation of the London School of Economics and Political Science in 1895, in order to provide an adequate opportunity for the study of economics and allied subjects. The Webbs themselves chose the first four Directors of the London School. Of the four, Beveridge tells us, the first two became Conservative Members of Parliament, the third had socialist sympathies, and the fourth (Beveridge himself) was a Liberal. The Webbs, Beveridge says, "believed that the impartial study of society would further the Socialism which was their practical aim, but they were prepared to take the risk of being wrong in that belief."

The Fabian technique of trying to reduce apparently irreconcilable differences of principle to negotiable disagreements over facts is no invention or novelty, but is implicit in the very nature of the democratic society. We have peace in a free society to the extent that people are willing to keep to themselves conflicting fundamentals in religion, morals, and philosophy. Separation of state and church in the United States was effected and has been maintained not because Americans are indifferent to religion, but because the framers of the Constitution felt it to be wiser to keep a fundamental issue like religion out of politics and to concentrate on issues in which people of all religions can cooperate without injury to their religious belief.

Fabianism has frequently been described as reform without resentment, social reconstruction without class war, political empiricism without dogma or fanaticism. Despite its small size (its membership never exceeded a few thousand), the Fabian Society has had an enormous impact. In the 1945 election, which led to the first Labor government based on a substantial parliamentary majority, 229 of the 394 Labor Members of Parliament were Fabians, and more than half of the Government, including Attlee (the Prime Minister from 1945-1951), was Fabian. Hugh Gaitskell, who succeeded Attlee as Leader of the Labor Party, was also a Fabian of long standing, as is Gaitskell's successor, Harold Wilson.

(4) *Liberalism* has become an increasingly important source of socialism, particularly since Liberal parties have dwindled to insignificance in many countries. In England, the Liberal Party has virtually disappeared and the Labor Party seems to have inherited about one-third of the estate. Temperamentally, many Liberals do not find it easy to join a socialist movement; the passion for individual liberty and individual difference is still the most distinguishing trait of the Liberal.

Apart from the tendency toward red tape and regulation for the sake of regulation, there is also in socialism a tendency toward the state, the mass, and collectivity. Both tendencies are repugnant to the true Liberal, the man who occasionally still likes to be himself and not just a number in the National Register. Yet, during the last thirty years, more and more Liberals have joined the Labor Party. Why?

In the first place, the weakness of the British *Liberal Party* is due to the fact, not that it has failed, but that *its success has made it unnecessary*. Both the Conservative Party and the Labor Party are now thoroughly committed to the Liberal principles of respect for individual freedom of worship, thought, speech, and association. Liberalism as a protest against clericalism is no longer a live issue in England (or in most other countries).

Free trade, another great ideal of nineteenth-century British Liberalism, no longer arouses passionate political interest, and is now the concern of experts rather than politicians. With both Conservatives and socialists committed to some form of tariff protection, even the Liberals realize that free trade no longer has the importance it once had.

The specific issues gone, many Liberals have joined the Labor Party, or vote Labor, or think of themselves as vaguely socialist. Liberalism has generally been to the Left of the Conservatives, and in a country with a two-party system, like Britain, if one wishes to stand to the Left of Conservatism, the Labor Party is now the only platform to stand on.

On issues of public ownership, the Liberal elements in the Labor Party are opposed to doctrinaire policies of nationalizing for the sake of nationalizing—*i.e.,* the Liberals in the Labor Party generally are on its Right wing, just as the Liberals in the Conservative Party are its Left wing. The Right-wing Laborite is so close to the Left-wing Conservative in mentality, outlook, temperament, and policies that it takes a pencil of electronic sharpness to draw the line of demarcation between the two. The London *Economist* has coined the word "Butskell," a composite of R. A. Butler, a leading Conservative of reformist leanings, and Hugh Gaitskell, the late moderate Labor leader. "Butskellism" is a symbol of the closeness of both major British parties on major issues.

Liberalism has contributed much that is lasting in British socialism. Because of the Liberal influence, socialist leaders are more moderate and less doctrinaire than they might otherwise have been, and have a deeper respect for individual liberty. Liberalism has turned the Labor Party into a national party rather than one based on class, and it has bequeathed to the Labor Party the Liberal message that there can be reform without bitterness and hatred.

SOCIAL-ECONOMIC
CHANGES
AND REFORMS

The victory of the democratic nations in World War I provided a strong stimulus for the growth of socialist parties throughout the world. The war had been fought in defense of the ideals of liberty and social justice against the authoritarian imperialism of Germany and her allies, and during the war promises were made to the peoples of the major democratic belligerents that military victory would be followed by the establishment of a new social order based on greater opportunity and equality.

In England, the Labor Party reflected in its growth and development the protest against the old social order. Founded in 1900, the Labor Party polled only two seats in the Parliamentary elections of that year. By 1910 forty Laborites sat in the House of Commons, and the party had ceased to be a negligible factor. In 1918 the parliamentary representation rose to 57, and in 1922 the Labor Party obtained 142 seats out of 615, replacing the fading Liberal Party as the second strongest party in the country. In 1924, the Labor Party, though still a minority, formed a government with the tacit support of the Liberal Party, but the experiment lasted only for ten months, because the Liberals finally decided that they could not go along with a socialist program.

In 1929, the Labor Party became for the first time in its history the largest single party in Britain, obtaining in the general election 288 out of 615 seats in Parliament. Although lacking an absolute majority in the House of Commons, the Labor Party formed a government that lasted until the summer of 1931. The coming of the world depression in 1929 weakened Britain economically, and the Labor government, being unable to follow socialist policies to cure the depression and unwilling to adopt conservative remedies, resigned in the summer of 1931. In the ensuing election the parliamentary representation of the Labor Party dropped to 52 out of 615, but by 1935, the last election before World War II, its strength in the House of Commons had risen again to 154. As long as the shadow of Nazi-fascist aggression hung over Britain, however, there was little chance for embarking upon a major experiment of social and economic reform.

Between 1935 and the end of the war in Europe there was no general election. In the first postwar general elections, held on July 5, 1945, the Labor Party obtained 394 out of 640 seats, with the result that for the first time in British history a Labor government was formed with a clear majority in the House of Commons. In 1950, the

Labor majority fell to a bare 315 out of 625 seats, and because of the narrow margin and the resulting instability of government, a new election was held in 1951. Although the Labor Party received more votes than the Conservatives in the 1951 election, it lost its parliamentary majority to the Conservatives, 321 seats to 295. In the elections of 1955, the Conservatives polled more votes than Labor, winning a comfortable parliamentary majority of 345 seats against Labor's 277. In the elections of 1959, the Conservatives won 365 seats, as against Labor's 258 seats. Labor's defeat in 1959 was particularly humiliating. First, its share in the popular vote had dropped three times in a row; in 1951, Labor obtained 48.8 per cent of the popular vote, in 1955, 46.4 per cent, and in 1959, only 43.8 per cent. Second, this was the first time in a century that a government in power had been able to increase its parliamentary representation in three successive elections.

Between 1900 and 1918, the Labor Party was not officially committed to socialism, although it included, of course, many individual socialists. In 1918, when the party adopted socialism in its program, its commitment to the nationalization of industry was just about complete. But as the party learned the facts of life it changed its outlook drastically, and urged nationalization only where it had been proved pragmatically that public ownership would do more for the welfare of the nation than private ownership. In the election of 1945, for example, the Labor Party did *not* enter the campaign with a program of "socialism" in the abstract, but promised to nationalize specifically listed industries and services, if elected to office.

In each case, it explained why nationalization was necessary. For gas and light, water, telephone and telegraph, and other utilities, the criterion of nationalization was the existence of a *natural monopoly*. On the coal industry, there was general agreement in Britain, regardless of party, that the industry was so sick and inefficient that it could not be put on its feet except through nationalization. The iron and steel industries were declared to be so *vital to the nation,* in peace and in war, that their management could not safely be subject to the decisions of private persons. The nationalization of all inland transportation, by rail, road, and air, was proposed on the ground that *wasteful competition* could best be avoided by a *coordinated scheme* of transportation owned and managed by public authorities. The Bank of England was also proposed for nationalization on the ground that its purpose was so obviously public. Finally, the election program of 1945 also promised the setting up of a National Health Service, so

that the best possible health and medical facilities might be available
to every person without regard to his ability to pay.

After the electoral triumph of 1945, the Labor Party methodically
carried out its program. With one exception, there was little argument
over nationalization. On the exception, iron and steel, the Conservatives argued that the industry was highly efficient, and that the needs of
the national welfare could be accommodated without nationalization.

Reproduced by permission of the Proprietors of Punch

Round the Corner

The attitude of the British public toward nationalization was generally one of indifference. The exception was, and is, the National Health Service, because of its direct effect on the everyday life of the individual citizen. Although no one was compelled to join the National Health Service, 97 per cent of the population and over 96 per cent of the doctors and physicians are in it. At first there was considerable delay and confusion arising out of the administrative and technical difficulties experienced in setting up the necessary machinery, and a number of barbs—some good-natured, others not so good-natured—were leveled at the program by the press of Britain (see cartoon) and the United States. As the program began to hit its stride, however, adverse criticism (in Britain, at least) died down; now the National Health Service seems to have established itself as a part of British life. The Conservative Party, like the Labor Party, is fully committed to the program.

The Labor government elected in 1945 also set up a comprehensive cradle-to-grave scheme of social security. The system provides protection against sickness, unemployment, and old age, supplemented by maternity grants, widows' pensions, and family allowances. Social security as set up by the Labor government was no invention of the Labor Party, but the culmination of several decades of social legislation enacted by Conservative and Liberal governments. A fully integrated system of social security was first proposed during World War II in the *Beveridge Report* (1942); in the middle of the war, both the Conservative Party and the Labor Party pledged themselves, if elected to office after the war, to introduce a comprehensive system of social security.

A further policy of the Labor government in the years 1945-1951 aimed at greater social equality. The setting up of the basic institutions of the welfare state in itself contributed to greater social equality, by bringing within the reach of large sections of the population many facilities and services that hitherto had not been available to those sections. *Educational opportunities* on the secondary and university levels, for example, were made available to children of lower-income families.

Taxation was the greatest leveler. Thus, a person with an income of £100,000, retained in 1910, after payment of taxes, about £94,000. In 1963, the net income on £100,000 after payment of taxes had shrunk to about £17,000. Inheritance taxes took about 50 per cent of bigger fortunes in 1938, about 80 per cent after World

War II. In 1938, the last normal prewar year, there were 6,600 persons in Britain whose income was over £ 6,000 after payment of taxes. By 1949, that number had dwindled to 60, but rose again to 3,000 in 1960, although the value of the pound had been cut to about one-third of its prewar purchasing power. At the same time, there was a sharp increase in the middle-income groups.

Putting the trend toward equality in Britain in another way, it can be seen that the proportion of the national income paid in wages and salaries was 60 per cent in 1938 and rose to 69 per cent in 1955 (after payment of taxes), whereas the share of dividends and interest in the national income dropped from 34 per cent to 20 per cent during the same period. Although all these policies have by no means brought about absolute equality, they have gone a long way toward the elimination of extremes of inequality.

One of the remarkable results of the victories of democratic socialism was the elimination of communism as an important factor in British politics. In the years between World War I and II, the communists usually had one representative in the House of Commons; in the election of 1945, the communists obtained two seats out of 640 in the House of Commons; in the election of 1950, after five years of vigorous Labor administration, the communists were unable to elect a single candidate, and they repeated this failure in 1951, 1955, and 1959. *Far from being the first step to communism, democratic socialism thus proved itself to be the high road to the grave of communism.* In contrast, where socialism declined after World War II, as in France and Italy, communism gained control of organized labor, thus threatening the very existence of state and society.

The record of the Labor government in the years 1945-1951 does not conclusively prove or disprove whether nationalization, or how much nationalization, is the cure for the social and economic ills of modern industrial society. The British voting public has been more impressed by the greater social equality of the welfare state than by nationalization. Apathy rather than extreme enthusiasm or extreme opposition has been the characteristic reaction of the British people to past nationalization. In a public opinion poll in 1960, 33 per cent of British voters thought nationalization had been a success, 28 per cent thought it was a failure, 12 per cent did not care, and 27 per cent did not know. What was more remarkable still, even among Labor voters only 40 per cent thought nationalization was a success, 20 per cent said it was a failure, 11 per cent felt it made no difference, and 29 per cent had no opinion. (Mark Abrams and Richard Rose, *Must Labour Lose?*, 1960, p. 32.) Even if it were conceded that the nationalized industries and services seem to have worked out fairly satis-factorily on the whole, no one claims that they have significantly contributed to Britain's basic economic problem of earning enough abroad with which to buy the foodstuffs and raw materials necessary to maintain her industries and feed her people. Before embarking upon further measures of nationalization, the British people want to see how the industries and services so far transferred to public owner-ship will work out, and the Labor Party reflected these doubts by proposing only very moderate schemes of nationalization in the elec-tions of 1950, 1951, 1955, and 1959.

Dropping much of the traditional socialist belief in nationalization, the Labor Party has come close to the Conservative Party, which in turn no longer opposes the basic principles of the welfare state. Inas-much as both parties seem to be united on kindred principles of social policy, and because so much of the British economy depends upon factors external to it (such as prosperity in the United States), there is little room left for such differences in principle as characterized the classic nineteenth-century struggles between the Whigs and the Tories.

In the nineteen sixties, British politics thus gives the impression of ideological peace and near-uniformity. The Labor Party, in particular, is in search of a new program and set of principles that can inspire the country, for the *impulse of early socialism*—nationalization plus social security—*has been largely spent*. The very success of the wel-fare state has thus become the main source of socialist hesitation and stagnation.

On the European Continent, the Scandinavian countries have had the most impressive record of social reform, both in the interwar years and after World War II. From the early nineteen thirties onward, the Scandinavian countries have been governed by socialist administra-tions based on parliamentary majorities, and as a result communism has been kept down to minor proportions in all three countries (Nor-way, Denmark, Sweden). The Scandinavian socialist movements have emphasized economic development and social security rather than nationalization, and their economic policies have been centered on fiscal measures (such as cheap money) and taxation rather than on public ownership. Full employment is a major point in Scandinavian (as in British) socialism.

One of the important lessons of the social and economic reform in Scandinavia in the last thirty years is the emphasis on *socialization rather than nationalization*. One of the most serious political weak-nesses of the British program of economic change has been the tendency to substitute *state* ownership and management for private

ownership, thus increasing the tendency toward governmental centralization. In contrast, the Scandinavian reform programs have ex-
perimented with other types of social ownership in lieu of private
ownership.

The most significant contribution of Scandinavia to social reform
is the use of the *cooperative movement* rather than the state as the
agent of social and economic reform. Whereas in Britain the cooperative movement has been largely confined, as in most other countries,
to retail and wholesale trading in a selected group of articles, the
Scandinavians have set up cooperatives for slum clearance, health
insurance, and industrial production. This Scandinavian *middle way*
avoids the evils of unbridled capitalism, and avoids, at the same time,
the dangers of statism.

PROBLEMS **OF** **NATIONALIZATION**	Socialist theory and practice have un- dergone drastic changes on the issue of nationalization in the last forty years. When the British Labor Party adopted a socialist platform in 1918, it de- manded (in Clause IV of its revised

constitution) "the common ownership of the means of production,
distribution, and exchange." At that time, this formula expressed the
prevailing socialist orthodoxy.

Today, there is not a single socialist party in the world, nor a single
socialist leader of repute and responsibility still adhering to the old
formula of nationalizing *all* the means of production, distribution, and
exchange. In July 1951, the Socialist International, speaking for over
thirty socialist parties throughout the world, adopted a program that
specifically rejected the older doctrine of total nationalization, and
conceded that socialist planning is compatible with private ownership
in agriculture, handicrafts, retail trade, and small and medium-sized
industries.

In 1959, the German Social Democratic Party, the largest democratic socialist party on the European Continent, adopted a new program, in which freedom, justice, and respect for the individual are
declared as its highest values. As to nationalization, the program
specifically states that "efficient small and medium-sized enterprises
are to be strengthened to enable them to prevail in competition with
large-scale enterprises." Only where, for natural or technical reasons,
competition is impossible, public ownership becomes a necessity.
The following two general principles are included in the new program:

"Private ownership of the means of production is no longer identical with the control of power"; and "Every concentration of economic power, even in the hands of the state, harbors dangers."

Moreover, nationalization is now increasingly rejected as the only alternative to private capitalism. In his *Democratic Socialism: A New Appraisal* (1953), Norman Thomas, the leader of American socialism during the last thirty years, writes that "the state under the most democratic theory and practice will become too huge, too cumbersome, if it seeks to control directly all economic activity." Thomas speaks of the *dangers of statism* inherent in total nationalization, and like most thoughtful socialists today he stresses that the alternative to private capitalism is *socialization, not nationalization.*

Freedom is inextricably linked to the *diffusion of power;* this truism has always been admitted by socialists to apply to political government. They are now finally coming around to the idea that *in the economic realm, too, there can be no freedom unless there is diffusion of economic power.*

Total nationalization—even under the most democratic safeguards —is bound to lead to the all-powerful state, and such a state is a threat to liberty even if it uses its powers benevolently.

The concept of socialization, in contrast, implies the diffusion of publicly owned property. Property is owned and managed not by the state but by producer or consumer cooperatives, trade unions, churches, educational institutions, public corporations, and other organizations, and these organizations derive their powers from voluntary association rather than from the sovereign authority of the state. In such organizations, there is also much more room for the direct representation of workers and consumers than in nationalized industries and services.

This approach has been successfully tried in Israel as well as in Scandinavia. In Scandinavia, most public housing has been built, not by the state, but by corporations that combine individual ownership and management with financial assistance from housing cooperatives and municipal agencies. In Scandinavia, too, as mentioned earlier, cooperatives are not confined to the retail business as in many other countries, but are common in the field of manufacturing and wholesaling. In Israel, the Federation of Labor is the largest employer in the nation, and it has a considerable share in the ownership and control of such basic industries as transportation, building, foundries, heavy machinery, cement, glass, and rubber. Also, a sizable proportion of Israel's agricultural production is in cooperative farm communities.

None of these solutions are final, and mistakes are constantly made, but these forms of socialization do seem to their advocates to avoid the worst evil nationalization, monopoly, and the resulting concentration of economic and political power. In a capitalist democracy, the economic power of private monopolies can at least be opposed by the political power of the state. *When the monopolist is the state itself, who will protect the citizen against the state?*

Today, then, no socialist party advocates any longer that *all* industries be collectivized; nationalization is recommended only for *some* industries. How many is some? There is no clear-cut answer, but there seems to be universal acceptance among socialists of the idea that natural monopolies in the public utilities field be publicly owned and managed. The concept of the "sick industry" (*e.g.,* the British coal industry) and the criterion of the "key industry" (*e.g.,* the British steel industry) have also been widely accepted as standards upon which nationalization may be based.

As has been seen in the case of British steel, the difference between the socialist and nonsocialist viewpoint is less real than both parties believe it is. The socialists were willing to make one big concession when they nationalized steel, to leave the individual steel firms intact, so that their name, management, and traditions might be preserved in a highly competitive market in which intangible assets are important. The only major change in the steel industry would have been that the stockholders of steel companies would *exchange their shares for state bonds with fixed income.*

When the Conservatives got into office, they were willing, on their part, to make a big concession: while "denationalizing" the iron and steel industry and returning the property to private ownership (thus transforming bonds again into shares), they set up a national *Iron and Steel Board,* designed to protect the national interest. On this board, in addition to the representatives of management, there are representatives of the state and of the steel workers (a former secretary of the steel workers' union was appointed as the first vice-chairman of the board).

The Labor Party has announced that, when next in office it would "renationalize," or "un-denationalize," the steel industry. It remains to be seen whether the limits of English language will be reached before the patience of the English voters is exhausted.

It appears that *nationalization lends itself best to industries or services that are highly standardized—i.e.,* where *uniform rules of administration* can be easily applied (this is the thesis of "gas and water socialism"). On the other hand, in industries that demand high adaptability to changing conditions, industries, for example, producing largely for export, or industries operating with a considerable element of risk, the case against nationalization or socialization is strong. The tendency of a bureaucratically run enterprise to put security above adventure and risk is incompatible with rapid industrial expansion. The automobile industry a generation ago and the air-conditioning industry today are the products, not of the pre-existing giant enterprises, but of relatively small corporations that were willing to put risk capital into new products.

It remains to be proved that this same spirit of adventure, risk, and experimentation can be shown by publicly owned enterprises. After all, it is one thing to risk, and speculate with, one's own money, and quite another thing to use the public treasury for questionable ventures.

The traditional concern of socialists has always been with *distribution* rather than *production*. The most creative contribution of socialism has, therefore, been its revision of the internal social structure of nations in the direction of equality. Many countries with strong socialist parties exhibit a tremendous internal cohesion and unity, the direct result, according to socialist leaders, of a high degree of social justice based on the concept of "fair shares for all." In contrast, these leaders point out, where socialism has recently been weak, as in France and Italy, the people are torn and disunited among themselves, and there is a general feeling of frustration, resentment, and stagnation.

It has not been shown so far that publicly owned enterprise is any more efficient in production than private enterprise, or that it has materially increased the people's standards of living. C. A. R. Crosland, a leading British economist and Labor M.P., makes important concessions on both points. First, he admits that the performance of nationalized industries in Britain has not been conspicuously better than that of private enterprise and that nationalized industries have been plagued by "bureaucratic centralization." Speaking of living standards, he argues that further nationalization "cannot be said to be necessary to full employment and prosperity, for these exist already." (*The New Leader,* February 29, 1960.) Crosland also points to the fact that average consumption standards in Britain "scarcely moved" between 1945 and 1951, whereas they rose by 20 per cent in the years 1951 to 1959 (*Can Labour Win?,* Fabian Tract No. 324, 1960).

The spectacular boom in Western Europe in the nineteen fifties and sixties has particularly benefited the lower-income groups; as in the United States a generation ago, the Western European worker is aggressively adopting middle-class habits and living standards, characterized by the ownership of a home, car, and consumer durables like refrigerators and dishwashers. As living standards have risen sharply in Western Europe, people now care much less about inequality than they did before World War II. Misery and inequality are, therefore, no longer the factors that can give socialist parties electoral victories in a prosperous world.

From the very beginning, public enterprise has found that three specific difficulties hamper its over-all performance. First, there is the *managerial problem* of administering vast public enterprises with flexibility and initiative, and at a low cost. The excessive tendency toward centralization and playing it safe is a serious matter. Moreover, it is not certain that the managerial situation will improve as nationalization continues. In the first phase of public ownership, the public corporation can draw upon managerial talent which has been trained in the tough environment of private competition, but if nationalization goes on, management of public enterprises will have to draw its top personnel from among its own ranks. It will then be seen whether persons trained and bred in the secure, sheltered atmosphere of bureaucratic monopoly will possess as great a capacity to operate large undertakings as is shown by graduates from the hard school of private, competitive business.

This problem is closely tied to a second problem. In private business, the *system of profits and losses* operates in a crude but effective way to keep efficiency at a relatively high level, and the threat of bankruptcy is always real. In a public enterprise, this system no longer operates to the same extent; if there are losses, no one goes bankrupt, and the losses of one division can be passed on to the whole enterprise. Even if the whole enterprise or industry is in the red, management can, because it has a monopoly, either increase prices or receive subsidies from general taxation.

Third, there is the *political difficulty*. How are public corporations to be related to the elected representatives of the people? If the public corporation is too closely supervised by parliament or congress, its management may become demoralized and lose efficiency. If parliamentary control is relaxed, on the other hand, up goes the cry that there is not much difference between the old and the new system (since if management can do more or less as it pleases, what has nationalization changed?).

Because of all these difficulties and complexities, many leading socialists are increasingly reconciling themselves to the virtually complete elimination of nationalization from the socialist program, emphasizing the concepts of equality and welfare instead. In a Fabian

Tract on *Socialism and Nationalization* (1956), Hugh Gaitskell, the late Leader of the British Labor Party, concludes that "the most vital question is how far greater social and economic equality can be achieved without more nationalization and public ownership." After the electoral catastrophe of 1959, Gaitskell went even further by publicly advocating that the Labor Party eliminate from its constitution Clause IV (which demands the common ownership of the means of production, distribution, and exchange).

A prominent spokesman of the right wing in the Labor Party, Denis Healey, goes even beyond Gaitskell. A generation ago, American writers like A. A. Berle said that in the American capitalist enterprise the real power is in the hands of professional managers rather than of the shareholders who legally own it. This viewpoint is now increasingly recognized by socialists as being equally applicable to publicly owned enterprise. "Industrial power in every large, developed economy now rests with a managerial class which is responsible to no one. The form of ownership is irrelevant. State control over nationalized industries is as difficult as share-holder control over private firms." (Denis Healey, *The New Leader,* August 17, 1957.) For a high-ranking socialist to say that the form of ownership is irrelevant marks a basic change of outlook.

As a way out of this dilemma between old dogmas and new facts, the Labor Party proposed in 1957 a new course: the next Labor government should not take over businesses or entire industries, but should buy shares of companies in the open market, achieving a controlling interest in some firms, and being satisfied with a minority interest in others. The companies affected by such a policy would continue to operate as in the past; the main purpose of this new method would be to let the nation benefit from capital gains and rising dividends in important industrial enterprises.

This new procedure was not tried out after the 1959 election, because the Labor Party lost again, as it had done in 1951 and 1955. The aversion to further nationalization was deeper than even the more moderate leaders of the Labor Party had assumed. Shortly before the 1959 elections in Britain, the results of a public-opinion poll on nationalization were made public. Two million voters were interviewed in one of the largest polls in British political history. Of those interviewed, 63.5 per cent wanted no further nationalization; 18.5 per cent wanted more nationalization; the rest had no opinion. More remarkable still, it was found that of Labor supporters 41.5 per cent wanted no more nationalization, 36 per cent wanted more, and 22.1 per cent had no opinion. (D. E. Butler and Richard Rose, *The British General*

Election of 1959, 1960, p. 244.) After the election, a poll in 1960 showed that 58 per cent of Labor Party supporters opposed further nationalization of industry, while only 21 per cent were in favor, and 21 per cent did not know. *If even among Labor Party supporters the opponents of further nationalization out-numbered its advocates,* it is not surprising that the Labor Party suffered a decisive defeat; such defeats will continue so long as the voters as a whole identify the Labor Party with nationalization.

At its annual conference in October 1963, the Labor Party stated that Britain's foremost problem was rapid economic growth. It proposed, if elected to office, vastly increased government aid to scientific research and greater government participation in creating *new* growth industries rather than taking over old ones. The emphasis thus shifted from accelerated social justice to accelerated economic growth.

Hostility to nationalization is not confined to Britain, but is a world-wide phenomenon, at least in the economically more advanced countries. Voters in fourteen countries throughout the world were asked whether they wanted to see big industries in their countries taken over and managed by their governments, or whether big industries should be left alone or merely regulated (but not taken over and managed) by government. The results were as follows (*Fortune,* February 1959):

ATTITUDES TOWARD NATIONALIZATION OF BIG BUSINESS

	Leave them alone or Regulate but don't manage	Take them over	No opinion
Australia	88%	5%	7%
Britain	84%	8%	8%
Netherlands	83%	5%	12%
Sweden	81%	5%	14%
Canada	81%	5%	14%
Austria	77%	13%	10%
Germany	77%	4%	19%
Norway	73%	3%	24%
Denmark	73%	4%	23%
France	72%	14%	14%
Belgium	66%	7%	27%
Italy	63%	19%	18%
Brazil	61%	10%	29%
Japan	45%	18%	37%

Countries that have been ruled by socialist labor governments for many years show extremely low figures of those advocating nationalization, as in Sweden (5%) and Norway (3%). The figures are higher where Communist parties are strong, as in Italy (19%) and France (14%). Yet it should be pointed out that normal communist voting strength in France and Italy is nearly twice as high as the percentage of those who favor nationalization. Apparently, even for communist voters nationalization is not the main reason why they vote as they do.

A leader of the Labor Party, Douglas Jay, has succinctly stated the reason why democratic socialist movements have swung away from nationalization toward the welfare state, economic security, and social justice: "Modern experience has proved that although governments are not always very efficient at producing goods, they are highly efficient at redistributing income and wealth." ("The Future of British Socialism," *New Politics,* Winter 1963, p. 97.)

THE IMPASSE
OF SOCIALISM
TODAY

Socialists today find themselves bewildered and uncertain of the future. For over half a century, the socialist movement was almost entirely devoted to propaganda and organization outside the framework of governmental responsibility. Now that so much of the socialist program has been realized, however, socialism faces a fate similar to that of organized political Liberalism.

Just as political Liberalism has passed away largely because some of the causes it championed have died a natural death while others have been solved by conservatives and socialists along liberal lines, socialism too may gradually pass away, as far as its original program is concerned, even though political parties with the socialist label may continue for a long time.

In the field of international politics, the main weakness of socialists has been the *failure to understand the role of power.* This intellectual failure was based on an admirable emotion: the desire to remove power from the society of nations and establish a world commonwealth based on peace and justice. Desirable as this goal may be, however, specific international problems cannot be solved by it or any other abstraction. Moreover, the practical realities of national economic planning have frequently given socialist foreign policies a strong element of *isolationism,* which is in sharp contrast with the traditional socialist slogan of international brotherhood.

Thus the foreign policy of the Labor government during the years 1945-1951 was discouraging to all those, in Europe and America, who believed that Britain would be the natural leader in a movement for a united Europe. In fairness to the Labor government, however, it should be noted that the Conservative government that followed it vacillated for years on the issue of joining the Common Market. Britain finally applied, but was turned down by the opposition of France led by de Gaulle. Yet this French attitude in 1963 would have been ineffective if Britain's commitment to European unity had been less half-hearted and less hedged with ifs and buts. The division of public opinion in Britain on the Common Market was not based on party. Although the Conservative Party, as a whole, was a little more receptive to the idea of European integration than was the Labor Party, the main line of division was within each of the two major parties. It is, therefore, at least conceivable that when British public opinion more vigorously embraces the idea of European unity, a Labor government may well lead Britain into the Common Market, just as a Conservative government almost did so in 1963.

In Norway, the socialist government has been in favor of a strong alliance with the North Atlantic treaty powers, whereas in Sweden the socialists have been in favor of neutrality and avoiding advance commitments. In the Middle East, the socialist-dominated government of Israel is strongly associated with the United States and her allies, but India's Premier Nehru, also a socialist, is trying to maintain "non-alignment" between East and West. All these policies have little to do with socialism and are based primarily on national interests, attitudes, and traditions.

In sum, therefore, it can be said that from the viewpoint of ideology the pacifist heritage of socialism has frequently paralyzed its ability to solve international problems realistically, and that, taking the picture as a whole, the foreign policies of socialist governments in recent years have been no better and no worse than those of non-socialist governments in the same countries. The quality of a particular government depended on how intelligent and far-sighted that particular government was, rather than on whether it was socialist, liberal, or conservative.

In July, 1951, the Socialist International was re-established. At its first congress, over thirty socialist parties committed themselves to support the rearmament of their countries for collective defense against communist aggression. Meeting again in June, 1962, in Oslo, the Socialist International rejected the idea that the democratic nations should disarm unilaterally. As to the causes of the cold war, the Socialist International stated that the "East-West rivalry has largely been imposed upon an unwilling world by the communist leaders." These resolutions, an expression of realism and common sense rather than of socialism as such, are primarily of interest as reflecting a definite change of socialist outlook on the nature of war.

A generation ago, socialists looked upon capitalism as *the* cause of war, and upon universal socialism as the only guarantee for peace. From experience with both fascist and communist imperialism, socialists have learned that war is a much more complex problem, and that the forces of imperialism can be tied to any system of economic organization, not just the capitalist system.

The present difficulties of the economic program of socialism are not likely to be resolved so soon. One great objective of socialism, the *welfare state*—i.e., the responsibility of the community for a minimum standard of social and economic security for every person— *is no longer a monopoly of socialist parties.* All other parties in democratic nations, with the exception of ultraconservative diehards, are also in favor of the welfare state. Some parties are more warmly for it than others, and some parties recommend more benefits than others, but as a general principle, the welfare state (in the minimum sense) is accepted by reasonable persons in all parties, and is no longer a matter of partisan controversy.

The concept of the welfare state no longer requires a separate political party. In fact, much of the welfare state in England was historically the work of the Conservative Party, and the limits of the welfare state are increasingly set by the ability to pay for its benefits rather than by differences of ideology.

The very fact that after two generations of socialist propaganda and accomplishment the main principles of the welfare state have been accepted by all parties in democratic states has created a real dilemma for the future of socialism. If it keeps on trying to convert the converted, it will lose the old fire and enthusiasm that made it a distinctive movement in the Western world in the last three generations. If its leaders are unable to formulate a new program, adapted to the needs of the second half of the twentieth century, the party may simply settle down to a fixed position slightly to the Left of the conservative parties, separated from the latter not by a basically different economic or political philosophy, but simply by its own concentration on translating the conception of the welfare state into a reality at the earliest possible moment.

The distinction between socialism and communism is of particular importance in the underdeveloped countries. The overriding political fact in poor nations is the desire to attain rapid economic growth. Without such economic progress, the newly emerging nations feel, there can be no genuine political independence or international leadership. Domestically, rapid economic growth is the only means of satisfying the yearning of the people for better living standards, health, and education.

The history of the last two centuries has shown two methods of rapid economic development: first, that of the most advanced Western nations (northwestern and central Europe, North America, and Australia and New Zealand), in which the free market was the main instrument of producing rapid economic growth. While it is true that government greatly aided this process (tariffs for infant industries; land grants for railways and educational institutions; legislatures, executives, and courts favoring the employer rather than the employee), it is still true that private initiative and capital were primarily responsible for the economic progress of the Western nations in the last two centuries. Without any government-sponsored five- or ten-year plans, private individuals decided how available resources—labor, capital, land, raw materials—were to be used, and individual consumers decided how much of their income was to be consumed and how much saved. Economic growth in these Western nations was greatly favored by factors that are largely absent in underdeveloped nations today: a stable government, a fairly efficient civil service, relatively high levels of education, means of transportation and communication (highways, canals), and—perhaps most important of all—a considerable level of technological and entrepreneurial skill and initiative. Some nations—such as Great Britain, Scandinavia, or the United States—even had the good fortune of having developed political institutions of free government before rapid economic expansion took place. As Alexis de Tocqueville noted in his *Democracy in America* (1835), "democracy is favorable to the growth of manufacturing, and it increases without limit the numbers of the manufacturing classes." His prophecy has come true. Equality of opportunity, the rule of law, the right to pursue happiness—these are but a few principles of democracy which have been favorable to economic expansion.

The second historically proved method of rapid economic growth has been through totalitarian communism. In this method, the state owns the means of production, and the state sets an over-all goal—such as a five-year plan—of what is to be produced, and how the available resources of labor, land, and capital are to be employed. The freedom of the consumer, worker, and producer is replaced by the dictate of the police state. Because the communist state possesses totalitarian power, it can generally ensure that the plan is translated into reality. This may take a few decades, and millions of people may pay with their lives, but eventually a modern industrial economy does develop at a rapid pace. It is important to note that no nation has so far freely chosen the path of communist economic development: communism has either been imposed by internal revolution or civil war (Russia, China, Yugoslavia, Cuba) or by external armed force (the Soviet satellites in eastern Europe, and North Vietnam and North Korea in the Far East). Every nation that has been subjected to communism by internal force was characterized by economic backwardness, low levels of education, corruption or inefficiency in the public service, and traditions of authoritarian government.

In facing the problem of economic development, underdeveloped nations today generally do not wish to imitate either the Western capitalist process of development or the communist path of complete state planning and ownership based on political terror. Nearly every underdeveloped nation likes to think that its economic and social problems can be solved through methods which are different from both Western capitalism and Soviet or Chinese communism. The label which is attached to this "third way" is that of socialism. In the context of underdeveloped countries socialism means many things to those who profess it.

First, socialism in the underdeveloped world stands for the ideal of social justice. In underdeveloped countries, the differences between the rich and the poor are proportionately greater than in the wealthier countries. Socialism, then, stands for the commitment to raise the poor masses to a higher level and to narrow the gap between the thin upper class of the privileged and the vast mass of the dispossessed. Socialism means more welfare services for the poor, more schools for the uneducated, and more human dignity for the traditionally underprivileged. Where tribal organization of society is still alive, socialism is but a new term for traditional tribal loyalty and solidarity. Thus, African socialism is defined by a leading Tanganyika statesman as follows: "The foundation, and the objective, of African Socialism is the Extended Family. The true African Socialist does not look on one class of men as his brethren and another as his natural enemies. He does not form an alliance with the 'brethren' for the extermination of the 'non-brethren.' He rather regards all men as his brethren—as members of his ever extending Family." (Julius K. Nyerere, *"Ujamaa": The Basis of African Socialism,* 1962, p. 8.)

Second, the term socialism in underdeveloped countries often stands for the ideal of human brotherhood and world peace through law. As a result, socialists in underdeveloped nations frequently advocate nonalignment between the two sides in the cold war. Even where, as in India, the reality of Red Chinese invasion has made nonalignment a pure ideal or illusion, socialists still cling to it as a hope for the future. In Africa, the view is held that the world is divided, not between capitalist and communist countries, but between rich and poor countries, and the poor countries "should be very careful not to allow themselves to be used as the 'tools' of any of the rich countries of the world," whether such rich countries are capitalist or communist. (Paul E. Sigmund, ed., *The Ideologies of the Developing Nations,* 1963, p. 208.)

The third meaning of socialism in underdeveloped countries is the commitment to planning. Because underdeveloped countries look upon economic growth with a sense of urgency, they feel that the functioning of the free market may not ensure the kind of rapid economic expansion and growth that are called for. Some basic elements of a modern economy—highways, means of transportation, hospitals, low-cost housing, schools—cannot, in the very nature of things, attract private enterprise, since they are the framework within which private enterprise and profits can be generated, but which in themselves generally do not create such profits. Second, there is the kind of basic enterprise, such as the manufacture of steel, for which there is either not enough private capital available, or which cannot hope to compete with foreign established enterprises. Only the state can build the foundations of a modern economy (highways and the like), and only the state can assume the risks of profitless enterprise over a number of years, if such enterprise is necessary for the economy as a whole. In 1963, for example, India had five steel plants, of which three were state-owned. With a population of over 430 million, India produced only 5.6 million tons of steel in 1962, as compared with nearly 100 million tons produced in the United States. Yet even at her low level of development, India needed in 1963 at least 10 million tons of steel. As a step toward this goal, she asked American aid for the building of a sixth steel plant, to be state-owned, which would eventually produce about 4 million tons of steel. Yet after several years of negotiation, the United States finally turned India down, largely because the projected plant would be state-owned. Indian businessmen, opposed to socialism as a general principle, publicly regretted the American position, because, in the words of the Indian Chamber of Commerce, the American refusal "could also hurt the private sector of Indian industry, which is badly in need of more steel." (*The New York Times,* September 8, 1963.)

Yet the need for planning, to which all underdeveloped countries are committed, does not imply over-all, or even large-scale nationalization of the means of production. Here, India again provides a good illustration, as Nehru is a life-long socialist, and his nation is committed to the general idea of socialism. If planning can be measured by the extent to which a country's gross national product is controlled and disposed of by the government, we find that the figure is about 20 per cent for the United States, but only 13-14 per cent for India. (John K. Galbraith, *Economic Development in Perspective,* 1962, p. 33.) Where rapid development was necessary in the United States —as recently in atomic energy, jet aircraft, supersonic planes, space technology—the planning and financing have come almost entirely from the government, since in each of these areas the initial job was too big, too costly, and too profitless for private enterprise or initiative. What atomic energy or space technology in their beginning stages are for the United States, steel or railroads may be for India or any other underdeveloped country.

In the economic field, socialism in underdeveloped countries thus means an economic structure in which some industries are completely private (such as farming, handicrafts, small business), in which others have both a private and a public sector (as in heavy industry), and finally, in which the public sector dominates (transportation, public utilities). While this is the general meaning of socialism in the economic sphere in underdeveloped areas, the practical application varies in different countries. In general, it can be said that nationalization has gone furthest where political democracy is weak or nonexistent, as in Nasser's Egypt, in Ben Bella's Algeria, or in Nkrumah's Ghana. Where constitutional government is a reality (as in the Philippines, India, Nigeria, Israel, Chile), private enterprise is encouraged or at least tolerated.

Thus, we see that the meaning of socialism in underdeveloped countries differs from that in the wealthier countries, because the historical situation is different. In the West, socialism has meant, not how to industrialize a backward country, but how to distribute the fruits of a wealthy society in a more equitable way. As a result, the concept of the welfare state has virtually absorbed the idea of socialism. By contrast, socialism in underdeveloped countries is confronted with the task, not so much of distributing the fruits of an industrial economy which hardly exists, but to build an industrial economy, so as to raise the economic and intellectual level of the masses of the people. For the same reason, while socialism in Western countries has generally developed best within a framework of established constitutional government (as in Britain or Scandinavia), socialism in underdeveloped countries frequently develops within a tradition in which authoritarian rule by foreign imperialists or by native power-holders has been the rule. It is, therefore, to be expected that socialism in some underdeveloped countries will show a greater tolerance for authoritarian practices than has generally been true of Western socialism.

Yet, in the final analysis, socialism in the underdeveloped countries tries to imitate neither the Western capitalist pattern *in toto,* nor the communist totalitarian pattern. From communism, the underdeveloped nations (regardless of their commitment to socialism) have borrowed the idea that economic development can be planned, and in some cases must be planned, by the state. Yet, the peoples of the underdeveloped countries, particularly the leaders among them (India, Nigeria, Mexico, Brazil) have decided that they want planning without the totalitarian police state of communism. As to the capitalist West, the underdeveloped countries, and particularly the socialist elements in them, greatly admire its technological efficiency and spirit of progress, as exemplified in particular by the United States. Yet the great disparities of wealth as produced by the relatively freely functioning capitalist economies of the West seem a less worthy object of imitation in underdeveloped countries. The most important aspect of Western nations that appeals to underdeveloped nations is the political idea of self-government based on the rule of law. Whether the underdeveloped nations will be able to merge, under their concept of socialism, the Western political idea of liberty with the economic concept of planning, largely borrowed from the practice of communism, still remains to be seen. If the underdeveloped nations should fail in their attempted synthesis of constitutional government and economic planning (including partial government ownership of industry), there is the possibility that they (or some, at least) may consider constitutional government expendable, but not rapid economic development through full-fledged planning and public ownership of industry.

Abrams, Mark and Richard Rose, *Must Labour Lose?* Baltimore: Penguin Books, Inc., 1960.

Attlee, Clement R., *As It Happened.* New York: The Viking Press, Inc., 1954.

Bernstein, Eduard, *Evolutionary Socialism.* New York: Schocken Books, 1961.

Buber, Martin, *Paths in Utopia.* Boston: Beacon Press (Beacon Paperbacks), 1960.

Cole, G. D. H., *A History of Socialist Thought,* 5 vols. New York: St. Martin's Press, Inc., 1953-1960.

Cole, Margaret, *The Story of Fabian Socialism.* Stanford: Stanford University Press, 1962.

Crosland, C. A. R., *The Future of Socialism.* New York: The Macmillan Co., 1957.

———, *The Conservative Enemy: A Program of Radical Reform for the 1960s.* New York: Schocken Books, 1962.

Datta, Amlankusum, *Socialism, Democracy, and Industrialization.* London: Allen & Unwin, 1962.

Durbin, E. F. M., *The Politics of Democratic Socialism.* London: George Routledge & Sons, Ltd., 1940.

Ebenstein, William, *Great Political Thinkers,* 3rd ed., chap. 24. New York: Holt, Rinehart & Winston, Inc., 1960.

———, *Modern Political Thought,* 2nd ed., chap. 11. New York: Holt, Rinehart & Winston, Inc., 1960.

———, *Political Thought in Perspective,* chap. 21. New York: McGraw-Hill Book Co., Inc. (McGraw-Hill Paperbacks), 1963.

Egbert, Donald D. and Stow Persons, eds., *Socialism and American Life,* 2 vols. Princeton, N.J.: Princeton University Press, 1952.

Fisher, Margaret W. and Joan V. Bondurant, *Indian Approaches to a Socialist Society.* Berkeley, Calif.: University of California Press, 1956.

Freemantle, Anne J., ed., *This Little Band of Prophets: The British Fabians.* New York: New American Library (Mentor Books), 1959.

Gaitskell, Hugh, *Socialism and Nationalization.* London: Fabian Society, 1956.

Galbraith, John K., *Economic Development in Perspective.* Cambridge, Mass.: Harvard University Press, 1962.

Hayek, Friedrich A., *The Road to Serfdom.* Chicago: University of Chicago Press (Phoenix Books), 1960.

Heilbroner, Robert L., *The Great Ascent: The Struggle for Economic Development in Our Time.* New York: Harper & Row (Harper Torchbooks), 1963.

Hoover, Calvin B., *The Economy, Liberty, and the State.* New York: Twentieth Century Fund, 1959.

Jay, Douglas, *Socialism in the New Society*. New York: St. Martin's Press, Inc., 1963.

Landauer, Carl, *European Socialism*, 2 vols. Berkeley, Calif.: University of California Press, 1959.

Lewis, W. Arthur, *The Principles of Economic Planning*. Washington, D.C.: Public Affairs Press, 1949.

Man, Henri de, *The Psychology of Socialism*. London: Allen & Unwin, 1928.

McBriar, A. M., *Fabian Socialism and English Politics, 1884-1914*. Cambridge: Cambridge University Press, 1962.

Mises, Ludwig von, *Socialism*. New Haven, Conn.: Yale University Press, 1951.

Morris, William D., *The Christian Origins of Social Revolt*. New York: The Macmillan Co., 1959.

Nyerere, Julius K., *"Ujamaa": The Basis of African Socialism*. Dar Es Salaam. Tanganyika: (no publisher given), 1962.

Owen, Robert, *A New View of Society*. Glencoe, Ill.: The Free Press, Inc., 1948.

Perlman, Selig, *A Theory of the Labor Movement*. New York: A. M. Kelley, Inc., 1949.

Pigou, A. C., *Socialism versus Capitalism*. New York: The Macmillan Co., 1937.

Rivkin, Arnold, *Africa and the West*. New York: Frederick A. Praeger, Inc. (Praeger Paperbacks), 1962.

Robson, William A., *Nationalized Industry and Public Ownership*. London: Allen & Unwin, 1960.

Rose, Saul, *Socialism in Southern Asia*. New York: Oxford University Press, 1959.

Rosenberg, Arthur, *Democracy and Socialism*. New York: Alfred A. Knopf, Inc., 1939.

Rostow, W. W., *The Stages of Economic Growth: A Non-Communist Manifesto*. New York: Cambridge University Press, 1960.

Schapiro, J. Salwyn, *Movements of Social Dissent in Modern Europe*. Princeton, N.J.: D. Van Nostrand Co., Inc. (Anvil Books), 1962.

Schumpeter, Joseph A., *Capitalism, Socialism, and Democracy*. New York: Harper & Row (Harper Torchbooks), 1962.

Shannon, David A., *The Socialist Party of America: A History*. New York: The Macmillan Co., 1955.

Sigmund, Paul E. (ed.), *The Ideologies of the Developing Nations*. New York: Frederick A. Praeger, Inc. (Praeger Paperbacks), 1963.

Sturmthal, Adolf, *Unity and Diversity in European Labor*. Glencoe, Ill.: The Free Press, 1953.

Titmuss, Richard M., *Income Distribution and Social Change*. London: Allen & Unwin, 1962.

Ward, Barbara, *India and the West*. New York: W. W. Norton & Co., Inc., 1961.

Weiner, Herbert E., *British Labor and Public Ownership*. Washington, D.C.: Public Affairs Press, 1960.

Index